THE

FOUNDER

OF

QUAKERISM

(1922)

A PSYCHOLOGICAL STUDY
OF THE MYSTICISM OF GEORGE FOX

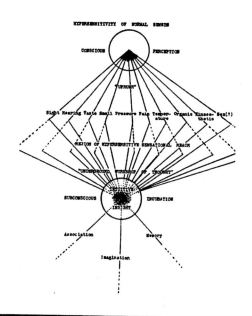

Rachel Knight

ISBN 0-7661-0021-9

THE FOUNDER OF QUAKERISM

A PSYCHOLOGICAL STUDY OF THE MYSTICISM OF GEORGE FOX

BY

RACHEL KNIGHT, PhD.

LONDON: THE SWARTHMORE PRESS LD.
RUSKIN HOUSE, 40 MUSEUM STREET, W.C.1

GEORGE FOX
FROM A PAINTING BY SIR PETER LELY

R0405868261

To

MY TEACHER AND FRIEND,

.EDWIN DILLER STARBUCK

SCIENTIST, PHILOSOPHER, QUAKER, MYSTIC,

AND MASTER IN THE ART OF LIVING,

I DEDICATE

WHATEVER IS OF VALUE IN THIS WORK, OF WHICH HE

HAS BEEN THE SYMPATHETIC AND UNTIRING

INSPIRATION, GUIDE, AND CRITIC.

THE FAULTS IN IT ARE ALL

MY OWN.

First published in 1922

Printed in Great Britain by
UNWIN BROTHERS, LIMITED, PRINTERS, THE GRESHAM PRESS, LONDON AND WOKING

INTRODUCTORY NOTE

THE author of this psychological study of George Fox died a year ago, before she had finished preparing the MS. for publication. Her executors accordingly asked me to see her book through the press and to write a few words of introduction.

The book was written as a thesis for the degree of Doctor of Philosophy at the University of Iowa, an honour which was conferred on its author in 1919. Dr. Knight had received her previous education at the Friends' Central School, Philadelphia, and George School, Bucks County, Pennsylvania, and had obtained her M.A. degree at Swarthmore College, and she had also studied in England at the Woodbrooke Settlement for Religious and Social Study. For five years she taught in private schools and for nine years was Principal in one of the Philadelphia public schools. In 1917 she held a fellowship at the University of Iowa and in 1919 at the Wistar Brown Graduate School at Haverford College, Pennsylvania.

After receiving her doctorate she was appointed Research Assistant at the University of Iowa, which she left to become Professor of Psychology and Dean of Women at the State College of South Dakota. Here she had spent one session (1920–21), and looked forward to a widening sphere of work and influence, when she died after an operation in September, 1921, at the age of 43.

She was a leader among the younger members of the Society of Friends in America. Belonging herself to the " Liberal " branch, she had a great number of friends in all branches of the Society in America, and also in England, to which she paid her last visit as a delegate to the All Friends' Conference held in London in 1920. Her sympathetic and forceful personality made her a fine teacher and leader, and it was in this capacity rather than in the sphere of scholarship that she did her best work and promised still greater achievements.

Her thesis contains some crudities and extravagances that a later and riper judgment would doubtless have pruned away, but it is published as the author left it, and it is a suggestive piece of experimental work in the largely unexplored field of the psychology of religion. There are obvious instances throughout the work in which the author has given a needlessly elaborate psychological or even physiological interpretation of expressions used by Fox which bear a simpler explanation, but despite the author's temptation to bring every feature of Fox's character and experience under some head of the so far accepted classification of psycho-physical tendencies, her work throws new light on the great founder of the Quaker movement.

The great mystics elude all attempts at analysis and classification, but Dr. Knight was not unaware of this. She has indeed done more than analyse and classify the experience of Fox and his several " openings " and " states "—she has presented the man himself anew to us with a sympathy and insight that bear witness to the degree to which she herself entered into the deep experience out of which he spoke. For the teaching and example of Fox brought her, like many another, " to sit under her own Teacher," and so to be an inspired and inspiring teacher of others.

A. BARRATT BROWN.

FOREWORD

THE problems of religion have been persistent problems to me. To study religion best I believe we must turn for our material to those for whom religion is real and vital and constitutes wellnigh the whole of their lives. George Fox had long interested me as a picturesque character and as the founder of a religion of life. Ever since one summer day in 1912 when I had fingered through the original manuscript of his Journal in the Library at Devonshire House in London, chancing on one interesting episode after another that made him a real and living personality to me, I had wanted to know him better and understand the source of his power and personality.

The original Journal was written mostly from dictation, and is not in his own handwriting. But occasionally there are special notes and interlinings from his own pen. The ragged year-worn pages of the Journal have now been incrusted into new margins with all the skill of the modern bookbinder's art, and the whole is bound into a ponderous volume. From it no accurate and complete reproduction was made until 1911. It is a matter of interest that then it was from the very University whose students had treated him so rudely two centuries before that this Cambridge Edition of his *Journal* was issued.

Other and earlier editions had always eliminated

most carefully the more abnormal features,—the very items which are often of most use to the psychologist. For purposes of general use, however, I have found Rufus M. Jones's edition, *George Fox : An Autobiography*, which is a condensed form of the Journal with its spelling modernized, a more workable volume. It is to this that most references are given. It is perhaps well to state that I have retained much of the phraseology of Fox ; for instance, such words as priest and professor. For him a priest was an ordained minister of any sect whatever. A professor was one who professed Christianity, often a mere nominal Christian.

It has been a peculiar joy to me to have been able to do this work at the University of Iowa, where the atmosphere is not only one of sincere and honest scholarship, but also one of delightful friendliness and comradeship. My most heartfelt thanks are therefore due to the President of the University and to the Dean of the Graduate School, as well as to all the members of the Department of Philosophy and Psychology. Especially do I wish to acknowledge my debt to Dr. Mabel Clare Williams, who has read my entire manuscript and given much helpful criticism.

University of Iowa,
July 1919.

CONTENTS

CONTENTS

PART FIVE

APPENDICES

OF GEORGE FOX

WILLIAM PENN : " I can say I never saw him out of his place, or not a match for every service or occasion. . . . I have done when I have left this short epitaph to his name : ' Many sons have done virtuously in this day, but, dear George, thou excellest them all.' "

CHARLES LAMB : " Reader, if you are not acquainted with it, I would recommend to you, above all Church narratives, to read Sewell's *History of the Quakers*. It is in folio, and is the abstract of the journals of Fox and the primitive Friends. It is far more edifying and affecting than anything you will read of Wesley and his colleagues. Here is nothing to stagger you, nothing to make you mistrust, no suspicion of alloy, no drop or dregs of the worldly or ambitious spirit."

JOSIAH ROYCE : " George Fox . . . was not a typical mystic. . . . Contemplation was compatible with work ; and the Light was still with him in the company of his Friends. . . . Above all the Light taught this unresting soul how to labour amid all the storms and the lurid hatreds of his day, not in vain, but humanely, valiantly, and beneficently."

WILLIAM JAMES : " Every one who confronted him personally, from Oliver Cromwell down to county magistrates and jailers, seems to have acknowledged his superior power."

RUFUS M. JONES : " Almost more remarkable than the truth which he proclaimed was the fervour, the enthusiasm, the glowing passion of the man. He was of the genuine apostolic type. . . . It is this courageous fidelity to his insight that made him a social reformer and a religious organizer. He belongs in this respect in the same list with St. Francis of Assisi. They both attempted the difficult task of bringing religion from heaven to earth."

RALPH WALDO EMERSON : " An institution is the lengthened shadow of a man, as Quakerism of George Fox."

PART ONE
GEORGE FOX

I

GEORGE FOX THE MAN

GEORGE Fox, born in Leicestershire in 1624, died in London in 1691. Thus his life extended through the period of political and religious readjustment in England, from the last year of the reign of James I, through the Protectorate, into the Restoration of the Stuarts. Religious toleration was not obtained until 1689 ; so Quakerism arose in the last strenuous days of severest persecutions.

Fox's parents were people of worth and substance. His father, a weaver, was known as " Righteous Christer." Of his mother William Penn said that she was a woman " accomplished above most of her degree in the place where she lived." [1]   George, a sober and more than ordinarily religious child, was early apprenticed to a shoemaker and dealer in wool, where he earned a reputation for strict veracity.

Between the ages of nineteen and twenty-four he had no fixed occupation, but sought the truth and strove for satisfaction of mind and heart by wandering from place to place, consulting all whom he thought might aid him.   It was a liberal, though not a scholastic, education.   The Bible was his constant companion in

[1] William Penn : Preface to Fox's Journal, in *George Fox : An Autobiography*, edited by Rufus M. Jones, vol. i, p. 46.

these wanderings. His knowledge of it became so thorough that his contemporaries said that if every Bible in England were destroyed George Fox could reproduce it from cover to cover.

His temperamental response to ideational rather than to objective stimuli led him to find real fellowship with no one in those years during which he was developing his deep conviction of the principle of immediate Divine Guidance through the Indwelling Christ, the Inner Light. This principle found expression in his life in consistent testimonies which often brought him into sharp conflict not only with leaders of the Calvinistic sects of the Commonwealth days, but also with the authorities of the State. Seven times at least, for periods extending over a year at a time, he was imprisoned on various just and unjust charges in prisons of disgusting filth and morale. In spite of weakened health, he continued unfalteringly in the preaching of the Truth as he saw it.

Nothing was farther from his intention than founding a new sect. But the circumstances of the times and the persecutions led to an organization which is one of the purest examples of true democracy in existence. Within six years of his initial activity in the ministry his prophetic message and apostolic vigour had drawn a group of more than sixty virile young men of the North to share with him the task of spreading the Truth as *free* ministers of the Gospel. Women shared equally in this ministry from the very beginning. So closely were these knit into harmony by similar experience of Divine Guidance that they all spoke the same religious language and suffered persecution in the same spirit of toleration and loving forgiveness of their persecutors. The Conventicle Acts and a special Quaker Act in 1662 led to such severe persecution that there were said to have been four thousand two hundred Quakers, men and women, in prison in England at one time. Others were banished to Barbadoes and to New England. After thirty years of service, the followers of Fox had become an organized society of sixty-six thousand members. These were drawn from all degrees of social standing. Workmen and tradesmen of the country-side and small villages mingled with the scholarly Robert Barclay, the aristocratic Isaac Penington and the courtly William Penn.

In spite of a physique that was vigorous yet peculiarly sensitive and liable to psychic disarrangement, and in spite of a constitution weakened by exposure and imprisonment, Fox continued active, travelling in the ministry for nearly forty years. He spent two years in the wilderness of America, and also went on missionary journeys to Ireland, Scotland, the Bermudas, Holland and Germany. He inspired his followers also to go as missionaries to Italy, to the Sultan of Turkey, and into " Prester John's country "—Abyssinia. Others sought an opportunity to go to China, that the message might be carried to all men and all races, that all alike are born of God and are capable of becoming sons of God. Superstitious seamen, however, refused to carry Quakers, and they were halted in their journeyings by lack of means of conveyance.

At the age of forty-five Fox married Margaret Fell, one of his earliest converts, who had been his fellow-worker through many years. This marriage with the widow of Judge Fell, ten years his senior, proved to be one of rare sympathy and community of purpose.

On January 11, 1691, he attended a large Meeting for Worship in London, preached a long and powerful sermon closing with prayer. As he left the meeting he "felt the cold strike to his heart."[1] Later he said, "All is well ; the Seed of God reigns over all, and over death itself. And though I am weak in body, yet the power of God is over all."[2] Two days later he died.

His unwavering zeal and energy resulted, not alone in his public ministry, but also in untiring effort to spread the truth through the written Word. Untutored and untrained he was. His Journal, nevertheless, is a remarkable and direct account and record of personal experience of "the dealings of the Lord"[3] with him. It bears little resemblance to the typical mystic's account of "that wondrous journey which he believes leads Godward."[4] His treatises, epistles, etc., have been collected into eight stout volumes. These are neither philosophical argumentations nor theological dissertations. They are generally earnest and urgent pleading for a type of life that is consistent with the principles which, by many repetitions and varying methods of presentation, he tries to impress upon his readers.

This man of rugged appearance, of crude presentation of his thought, of numerous repetitions in his writings, is so fired with his prophetic message that he carries with him a tremendous conviction. It requires that one have the sincerest respect for the virtues of the

---

[1] *George Fox : An Autobiography*, edited by Rufus M. Jones, p. 578. (Note : In referring to this shorter edition of the Journal of George Fox, hereafter I shall speak of it simply as " Journal.")

[2] *Journal*, p. 578.   [3] Ibid., p. 65.

[4] Josiah Royce : Article, " George Fox the Mystic," in *Harvard Theological Review*, January 1913. p. 37.

man, and love for his personality, even if one does not accept in full, with all its implications, his message of the truth of a divinely endowed humanity that is capable of becoming sons of God, joint-heirs with Jesus Christ.

II

GEORGE FOX THE MYSTIC

AT a few places in the world's life there develop rare
souls who have a mighty sense of their immediate
rapport with a Divine Being. Such we shall call by
the name of mystic.[1] Among such mystics I would
class George Fox, a man of dominating and gripping
personality, strong, rough-hewn, fearless, stern, pas-
sionate in exhortation and in rebuke ; and yet withal
of a purity, a rare sensitivity and a gentle sweetness
that led his friends constantly to refer to him in life
and after death as " dear George." He was a man
of censoriousness and antagonism toward those who
assailed *his truth*. At times he showed a sort of failure
to trust in the ultimate awakening of those whose
hearts seemed hard or closed to " that of God " which

[1] Many would include as mystic all those who experience a state of
ecstasy in communion with any object of beauty or truth, whether that
object be such an abstract thing as natural law or space, or concrete as
the person of the beloved. From such a point of view artists, poets,
musicians, scientists, inventors, lovers, would be called mystics. The
mathematician or the inventor who reaches out into the unknown and
grasps by immediate intuition some new truth would be classed as mystic.
So, too, would any who through mere subjective reference reaches to
that state of ecstasy. Although psychologically the description of this
experience and that of the religious mystic in communion with his God
may be the same, I believe that it is truer to limit the conception of a
mystic to those whose religious experience includes the mighty sense of
rapport with a Divine Being as object for his communing.

he believed was to be found in all men. Yet he had ever a forgiving spirit toward those who harmed him personally and a boundless love even toward his persecutors.

Is this man, then, with all his vigorous, vital activity, rightly classed with those whom the world has ever called the mystics? The Bible, which had been put into the hands of her people by Queen Elizabeth, was his constant companion through many days in the fields and nights of restless waking. His mind became so filled with its spirit that his own experience was couched largely in its terms, and he came to live constantly and consciously in the spirit of those who gave it forth.

St. Paul and Fox.

We find that Fox's mysticism is in type most like that of St. Paul. Both felt the unity of their lives with God, a unity that arose from their mutual sense of their immediate personal experience of God through that inward possession which Paul calls " Christ in you "[1] and Fox calls " the divine light of Christ "[2] or " the seed of God."[3] Both men were somewhat similarly constituted mentally, with a capacity for physical response that became almost, if not quite, pathological at times. Both entered upon their life-work of ministry after a marked psychical experience. Paul was blinded by a vision on the road to Damascus, and went into the wilderness for a period of preparation. Fox, after the death of " one Brown," who prophesied on his death-bed of Fox's future work, lay as one dead for about fourteen days, " much altered in countenance and person," as if his body were " now

[1] Colossians i. 27.　　[2] *Journal*, p. 101.　　[3] Ibid., p. 88.

moulded or changed." [1]   He came out of the experience with a sense of having been brought by the eternal power of God through " the very ocean of darkness and death " into the " greatness and infinitude of the love of God which cannot be expressed by words." [2] In the reaction after the ecstatic experience, a temptation to despair came to Fox. Then it was Paul's condition that came to his mind. After Paul " had been taken up into the third heaven, and seen things not lawful to be uttered," a temptation had come to him also. So, " by the power of Christ," [3] Fox, too, overcame his temptation. But neither for Paul nor for George Fox did mysticism lie in ecstatic visions so much as in the normal experience of daily living in heavenly places. The proof of their inward co-ordination lay not in ecstasy, but in the steady manifestation of their love for humanity. The form of expression which Fox's experience took was no doubt influenced by his familiarity with the Scriptures during his formative period. Undoubtedly, too, his unusual missionary zeal for foreign lands arose partly from his reading of Paul's life, though his own active temperament made him ripe fruit for it.

The Montanists and Fox.

Montanus also was subject to trance and ecstasy ; but, unlike Fox, he and his followers depended upon such manifestations for their sense of immediate contact with God. Fox believed that there *is that of the Spirit of God inherent in every one*, rich or poor, saint or reprobate, that may be immediately perceived and realized by every one. The Montanists believed rather that the

1 *Journal*, p. 87.   2 Ibid., p. 88.   3 Ibid., p. 89.

Holy Spirit *might come upon* any person, no matter what the rank or sex. Fox's mysticism was a return to the New Testament type of prophecy and experience, the prophetic exponent of which is a highly gifted, spiritually developed person who lives on a lofty level of experience and practises the truth which he sees. The Montanist was not a return to the New Testament type of such a heightened personality. The recipient of the " power " with them must be a mere *passive* instrument to be played upon. A man must be " out of himself " and his body " possessed by " God. Fox was no such instrument of an outside force, but rather the organ of an inward Spirit who had become the Life of his life, who flooded his faculties with energy. He did not suppress his reason ; and differed from others only in that he co-operated better than they with the Divine Spirit to whom his life was consciously allied. He therefore showed in his public prayer, as William Penn said of him, that " he lived nearer to the Lord than other men." [1] What he felt was true of himself he believed to be possible for all men. He placed a fuller value on human personality than the Montanists, though he agreed with them in their belief and emphasis on the continuous and developmental character of revelation.

Socrates and Fox.

Socrates seems to distinguish between the " command of the Lord " which guides the general tenor of his life and the inhibitory power, the " sign " which he calls his Dæmon, " which is a kind of voice " that came to him first as a child and which, he said, " always forbids but never commands me to do anything that

[1] William Penn : Preface to *Journal*, p. 54.

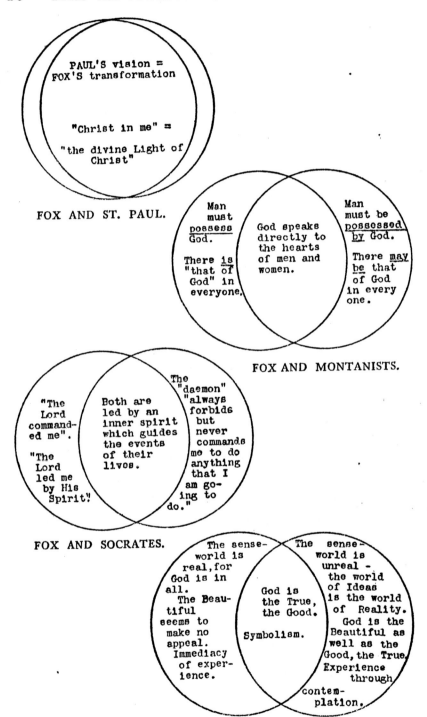

PAUL'S vision = FOX'S transformation

"Christ in me" = "the divine Light of Christ"

FOX AND ST. PAUL.

Man must possess God.

There is "that of God" in everyone.

God speaks directly to the hearts of men and women.

Man must be possessed by God.

There may be that of God in every one.

FOX AND MONTANISTS.

"The Lord commanded me".

"The Lord led me by His Spirit."

Both are led by an inner spirit which guides the events of their lives.

The "daemon" "always forbids but never commands me to do anything that I am going to do."

FOX AND SOCRATES.

The sense-world is real, for God is in all. The Beautiful seems to make no appeal. Immediacy of experience.

God is the True, the Good.

Symbolism.

The sense-world is unreal - the world of Ideas is the world of Reality. God is the Beautiful as well as the Good, the True. Experience through contemplation.

I am going to do." [1] To George Fox the " voice of the Lord " was ever dynamic and motor, *moving* him to *do* some act, to *perform* some service, or to *go* to some definite place. Even in deterring action it took the form of a definite and positive command. Although it differs thus in form, Socrates and George Fox have in common a sense of the spiritual guidance of a Supreme Power in even the smallest events of their lives.

Plato and Fox.

Though Fox undoubtedly dwelt more upon the manifestations of God in human personality, he is keenly sensitive to the sense-world. In Plato, as is evident in his myth of the cave, there is a tendency to treat the sense-world as unreal, shadowy and un-divine. To Plato, Reality was not alone the True, but the Good and the Beautiful as well. The soul has in itself an eye for Divine Reality and the mind a native capacity for the beatific vision. In Fox there seems to be very little appreciation of the Beautiful as a definite element in his appreciation of the deeper values. The aspiring lines of a Gothic cathedral but " struck at his life " because to him they represented and symbolized an empty show of a religion that was not sincere. England was largely Calvinistic in his day, but he must have had some opportunity to hear inspiring music in the cathedrals at least. However, music made no appeal to him unless it expressed spontaneously the exhilaration of one's spirit. While still a seeker and despairing, a priest had advised that he sing hymns and use tobacco, but " psalms he was not

[1] Plato: *The Apology*, trans. by Jowett (3rd ed.), vol. ii, p. 125.

in a state to sing." [1]   Later, however, he could appreciate that Friends were making music in their hearts,
and a few times even he himself was led to sing.   Had
Fox gone to school to Plato as well as to the apostles,
there would no doubt have been a richer content of
æsthetic value in his mysticism and in the lives of those
who became his followers in manner of life as well as
in thought.   Both Plato and Fox used a symbolism ;
but to Plato thoughts and things became symbolic
through contemplation and through intellectual associations, while to Fox the symbolism was so immediate
that he was hardly aware that it was symbolic at all.

Aristotle and Fox.

Aristotle cannot be classed as a mystic.   Yet he was
a strong influence in the direction of a negative mysticism
with whose emphasis Fox had little in common.   To
Aristotle " God exists beyond the heaven ; He is the
Motionless First Mover, who by the mere power of
His thought causes the heaven to revolve, and through
it transmits the stream of energy to the farthest recesses
of the material universe." [2]   Each man is thus but
" a copy of God's thought of the perfect human being ;
each one perishes, but the species ' Man ' never perishes,
because God's thought is eternal." [3]   One might say
that to Aristotle there is no avenue of approach to
God, although he nowhere defines the relation between
God and the " Natures " that compose the universe.
To him the " vital force " which seems to be inherent

[1] *Journal*, p. 72.
[2] William Romaine Newbold : " The Spell of Aristotle," in *Old
Penn* (Official Weekly Review of the University of Pennsylvania).
Reprint, p. 509.
[3] Newbold : " The Spell of Aristotle," p. 511.

in all living forms is more of a mechanical device than a soul akin to God, such as the " that of God " of which Fox so often speaks. Man's soul is to Aristotle, as Dr. Newbold says, like a " coiled-up spring set at birth to go off mechanically." So there could be no present help in time of need from such a God, even though He be indeed "the crown and head of the universe," the One *beyond* the Many. To Aristotle the soul attains vision only when, uncoiled, it leaves behind everything that could characterize the object of its vision, for God as Absolute Actuality has no describable characteristics save mere conscious existence. For Fox God is not thus away and beyond, but is very near ; indeed, is immanent in the very heart of the meanest person alive, and is to be immediately perceived and known there, and to be relied upon for guidance in all affairs of life.

Henry Suso and Fox.

With such mortification of the flesh and self-tor-turings as Henry Suso practised " out of the greatness of the love which he bore in his heart to the Divine and Eternal Wisdom "[1] Fox had nothing in common. His leathern suit—a form of dress not very usual at that time—was probably chosen for its durability, and not as a symbol. But he was quick to notice that it soon became a " dreadful thing " to the priests when " it was told them, ' The man in the leathern breeches is come.' "[2] Nor was it for any such cathartic effect as Suso's horsehair undergarment. The actual con-

---

[1] Henry Suso : *The Life of the Blessed Henry Suso* (trans. by Knox, London, 1865), p. 69.
[2] *Journal*, p. 139.

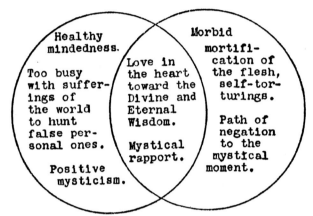

Healthy mindedness.

Too busy with sufferings of the world to hunt false personal ones.

Positive mysticism.

Love in the heart toward the Divine and Eternal Wisdom.

Mystical rapport.

Morbid mortification of the flesh, self-torturings.

Path of negation to the mystical moment.

FOX AND SUSO.

Man is the "temple of the living God".

Man's soul is "that of God" immediately present in the heart, and is moved and led and drawn by the Father of mankind.

God is the "teacher of His people Himself" in the heart of even the meanest of men.

Man is a "copy of God's thought".

Man's soul is a mechanical device like a "coiled up spring".

God is the Motionless First Mover, the "One Beyond the Many".

FOX AND ARISTOTLE.

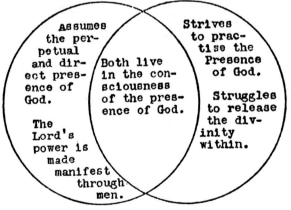

Assumes the perpetual and direct presence of God.

The Lord's power is made manifest through men.

Both live in the consciousness of the presence of God.

Strives to practise the Presence of God.

Struggles to release the divinity within.

FOX AND BROTHER LAWRENCE

ditions of the real world about him, the filthiness of the prisons in which he lay, the squalor and dirt and unrighteousness in Barbadoes, the earth and air of Ireland that smelled of the corruption of the nation, were too persistent as problems to be solved for him to occupy himself with such useless mortifications of his flesh as abstaining from a bath for twenty-five years. When necessary, he could sleep among the furze-bushes or on the bare ground out of doors. Indeed, he did so when superstitious fear closed for him the doors of inns in the English country-sides or when he was wandering in the American wildernesses. But he never had to seek to make his sleep uncomfortable by securing for himself, as did Suso, a door for " a most miserable bed, . . . hard pea-stalks in lumps under his head, the cross with the sharp nails stuck into his back, his arms . . . locked fast in bonds, the horsehair garment . . . round his loins, and the cloak . . . heavy and the door hard." [1]

To that great group of ascetic mystics who have painfully striven to find God by such a path of negation Fox certainly does not belong. Rather he belongs among those positive mystics who seek to realize the presence of God in this finite human life.

Plotinus and Fox.

With the fine and rational Plotinus Fox has in reality far more community of spirit. Plotinus, with scholarly insight, expresses his experience with more of philosophical charm. To Plotinus God is the " root of the soul," " the centre of the mind," " the divine centre of our being." He is " not external to anyone,"

[1] Henry Suso: Op. cit., p. 68.

but is " present even with those who do not know Him." [1]   Fox directly and simply, if daringly, speaks of " that of God in every one."   He calls it by varying names, this relationship that binds mankind so closely to God and to its fellow-men—this relationship which remains on God's side as an unbroken love and trust that " will not let one go," and on man's as a haunting and unceasing longing.

Fox and his Quaker followers employ but those figures and metaphors which have been used by all the great spiritual religions of the world to express their experiences :—the Light, the Seed of God, the Inner Life, the Inward Guide, the Christ Within. Usually Fox called it the Inner Light, which is the same analogy that Plato uses in the myth of the sun. Not a philosopher, he speaks out of his own immediate, intense and abundant experience : " God had given to us, every one of us in particular, a light from Himself shining in our hearts and consciences." [2]   Plotinus, more philosophical, describes God as the Universal Soul that enfolds in itself all individual souls, and the Universe as an unfolding of this Universal Soul.   That which Fox experienced intuitively he found not only alone in the fields at night, but also in the midst of crowds of his fellow-men in the market-place or in the quiet, alert waiting of the Friends' meeting.   He speaks of it with much simplicity and confidence. Plotinus is just as confident, but he achieves it through contemplation and surrender.   To him it is " the flight of the alone to the Alone," a " mode of vision

---

[1] Plotinus : Enneads VI, 9, 7. Bakewell : *Source Book in Ancient Philosophy* (New York, 1907), p. 388.
[2] Cf. *Journal*, pp. 100, 101, 137, 143, 148.

which is ecstasy," when the soul, " energizing enthusiastically, becomes established in quiet and solitary
union," until, " having surrendered himself to it, he
is one with it, as the centres of two circles might
coincide," until " there is no part left with which he
does not touch God." [1] Plotinus, like Fox's contemporary, the simple monk Brother Lawrence in his
scullery at the monastery, was ever voluntarily striving
to " practise the presence of God." When dying he,
who had ever " seemed ashamed of his body," exclaimed :
" I am struggling to release the divinity within me." [2]
Fox so intuitively took for granted that " God teaches
His people Himself," and that it was the " voice of
the Lord " that guided his every act, that he speaks
naturally and directly of acting " in the Lord's power,"
of " the Lord's power being made manifest " [3] through
him. At the close of his life, having followed this
inner leadership, he could say, " I am clear, I am
fully clear." [4]

Boehme and Fox.

Just at the time when Fox was undergoing his particular period of storm and stress in finding his higher
co-ordinations during his late adolescence, there began
to appear in England translations of the writings of
the German mystic, Jacob Boehme. Muggleton says
these books were the chief books bought by the followers
of Fox. [5] Rufus M. Jones thinks that Fox was more
directly influenced by Boehme than by any other mystic.

---

[1] Plotinus : Ennead V, 1, 2, 3, 4,; cf. Bakewell, op. cit., p. 389.
[2] Plotinus ; cf. Bakewell : *Source Book in Ancient Philosophy*, p. 390.
[3] *Journal, passim.* [4] Ibid., p. 578.
[5] Muggleton : *Looking Glass for George Fox* (2nd ed., 1756), p. 10.

In-
tui-
tion
and
con-
fid-
ence.

Both "energize
enthusiastically".

"The root of the soul
"not external to any
one", "present even
with those who do
not know Him."

"the Seed of God",
"that of God
in the
heart".

Con-
tem-
pla-
tion
and
sur-
ren-
der.

FOX AND PLOTINUS.

Lack of schol-
astic training.

Similar psychic exper-
iences.

Belief in the power of
Light.

God reveals Himself in
the human heart as
well as in the
world system.

FOX AND BOEHME.

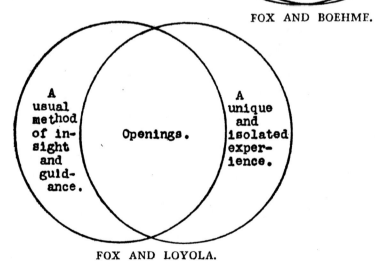

A
usual
method
of in-
sight
and
guid-
ance.

Openings.

A
unique
and
isolated
exper-
ience.

FOX AND LOYOLA.

He was a man without scholastic training even as Fox. Like Fox, he found his great illumination at the end of a period of long and earnest travail of soul " striving to find the heart of Jesus Christ and to be freed and delivered from anything that turned him away from Christ." [1] He had resolved to " put his life to the greatest hazard," when suddenly " the gate was opened." Then he " saw and knew the Being of Beings, the Byss and Abyss, the eternal generation of the Trinity, the origin and descent of this world and of all creatures through Divine Wisdom." [2] Fox, having it opened to him that he must "forsake all and be as a stranger to all," came to see that " there is one, even Christ Jesus, that could speak to his condition." [3] The " Lord gently led him along and let him see His love, which was endless and eternal, surpassing all the knowledge that men have in the natural state, or can obtain from history or books." [4] That love let him see himself as he was without God. It is not alone in such similarities of experience, however, that Fox and Boehme resemble each other. They both share a belief in the infinite power of Light which is at war with the principle of Darkness, and in the " doctrine that man is an epitome, a microcosm . . . possessed within by the same Spirit and Divine Reason that reveals Himself in large in the macrocosm or world system." [5] Fox shows a tendency to allegorize or spiritualize the Scriptures in much the same fashion as Boehme does.

---

[1] *Memoirs of Jacob Boehme*, p. 8. (trans. by F. Oakley, 1780).
[2] *Jacob Boehme : Second Epistle*, sect. 6–8.
[3] *Journal*, p. 82.   [4] Ibid., p. 83.
[5] R. M. Jones : *Studies in Mystical Religion* (London, 1909) p. 495.

Loyola and Fox.

Fox was at all times in his career subject to experiences which he called " openings." These were such direct and immediate revelations in his soul that his records of them are not statements of mere facts. They become principles of living truth which he himself sees. Other mystics have had similar experiences in their own degree and type, and also have described them by this same imagery of an opening of their spirits. For instance, St. Ignatius Loyola considered the profoundest spiritual experience of his life to have been one unaccompanied or expressed by any visual imagery : " On his way [to a church near Manresa] he sat down facing the stream, which was running deep. While he was sitting there, the eyes of his mind were opened so as to understand and comprehend spiritual things . . . with such clearness that all things were made new. If all the enlightenment and help he had received from God in the whole course of his life . . . were gathered together in one heap, these all would appear less than he had been given at this one time." [1]   But with Fox an " opening " was no such supremely unique and isolated fact. Though these openings varied in quality and importance, they continued more or less intermittently throughout his entire life.

Fox's Original Contribution to Mysticism.

However, as Josiah Royce points out, such " openings and the central mystical consciousness are decidedly different sorts of mental facts." [2]   It is this direct

[1] Loyola : *Testament* (London, 1900), pp. 91, 92.
[2] Josiah Royce : *George Fox as a Mystic*, op. cit., p. 52.

mystical consciousness of the presence of the Divine that is so central in his life. It is this which inspired and directed him into worship on the basis of silence, and which united him with the contemplative mystics. And yet there is in it somewhat of a new element. Such corporate waiting upon the Lord as a Friends' Meeting is not a mere collection of independent Quietistic worshippers each in his own heart worshipping and waiting for the voice of the Lord to speak individually with him in the silence. The group is rather a single unit, so conjunct and so interrelated and interacting that it becomes, not a summation, but a multiplication of active, alert, energizing seekers, so that when the corporate communion finds true expression in words, the words break not *into* the silence, but seem rather to be *breathed out of it*; and one speaks not alone for the edification of the others, but rather sums up and expresses the combined spirit of the gathering. It is as if all hearts present were expressing through the lips of the one speaker the consensus of the knowledge of God made evident in their own hearts. We do not wonder that George Fox simply records nothing of his own service in such ministry, realizing it is a power greater than his own that serves, and merely says, " The Lord's power was made manifest that day." Here is a new element, and different from those found in any other mystics, however wonderful their vision, however close their personal communion with their God may have been.

Fox as a Mystic.

Fox in his mysticism, then, was not of that ecstatic type evident in the Montanist group which found its philosophic exponent in Tertullian ; but, like St. Paul, he passed through his moments of ecstatic illumination into a normal mystical *life*, guided, as was Socrates, by a power within. He believed, with Plato, in a native capacity for beatific vision in the human heart, yet missed somewhat the wealth of beauty outside its human manifestations. " Energizing enthusiastically " as did Plotinus, he did so not so much for the purpose of reaching through contemplation the supra-rational union with the Divine, as to render manifest in the world " the power of the Lord," whose presence at all times he felt intuitively. He found no need in his life of many imprisonments for ascetic intoxicating self-torture as did Suso. He drew rather his forms of expression from healthier minds such as the Teutonic Boehme. He was active, positive, practical rather than passive, negative, theoretical ; intuitional rather than contemplative. He was emotional with his periods of ecstasy, but not merely so. He was intellectual—using in his arguments with opposers and oppressors the Scriptural authority most conclusive to them to back his more intuitive statements—but never primarily so. He was volitional, strenuously forging his way through any opposition to the goal he saw before him, and striving to know the will of God, yet doing so through an intense passivity, an opening up of all the channels of his being in an intense awareness, and waiting in the silence of the Meeting for the personal and corporate uprush of spiritual power that makes of normal daily living an abundant life of " normal joyous correspondence with the present God who . . . floods every act and impulse with constructive energy." [1]

[1] Rufus M. Jones : Introduction to *Children of the Light*, p. 3.

PART TWO

SOURCES OF FOX'S MYSTICAL INSIGHT

SOURCES OF MYSTICAL INSIGHT

I HAVE endeavoured to picture Fox's mysticism as it is in contrast to that of other mystics. My aim shall be now to tease out with somewhat of intensive analysis the sources which gave the value of truth to the practical vital religion of this seventeenth-century mystic. Josiah Royce, in *Sources of Religious Insight*, having dealt with individual and social experience and with the reason and the will as sources of religious insight, concludes : " The foregoing appear to leave us, after all, with no vital and positive religion." [1] Then he moves on to a discussion of loyalty as that which brings together these sources into the higher religious life. But I think we shall find that individual and social experience is a " big blanket " term that covers a myriad of sources, and that reason and the will play their part, not so much in giving the truth values to religious living, as in clarifying them in the consciousness and in putting them into practical operation.

[1] Josiah Royce: *Sources of Religious Insight* (New York, 1912), p. 166.

III

HYPERSENSITIVITY OF THE SPECIAL SENSES

ONE important source of the truth value of the mysticism of George Fox is the normal working of the normal conscious and subliminal perceptive powers. He differed not at all from his fellow-men save that he lived with greater fineness of discernment and with keener awareness than others. His special senses, with marvellous acuteness and delicacy, were registering differences which summed up and affected his judgments, even though unconsciously.

The hypersensitivity of his senses, though not cognizable, no doubt gave a richer content to his mental life, and I would count it as one of the several sources of his peculiar mystical insight. That he possessed such maximal perceptivity I believe we are warranted to claim. He heard and attended to sounds unnoticed by others. The plot of his jailers was foiled by his detecting their whispered plot to murder him.[1] His keenness of eyesight detected the ruffians hidden under the hedge in the dark to attack him.[2] His keenness of smell detected the differing smells of Ireland and England.[3] His gentle pitying touch upon the hair of John Jay, who had been thrown from his horse, found

[1] *Journal*, p. 261.　　[2] Ibid., p. 307.　　[3] Ibid., p. 464.

none of the rigidity of death and told him the neck was not broken but dislocated.[1] His combined senses saw in the bearing of Oliver Cromwell his approaching illness and death,[2] in the priest Lampitt his foul spirit,[3] in the shifting elusive expression of the face of the licentious woman the record of her life.[4] The insincerity of priests and laymen, who " professed that which they did not possess," [5] the unjust spirit that led to persecutions and to political warfare, to harmful social habits and to industrial injustice and inefficient service, were all matters of personal concern to him through his quick sensing of them.

Experimental studies of both animals and men have proven that our senses do record impressions of which we are not aware. The study of the stately horse of Berlin, Clever Hans, gives evidence for the animal world of a high degree of sensory keenness and great concentration of attention.[6]

---

[1] *Journal,* p. 513.   [2] Ibid., p. 325.   [3] Ibid., p. 160.
[4] Ibid., p. 185.   [5] Ibid., p. 69.

[6] Pfungst tells the story of Clever Hans: Hans had gained a reputation for keen intelligence. When, however, he was carefully examined by trained psychologists it was found that he required always some sort of visual aid, though that aid was not given intentionally. Laboratory measurements of involuntary head-jerks were found to average not over one millimetre, and the corresponding movements in the owner were even more minute. Mr. Pfungst, the psychologist, also succeeded in cultivating a control of his own movements, so that he became able to call forth at will all the various reactions of the horse by making the proper kind of voluntary movements, without asking any relevant question or giving any command. He met with the same success when he simply focused the mind attentively upon the answer desired, since in that case the necessary movement occurred whether he willed it or not. Thus they proved that Hans' accomplishments were founded upon his marvellous power of perceiving the slightest movement of the questioner and upon the intense and constant, though possibly involuntary, power of attention. Pfungst concludes: " Such

George Fox had such power of concentrated attention in looking at people that there are repeated allusions to the piercing quality of his eyes.[1]   So carefully did he read people, that he knew the thoughts of their minds.   He knew that the priests who came to visit him in jail would plead for the innate sinfulness and imperfection of humanity, even before they spoke.[2] He loved to wander through the fields, to lie upon a haystack, to climb into the trees even in his manhood days.   Thus reading the heart of Nature, he developed the power to read the hearts of men.   He saw that beggars were in real necessity, and ran after them to aid them.[3]   He cast an eye upon a woman and found an unclean spirit in her.[4]   He was keen to notice the attention, diligence and affection with which the people in the meeting listened to his preaching at Oyster Bay, Long Island.[5]   He heard the magistrates near Shelter Island saying among themselves that if they had money enough they would hire Fox to be their minister.[6]   The mosquitoes on the Rhode Island shore were very troublesome to him.[7]   His senses were more alert ; " all things seemed new and the earth gave another smell "[8] after a deep religious experience.   Smoke, whether of an open fire or of tobacco, was " offensive " to him, as well as were the lingering traits of it in his clothing.[9]   The earth and the air of Ireland smelt of the corruption of the nation, as if a foulness ascended

signs call for a high degree of sensory keenness and great concentration, but by no means ' an extremely high intelligence.' "   (Pfungst : *Clever Hans* (New York, 1911), p. 185.)

[1] *Journal*, pp. 187, 344, 557.   [2] Ibid., p. 122.
[3] Ibid., p. 157.   [4] Ibid., p. 185.   [5] Ibid., p. 505.
[6] Ibid., p. 508.   [7] Ibid., p. 509.   [8] Ibid., p. 97.
[9] Ibid., p. 439.

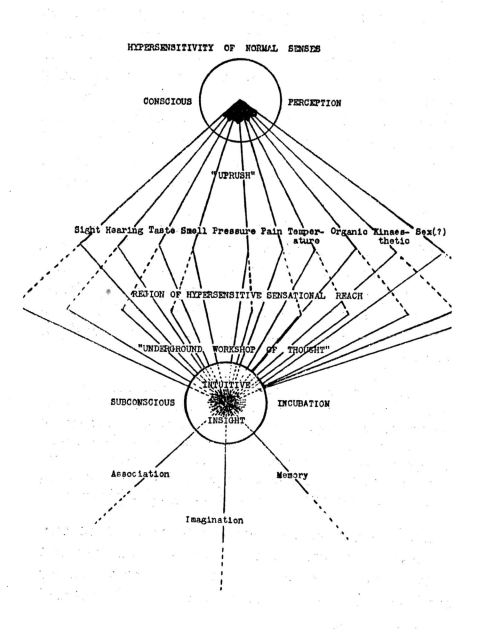

HYPERSENSITIVITY OF NORMAL SENSES

CONSCIOUS   PERCEPTION

"UPRUSH"

Sight Hearing Taste Smell Pressure Pain Temper- Organic Kinaes- Sex(?)
                                        ature   thetic

REGION OF HYPERSENSITIVE SENSATIONAL REACH

"UNDERGROUND WORKSHOP OF THOUGHT"

INTUITIVE

SUBCONSCIOUS   INCUBATION

INSIGHT

Association   Memory

Imagination

from the spilled blood of the Papist massacres there.[1]

Binet records an experiment upon a hypnotized girl which shows that the human touch is refined to just as marvellous an extent as any animal sense. On the back of her neck, where the touch nerves are supposedly quite sparsely located, he placed a coin which she had never seen. She was given a paper and pencil, and asked to draw whatever came to her mind. She had normally no skill in drawing, but she reproduced in size, and most creditably in design, the coin pressed to her neck.[2]

But not alone in hypnotized cases does one find conclusive evidence of the hyperæsthesia of the senses. We are constantly living better than we know. Retinal after-images are an everyday example of the normal way our sensitive mechanism is registering and recording unconsciously such minimal stimuli. Miss Washburn says : [3]

" Only the impression made on the sense organ, not in the least the impression made on attention, is the determining condition for the retinal after-image. We often note retinal after-images of objects which were quite unnoticed in our surroundings : with the eyes closed we see a green spot in the field of vision and trace it to a red object at which we have been looking with unobserving eyes, our attention occupied with something quite different."

But it is in its normal state that we find such delicacy of response in Fox, and not in any abnormal hypnotic state. His senses were perhaps no more innately sensitive than those of ordinary men. But bombarded

[1] *Journal,* p. 464.
[2] Binet: *Alterations of Personality* (New York, 1891), p. 214.
[3] Washburn : *Movement and Mental Imagery* (Boston, 1916).

on all sides by insistent stimuli, he had learned the use of them so that his sensory reach was more extensive and more accurate than theirs. The belief is prevalent that blind persons have better developed senses of touch and hearing than seeing persons. But this is not borne out by psychological tests. The apparent difference lies in the fact that persons handicapped by loss of sight and hearing learn to use their other senses to better advantage.[1] Helen Keller's normal senses are an excellent example of such skill.

In contact with any adequate stimulus, the nervous system is integrated for specific response in that direction. If, then, such a stimulus be repeatedly in control of the common pathway to consciousness, at such

[1] Dr. Seashore writes: "Through years of experience in the laboratory, the conviction has gradually grown upon me that a more radical distinction should be made between sensitiveness and ability to use a sense, i.e. between inborn sensory capacity and acquired ability and skill. From time to time I have taken the opportunity of comparing my own sensitiveness in touch and hearing with that of blind persons distinguished for ability in guiding themselves by hearing and touch; and in no case did I find that the blind possessed any significant superiority to myself in sensitiveness to touch and hearing, although some of the blind persons experimented upon were noted for their wonderful performances through hearing and touch." (C. E. Seashore: "Experimental Tests in Psychology," in *Journal of Educational Psychology*, 1916, No. VII, p. 81.)
A series of experiments upon compared groups of blind and seeing persons for localization of sound, for discrimination of intensity of sound, for lifted weights, for active and passive pressure, and for tactual space, resulted in the conclusion that "The blind who are skilful in the use of touch, muscle sense, and hearing are not more sensitive or keen in sensory discrimination than seeing persons when fundamental capacities are tested." Also that "Development of the use of a sense consists not in the heightening of sensitivity or sensory discrimination, but in the development of complexes and meanings in terms of these." (C. E. Seashore and T. L. Ling: "The Comparative Sensitiveness of Blind and Seeing Persons," in *Psychological Monographs, University of Iowa Studies in Psychology*, No. VII, p. 148.)

intervals that the nerve cells involved have not returned to the resting stage from the preceding stimulation, the rhythmic discharge of energy results in a sort of summation of power, a gradual ascent of efficiency until the maximum is reached.[1] Thus the brain threshold in that particular field is raised to its full capacity, and " the brain patterns that dominate at the close of the adolescent and at the beginning of the adult period fix and determine until death the life reactions of the individual. The action patterns thus formed in the plastic brain constitute the personality of the individual and make the reactions of the human mechanisms as inevitable and as true as are the reactions of a man-made machine."[2] The cruder character of the native endowments of the rough-hewn youthful Fox were refined till they fitted together perfectly into the mosaic of the mature brain pattern of his ripened personality. His keen perceptions drove themselves back more deeply into closer associations and co-ordinations until the inner heart of the man was highly integrated. In mature life he shows a personality so unified that one feels him as set apart from his fellow-men. It is as if there existed a chasm between the outer shell of his social contacts and the mighty inwardness of his soul's life with its God, which had been bridged, however, by an habitually consistent type of immediate response, that had been developed during the adolescent years of seeking and turmoil.

Fox's receptor nerves were acutely sensitive even in

[1] Cf. Crile: *The Origin and Nature of the Emotions* (Philadelphia, 1915), p. 30.
[2] Crile: *A Mechanistic View of Peace and War* (New York, 1915).

adult life. He had acquired skill in the use of his inborn capacity of sensory attention, and came to use all his senses to give point and power to his speech. The ambitious priest got the parsonage and " choked himself with it." [1] Fox " trampled under his feet " the offer of a captaincy in the national army.[2] Another priest was told that " his heart was rotten, and he was full of hypocrisy to the brim." [3] Fox " saw how God would stain the world's honour." [4]

Dr. Crile has demonstrated that the state of sensory threshold depends not alone upon the native physical inheritance of the sense mechanism, but also upon the continued use that has rendered permanently available in adult life the endowment of the child. We not only live better than we know, but we can by constant use and exercise keep our senses consciously functioning at the highest efficiency of their inborn capacity. So the threshold of sensory consciousness is much lower than we generally suppose, and also than we consciously draw upon in our daily living.

The hot-spot of his inmost life could then throw aside these sensations that were bombarding him so rigorously, and he could be indifferent to and independent of them all. He could pull himself away from them all until his judgments were no longer specific and direct as the result of them. Instead of being attentive to them, he could be more than normally indifferent. His judgments, then, on this higher level drew up into themselves all the richness of his sensory contributions and expressed themselves in general characterizations and spiritual conclusions.

[1] *Journal*, p. 119.
[2] Ibid., p. 128.
[3] Ibid., p. 164.
[4] Ibid., p. 245.

Love of Nature is apparent in his search for strength and consolation in the open fields and by the brooksides. It is in the solitude of Nature's heart that he most often finds guidance and uplift. Yet one fails almost utterly to find the least description of her beauty or wealth of tone and colour and form. Nor did he respond to the marvellous uplift that is to be found in the ascending aspiring lines of a Gothic cathedral. He could see in it only a symbol of a dead church which worshipped a " dead Christ." The sublime dignity and reverent appeal of a ritual had no meaning for him. No doubt he had many an opportunity to hear majestic music in the churches and cathedrals which he frequented in his early years, yet he seems to have had no sense of musical appreciation. It is the inner melodies in the hearts of men of which he is conscious rather than the harmony of their tones in singing. But he too could sing if the occasion demanded and he was " in a state to sing."

A false mystic, in getting superior associations and co-ordinations, and having raised himself to a higher level of spiritual efficiency, cuts himself loose from all sensory contributions. He takes the negative path and climbs to his mystical heaven by the ladder of purgation. Fox, truer it seems to me to a higher type of mysticism, carries with him all the wealth of his racial and personal genetic endowment, and, with all his senses functioning alertly, uses them all to gain an insight closer to the full life of a divine humanity.

It is the general effect of the stimulation of his senses that one finds rather than any one sense superior in its native endowment in giving specific sense impressions. He was feeling his way out into life on all sides with equal alertness rather than being a specialist in any one sense-activity.

Fox was affected by sights and sounds, odours and feelings unnoticed by others, and in a perfectly normal way these affected his judgments. By immediate inference he learned the power of discerning situations, and so could "see through" the conditions of his day. Passing from James Nayler, he cast his eyes upon him, and a fear struck him concerning him.[1] This fear later was justified. Nayler unfortunately "ran out into imaginations" and became for a time a part of a fanatical group. Again, Fox met Cromwell riding in Hampton Court Park at the head of his life-guard. Before he came to him he "saw and felt a waft [or apparition] of death go forth against him." When he came near him "he looked like a dead man."[2] The next day Cromwell was too ill to see visitors, and died shortly afterwards.

The source of the truth in judgments such as these is not any simple and direct sensation, but is either a combined reading of complex perceptions or it is due to the summation of sensations so slight as to be independently imperceptible. But so delicate and marvellous is the human mechanism that it does record and use impressions so slight as to be totally below the level of consciousness.[3] Fox thus summed up slight impres-

---

[1] *Journal*, p. 234.   [2] Ibid., p. 325.

[3] Breuckner has proven by slightly differing pressure upon nearby points of the arm with a finely adjusted mechanical device that two weights, each so slight that taken separately they gave no sensation, together gave a distinct though diffused sensation. Continuous experimentation thus proved that two qualitatively similar stimuli, each so slight that there is no consciousness of sensation, do sum up to make a perceptible impression. A zero plus a zero do somehow make a positive quantity. (Cf. Breuckner : "Die Raumschwelle bei Simultanreizung," in *Zeitschrift für Psychologie*, vol. xxvi, 1901, p. 33.)

sions and judged people at first acquaintance with much accuracy. He could appreciate Elizabeth Hooten's power at their first meeting.[1] A remarkable woman, she soon became the first woman Quaker preacher, and travelled extensively in the ministry. Rendered more than ordinarily sensitive by his unexpressed love for Margaret Fell, Fox could read the foulness of spirit of priest Lampitt,[2] who ministered at the church at Ulverstone which the Fell family attended.

An attempt was made at the University of Iowa to find if such imperceptible differences did not sum up to affect judgments.[3] It resulted in the conclusion that there may be some correlation between the feeling of certainty and correctness of judgment. Certainty alone is not a criterion of correct specific judgments, but it seems to be of correct general judgments.

We find Fox making unhesitating general judgments with an assurance of certainty. We find him recording on page after page : " The Lord led me " ; " The Lord drew me " ; " Through the Lord's power I spoke " ; " I saw." The testimony of such students as Seashore, Pfungst, Binet and Singer, as well as Titchener,[4] Prince,[5] Jastrow,[6] and others to whose

---

[1] *Journal*, p. 79.   [2] Ibid., p. 160.
[3] Cf. Appendix I.

[4] Cf. E. B. Titchener : " While the number of sensible qualities is fixed by the differentiation of the sense-organs, the number of affective qualities is indefinitely large." (*Psychology of Feeling and Attention*, (New York, 1908), p. 128.)

[5] M. Prince : *The Unconscious* (New York, 1914), p. 12.

[6] J. Jastrow : " Sensibility makes the man. It is the hub of the wheel into which the several spokes of our capabilities and interests are set ; together they make possible the encompassing conduct and achievement, the rim upon which we travel—child, youth and man—through our uncertain and irregular journey." (*The Qualities of Men* (New York, 1910), p. 142.)

work we have not referred, lead us to see that it is the normal, alert awareness of the native faculties of a man that can enable him to read accurately the conditions of men and affairs around him. It is not any occult sense.

Mystics have agreed whenever they have attempted to describe their experience—their sense of absolute immediate guidance—that it is ineffable, beyond the power of words to tell.

"Those to whom this heavenly love is unknown," wrote Plotinus, "may get some conception of it from earthly love, and what joy it is to obtain possession of what one loves most. It is a bold thing to say, but in the vision a man neither sees, nor, if he sees, distinguishes what he sees from himself, nor fancies that there are two—the seer and the seen. Having surrendered himself to it, he is one with it, as the centres of two circles might coincide. It follows that the vision is hard to describe. For how could a man report as something different from himself what at the time of his vision he did not see as different but as one with himself?"[1]

As naturally as Jesus is reported by John to have spoken when He said, "I and My Father are one";[2] "My Father worketh and I work";[3] "I must work the works of Him";[4] "I am in My Father";[5] "He that hath seen Me hath seen the Father,"[6] George Fox could say of his own preaching, "The Lord's power was made manifest that day." Because all mystics, like Plotinus and Fox and Jesus, have thus spoken, people have been tempted to think that they have some peculiar

[1] Plotinus ; cf. C. M. Bakewell : *Source Book in Ancient Philosophy*, (New York, 1907), p. 389 ; condensed.

[2] John x. 30.   [3] Ibid., v. 17.   [4] Ibid., ix. 4.

[5] Ibid., xiv. 20.   [6] Ibid., xiv. 9.

and special approach to the Father. Therefore they
have put into their scheme of things a special spiritual
sense. But a special spiritual sense would imply the
separation of a spiritual essence or substance from the
reality of things as they are, and would make the only
approach to be this Way of the Spirit as something
separate and different from the Way of Nature through
the senses. It is as if there were certain vibration
rates to which the human mechanism responds spiritually, as the ear responds to sound vibrations, or the
eye to light vibrations ; and as if the special organic
physical mechanism for recording these spiritual waves,
having not yet been located, they have agreed to place
it as a special sense in that mysterious region of the
" Subconscious." They have contended that although
the spiritual sense may be perhaps potentially the
inheritance of all men, it is developed in very few. As
Evelyn Underhill puts it : " In normal men the spiritual
sense lies below the threshold of consciousness." [1]
From the depths of the subconscious or subliminal
personality, which looms so large in modern psychological literature, this transcendental sense must emerge
as from a prison. It is the business of the mystic
" to bring it out of its hiddenness and unify himself about it as a centre, thus putting on divine
humanity." [2]

I do not believe that such a special spiritual sense
needs to be presupposed, and it leads to an interpretation of human experience and human nature, as well
as to a theology, that is out of harmony with Fox's
experience and that of other mystics. It was Fox's

[1] E. Underhill: *Mysticism* (London, 1911), p. 63.
[2] E. Underhill: Op. cit., p. 63.

great task in life to bring men to see and to know that God speaks directly to all men, that He is the Teacher of His people Himself, and that they need no mediator to stand between them and their God to show them some secret, hidden and mysterious pathway. The type of psychic reaction which Evelyn Underhill thus describes as a sort of supernatural source for mystical experience I believe is explainable in a naturalistic manner as but a more refined type of the normal psychic procedure, which functions in the subconscious as well as in the conscious realm, entirely in accordance with the normal laws of mental behaviour.

A special spiritual sense would imply a dualism in human nature, as well as a theology of a God set apart, transcendent, touching His created world only in rare spots. Fox did away with the use of all outward sacraments. He was not satisfied with such observances, although, as Canon Illingworth says, they carry with them the " promise, not that God may be found, but that He will definitely meet us, at the time and in the place of His appointment." The mystic Fox was not less, but more, sacramental than others. He knows experimentally that God is everywhere present and ready to be found, and that, being found, it is by no special sense of his, but, as Plotinus phrased it, "there is no part of him left with which he does not touch God." [1] His God is not the transcendental God of Plotinus, however, whom he reaches out to touch with some special organ or sense. He is immanent in the world and in his own life. Fox's life, it

[1] Plotinus; cf. C. M. Bakewell: *Source Book in Ancient Philosophy* (New York, 1907), p. 390.

seems to me, is in full accordance with Locke's [1] dictum that there is nothing in the life that is not in the senses. The rich soul-life of Fox is but the refined behaviour of the special senses.   Even the mystic seems to be usually aware of the truth of this.

[1] J. Locke: *Of Human Understanding : Locke's Philosophical Works* (London, 1892), vol. i, p. 135.

IV

THE INTIMATE SENSES OF "APPRECIATION" [1]

WHILE much truth arises in Fox, as in all men, from the harvesting of the littles in the world of discrete perceptions, there is another whole world of rich experience that can be described only through introspective evidence. It is so big and bulky and vague that you cannot prove that if we are fine at all, it is here that we are fine, but there is much material that can be brought to bear evidence that it is so. It is in the world of the more intimate senses, the so-called " lower senses," that I would find another source of Fox's truth values. By no experiment can one test his sensational sensitivity, but his journalistic records show through their direct references or through their imagery that his intimate senses were insistently lively. I count them in him, as in all religious living, the higher senses.

Half a dozen sentences will often show their overtones in a single paragraph, as, for instance, this from his Journal :

" On a certain time as I *was walking* in the fields, the Lord *said to me,* ' Thy name *is written* in the Lamb's book of life which

[1] For the thought and much of the phrasing and detail of this section I am especially indebted to Dr. Starbuck. I have taken the liberty of drawing upon my notes from his class lectures and from his conference and seminar discussions.

was before the foundation of the world ' ; and as the Lord *spoke* it, I believed, and *saw* in it the new birth.   Some time after the Lord *commanded* me to *go* abroad into the world, which was like a *briery, thorny* wilderness.   When I *came in the Lord's mighty power* with the *word of life* into the world, the world *swelled,* and *made a noise* like the great *raging* waves of the sea.   Priests and professors, magistrates and people, were all *like a sea* when I *came* to *proclaim* the day of the Lord amongst them, and to *preach* repentance to them." [1]

The spatial or relational senses of vision, audition and pressure, which have been thought of as the descriptive senses, gave to Fox indeed a rich world of spatial experience, as we have already seen.   But just as wonderfully developed were his intimate senses of appreciation ; even as in the ear or eye there are specialized nerve endings, thousands and millions of them, that are carrying to the consciousness messages of pain or temperature, of taste or smell, of the well-being of the inner organs, of the strains and tensions of joints and tendons, and of all the motor accompaniments involved.

In the words of Fox we can find portrayed the brain pattern of the man very clearly.   It is as if the human mechanism were a great organ with nine or ten kinds of receptors which record its experiences.   When struck by the master hand of emotion or religious fervour, it responds so delicately that it discloses the whole range of its experiences, both individual and racial. It is as William James says : " Religious language clothes itself in such poor symbols as our life affords, and the whole organism gives over-tones of comment whenever the mind is strongly stirred to expression." [2]

[1] *Journal,* p. 102.
[2] William James: *Varieties of Religious Experience* (New York, 1902), p. 11.

" The most natural explanation . . . for individual differences in types of imagery," writes Miss Washburn, " is that they depend on individual differences in the appeal of certain kinds of stimuli to the attention. . . . ' Imagery types ' and their variations and anomalies may, I think, be most readily explained as attention types, due to innate differences in sense discrimination and to habits formed by the nature of one's environment and work." [1]

Fox's language is indeed a " sign and symbol of his mental state," and even though it be a " clumsy tool," we have abundant proof in his Journal and other writings, not only that his special senses retained unusual keenness in his maturer years, but also that his entire organism responded most delicately to temporary conditions. As do so many of the finer souls, Fox uses less direct imagery of sight and hearing and smell than of the more intimate sense complexes. It is through his imagery that we must, as Miss Washburn says, detect his " attention types," and must also realize that these arose from some innate differences in his sense discrimination.

One of the more intimate senses that we can thus detect looming large in Fox's experience, as in the lives of many mystics, is that of pressure. Plotinus speaks of that condition wherein one draws so close to God that there is " no part left with which he does not touch God." [2] To Fox the very life of God seems to impinge upon the life of man and permeate it until man knows Him to be not only near by but within.

[1] Margaret E. Washburn: *Movement and Mental Imagery* (Boston, 1916), pp. 43, 44.
[2] Plotinus; cf. Bakewell: *Source Book in Ancient Philosophy* (New York, 1907), p. 390.

Controlled by Him, Fox lives and moves and works even as if it were God Himself working.[1]

Very definite in detail are some of the overtones of his experiences. Praise from a professor was "like a thistle"[2] to him, and the world was like "a briery, thorny wilderness."[3] One feels he is walking again among the prickly gorse of his northern moors when he speaks of the "abundance of thick cloddy earth of hypocrisy and falseness"[4] and of the "brambly, briery nature which is to be burnt up with God's word and ploughed with his spiritual plough."[5]

The sense of pressure is so inextricably interwoven with other sense functions that its significance often lies in its intimate organic connections. Titchener calls inner strains which are referred outward "touch-blends." These sensations, so closely related with organic sensations and general bodily feeling-tone, are interpreted as originating in some external presence. "The Lord's power and hand carried"[6] Fox over a difficult time. "The Father of life drew"[7] him to his task. The "drawings on his spirit"[8] led him to Scotland or to Holland. But let the task be completed, and he was "set at liberty"[9] or "felt himself clear."[10] At the close of his long and tremendously busy life he could say with triumphant joy, "Now I am clear, I am fully clear."[11]

Perhaps the most vivid of all the touch-blend experiences which he records unwittingly is one of telepathic interest. It shows the closeness with which his life

---

[1] *Journal*, pp. 82, 148. [2] Ibid., p. 184.
[3] Ibid., p. 102.   [4] Ibid., p. 316.   [5] Ibid., p. 316.
[6] Ibid., p. 313.   [7] Ibid., p. 83.   [8] Ibid., pp. 298, 571.
[9] Ibid., p. 228.   [10] Ibid., p. 133. [11] Ibid., p. 578.

was knit into the life of the Society of which he had been the unintentional founder, and which had become indeed a part of his corporate life. Even as the instinct of the mother compels her to feel the pull in the upraised arms of her babe and to hear the cry to which other ears are deaf, so Fox could feel in world conditions the need of the farthermost members of his flock. It came at the time of the martyrdom of some Friends (among them a woman, Mary Dyer) on Boston Common. He writes : " When these were put to death I was in prison at Lancaster, and had a perfect sense of their sufferings as though it had been myself, and as though the halter had been put around my own neck, though we had not at that time heard of it." [1]

Closer still to the inner springs of feeling experience is the thermal sense which in Fox was at times internally felt :—he burned " with the fire of the Lord," [2] or " the Word of the Lord was like a fire " [3] in him. At other times it was objectively referred. The word which he spoke was " as a hammer and a fire " [4] amongst his auditors. Von Hügel speaks of Catharine of Genoa as also having such thermal experiences which gave a feeling of immediacy and worth to her mystical union. He speaks of " that feeling of mostly interior, but later on also of exterior, warmth, indeed often of intense heat and burning, which comes to her ; the first as though sunshine were bathing her within and without, the second as though a great fire were enveloping her, and sometimes as though a living flame were piercing her within." [5]

[1] *Journal,* p. 373. [2] Ibid., p. 133.
[3] Ibid., p. 132. [4] Ibid., p. 167.
[5] Von Hügel: *St. Catharine of Genoa* (London, 1909), vol. i, p. 178.

At times Fox's whole feeling tone was written in terms of cold instead of heat. At the close of his life he told some Friends that he " had felt the cold strike at his heart " [1] as he came out of the London meeting where he had preached his last long and powerful sermon. Two days later he died.

In Fox one feels sure that the sense of smell does share in the task of forming his wisdom. The various scents in nature no doubt are a part of the God-experience for those whose early years are spent in the open country as were Fox's. Significant biologically in previous stages of evolution, we find the sense of smell still playing a large part symbolically in the life of the Church, as, for instance, in the use of incense and of flowers. In Fox this sense remained so strong that he not only smelled the corruptions of Ireland, [2] but he told the Catholic governor of the county in whose smoky jail he was imprisoned that it was his purgatory in which he was kept.[3] Perhaps part of the rebellion of his spirit against the churches as " dreadful places " [4] was due to the oppression that came from the heavy atmosphere of churches filled with incense and with windows closed to one whose nostrils had been nurtured for many years with the fresher scents of the damp earth and the grass and flowers. It is the " living, refreshing presence of the Lord " [5] of which he speaks as meaningful to him.

The Master's " hunger and thirst after righteousness " found its verification in his own " thirst after the Lord," [6] supplemented by his thirst for his fellow-men. He knew that his " words should be few and savoury

---

[1] *Journal*, p. 578.   [2] Ibid., p. 464.   [3] Ibid., p. 440.
[4] Ibid., p. 76.   [5] Ibid., p. 573.   [6] Ibid., p. 84.

and seasoned with grace," [1] in order that those whose hearts were touched might for themselves " taste and see that the Lord is good."

More humorous, however, is the imagery which led him to evaluate persons in gustatory terms. One covetous priest " got a parsonage and choked himself with it." [2] A very " malicious bitter officer " of the army, railing against " the Truth," was so " full of evil that he could not speak, but blubbered and stuttered." [3]

Fox was so conscious of being filled with the Lord's power that he never seems to feel any emptiness in himself, though he recognizes the hollowness of others. A certain priest was " like an empty, hollow cask." [4] He met a people with " empty, high notions." [5]

Where the Psalmist finds his heart the organ whereby he can best describe his highest feelings, Fox speaks more indefinitely of his spirit or soul or life. When, however, one of his greatest times of deliverance came to him after months of agonizing struggle to find help in his search for God, he exclaimed, " My heart did leap for joy." [6] In the relationship with his wife, in which there seems to be so little of sentimental passion and so much of deep understanding, love and spiritual companionship, however, he constantly addresses her as " Dear heart, to whom is my love." [7]

Pleasure-pain experiences as recorded by him were judged as evidences of God's immediate dealings with him. They were influencing factors in his sense of the worth of life. " Though my exercises and troubles

[1] *Journal*, p. 66 (cf. p. 523).   [2] Ibid., p. 119.
[3] Ibid., p. 255.   [4] Ibid., p. 72.   [5] Ibid., p. 78.
[6] Ibid., p. 82.   [7] Ibid., p. 560.

were very great, yet they were not so continual but that I had some intermissions, and I was sometimes brought into such a heavenly joy that I had thought I had been in Abraham's bosom. As I cannot declare the misery I was in, it was so great and heavy upon me, so neither can I set forth the mercies of God unto me in all my misery." [1]

Visceral sensations cannot be so clearly teased out into objective clarity, but by indirect means we can detect them. Cannon has told a full, clear story of the bodily changes that come as the result of emotional excitation.[2] There are several markedly pathological experiences in Fox's life which show how readily his circulatory system responded to such stimulation. They also show how delicately hung this man of strong body was between health and debility.

One of the priests to whom he went for counsel and inspiration gave him, instead of spiritual leadership, some physic, and attempted to let blood in accordance with the medical custom of those days.[3] So strong was Fox's aversion to this treatment that his delicate circulatory system responded with such vigour that his blood was driven back from the periphery of his body, and they could " get not one drop of blood either in arms or head," his " body being as it were dried up with sorrows, grief and troubles." [4] At times he gave further evidence of a richly flowing circulation, though probably with thin arterial walls, for he " bled exceedingly " when an angry priest struck him in the face with a Bible before the altar.[5]

[1] *Journal*, p. 80.
[2] W. B. Cannon: *Bodily Changes in Pain, Hunger, Fear and Rage* (New York, 1915), pp. 9, 12, 36, 44, 52–59, 62–63, 66, 73, 108, etc.
[3] *Journal*, p. 73.   [4] Ibid., p. 73.   [5] Ibid., p. 146.

These sudden responsive changes were very effective verdicts as to the evaluation placed upon events in his life. In early manhood, "one Brown" had "great prophecies" upon his death-bed of Fox, and spoke of what he "should be made instrumental by the Lord to bring forth."[1] Upon his burial, Fox fell into a trance-like state for about fourteen days, when he "was much altered in countenance and person, as if his body had been new moulded or changed."[1]

Very quick and sudden were these physical responses. He was "struck even blind" when he found the justices to whom he wished to speak gone to hold court in another town, and he did not recover his sight till he was on his way to find them.[2]

His eyes often glowed with the inner stimulation that comes from a virile blood supply and perhaps also from active glandular secretions. The power of them thus was undoubtedly a considerable element in his influence over others. A deacon, angry at his preaching, responded to Fox's sharp rebuke, "Do not pierce me so with thy eyes ; keep thy eyes off me."[3] He quieted a crowd at Lancaster by "looking earnestly upon them so that they cried, ' Look at his eyes ! ' "[4] In Holland the famous Mennonite, Galenus Abrahams, bade Fox keep his eyes off him, for they pierced him.[5]

At times his whole person responded with this radiance. Theological students at Cambridge, knowing him to be "against the trade of preaching, which they were there as apprentices to learn," gathered to attack

---

[1] *Journal,* p. 87.   [2] Ibid., p. 95.   [3] Ibid., p. 187.
[4] Ibid., p. 344.   [5] Ibid., p. 556.

5

him, but let him pass unharmed. "O," said they, "hee shines, hee glisters." [1]

Again, he had spoken as a stranger to a congregation at Beverley after the regular sermon. A woman present reported a day or so later that "an angel or spirit had come to the church and spoken the wonderful things of God, to the astonishment of all who were there,—they did not know whence it came nor whither it went ; but it astonished all." [2]

William Penn said of him, "The most awful, living, reverent frame I ever felt or beheld, I must say was his in prayer." [3] Thus did his life bear witness to the part which his bodily reactions as well as his keen senses played in adding a sense of immediacy and worth to his mystical reading of events.

Miss Washburn emphasizes repeatedly that there can be no sensation, no consciousness without motor response to stimulation, and that degrees of consciousness correspond to the ratio between the innervation of and the inhibition in the motor mechanism. [4] Higher mentality, then, comes out of motor response which is strongly initiated and not "halted" (Angell) by such wealth of inhibition that "hot-spots" (Starbuck) are caused in association activity. Such hot-spots, though due to inhibition in the more direct routes of motor response, result in the immediate though more indirect discharge which characterizes very rapid thinking. There is comparatively little conscious accompaniment and associative activity in such thinking. Such was

[1] *The Journal of George Fox* (Cambridge edition, 1911), p. 190.
[2] *Journal*, p. 136.
[3] *Journal*, Preface by W. Penn, p. 54.
[4] M. F. Washburn: *Movement and Mental Imagery* (Boston, 1916), pp. 17 ff., 30 ff.

the condition of much of Fox's mental life ; for him to think or to feel was to act. So immediate was the kinæsthetic response that he was essentially what may best be described as " motor-minded." Motor strains played an exceedingly large part in the direct guidance which controlled Fox's life. In the flux of the God-life within him he felt repeatedly a moving toward the accomplishment of its purposes. He felt the " power and the Spirit of God move " in him ; " the Lord led " him. But these were rarely merely subjective experiences. Almost invariably they were objectively referred and were dynamic forces that led to almost reflex action. The tension of constraint or compulsion turned the energy into some objective channel. He was constrained to go in sympathy to the sick. " The Lord led him," [1] " drew him," [2] " brought him over " [3] to some task. He must reprimand a priest for his " foul spirit " ; [4] must pray in such power that " the house seemed to be shaken " ; [5] " must part two desperate fellows fighting furiously " ; [6] must write to those in authority in the State or Church, to Oliver Cromwell or to the Pope. Yet so absolutely in all this he felt the immediate presence and guidance of the Lord that he speaks interchangeably, " The Lord led me to speak," or " The Lord spoke." [7] Fox is conscious that the very dynamistic and vitalistic energy which achieves his acts is indeed this God-life within himself. There is nothing strange in this divine reference for Fox. It is as it should be. With child-like belief, seconded by his own experiential evidence,

[1] *Journal,* p. 83.   [2] Ibid. p. 83.   [3] Ibid., p. 88.
[4] Ibid., p. 160.   [5] Ibid., p. 90.   [6] Ibid., p. 233.
[7] Ibid., *passim.*

he has taken literally the words, "It is God which worketh in you to will and to do of His good pleasure." [1]

When one records that he travelled into every county in England and Wales, into Scotland and through Ireland, to Barbadoes, a thousand miles and back through the wilderness of the American colonies, to Holland and Germany, one gets only a slight conception of the incessant activity and energy of the man. In these days of swift locomotion it does not seem at all unusual to find a man appearing successively day by day in the small towns of the countryside miles apart. But when one finds him walking across fields some eight or twelve miles on an errand of slight importance because of a mere inner tension, and when one remembers that roads in those days were of dubious excellence and safety, and that a horse was the one other means of travel, it assumes a somewhat different aspect. In addition to his preaching, his mind was as actively engaged as his body. He read, he studied, he wrote, he dictated, even as he travelled, epistles, messages and treatises.

In dealing with his kinæsthetic sense experiences, I have so far treated them as if they were direct experiences arising out of the conditions of the time. Such a consideration, however, is not adequate. The question arises whether or not these experiences were not many of them at least of the nature of hallucinations or of pure mental imagery, as were no doubt many of his visual and auditory experiences.

Miss Washburn is convinced that there can be no genuine motor or kinæsthetic images, because every

[1] Philippians ii. 13.

attempt to think of a movement results in the actual making of the movement in a tentative way. Thus the result is a kinæsthetic sensation instead of a kinæsthetic image. But while I find few psychologists, if any, who would quarrel with Miss Washburn when she says,

" In every centrally excited or image process there would be two components, one kinæsthetic and one of the modality to which the image is referred," [1]

one does find even so good a psychologist as Angell expressing his convictions thus :

" There seems to be no reason in the nature of the case why we may not have kinæsthetic images in a form definitely distinguishable from the kinæsthetic sensations to which they may lead ; and many observers insist that their introspection verifies the reality of these images." [2]

I must confess that personally I belong to that latter class of observers for whom a kinæsthetic image is as real and separate an experience from the motor accompaniment of it as is a visual image. Miss Washburn continues :

" These factors (the two component parts of the image process) need not, however, be for consciousness in any way distinct, since distinctness for consciousness involves the excitation of two different motor responses, and the kinæsthetic and non-kinæsthetic components of the process need not give rise to different motor responses." [3]

[1] M. F. Washburn : *Movement and Mental Imagery* (Boston, 1916), p. 43.
[2] J. R. Angell : *Psychology* (New York, 1904), p. 200.
[3] M. F. Washburn : loc. cit., p. 43.

Her further analysis has not convinced me that the simultaneous excitation of two different motor responses, both of the kinæsthetic modality, is impossible, and that one of these may be peripherally excited and one cortically ; that is, that one may be sensational and one of the nature of the image. She quotes Stricker as one who has

"... furnished psychology with a classic example of a person whose kinæsthetic processes are habitually clear in his consciousness ; who is in the habit of attending to them and can readily detect them by introspection. ... He says, 'When I imagine that a yellow object becomes blue, I can imagine the yellow and the blue side by side without thinking of a muscle. But when I think of the yellow as giving place to the blue I must have recourse to muscle feelings : the thing is done with the aid either of the eye muscles or the muscles of the back of the neck.' Now the possibility occurred to Stricker that these 'muscle feelings' which were so noticeable a part of his experience in general were the results of actual motor contraction, and that there is no such thing as a remembered or centrally excited kinæsthetic sensation.' " [1]

My own introspection leads me to differ radically from Stricker. I cannot imagine two colours side by side, any more than I can perceive them without feeling my eye muscles swing constantly back and forth from one to the other. So I would conclude that if there be imagery at all, a kinæsthetic image is as true a psychic experience as a visual or auditory one, but each has an ever-present motor accompaniment. When such motor accompaniment gets so vigorous that it gets an objective reference, it takes the form of a definite hallucination.

[1] M. F. Washburn : *Movement and Mental Imagery* (Boston, 1916), p. 50; quoting Stricker : *Studien uber die Bewegungsvorstellungen* (Wein, 1882), p. 18.

This long digression has been for the purpose of justifying the position that I take in regard to Fox. I believe that his kinæsthetic imagery of motor strains was thus objectified until he actually felt them as real. He felt that it was actually the "hand of the Lord" that led and drew him. Such wealth of kinæsthetic imagery as is evident in the large part played in his life by this type of "guidance" lends an immediacy to his religious experience that has much to do with creating in him the mystical temperament. At Reading in 1658 he "was under great exercises and sufferings, and in great travail of spirit for about ten weeks," [1] because he was disturbed over political affairs. At that time he had "a sight and sense of the King's return." [2] Here, it seems to me, the kinæsthetic motor process caused the cortical excitation of the visual centre calling forth such a visual image with its accompanying kinæsthetic feeling which he interprets as a sense of prophetic revelation.

Considering this kinæsthetic accompaniment which is found to be present in all sensory experience, every experience is found to be no simple isolated fact, but to involve a complex of sense elements and "feelings." Many of these are as yet irreducible to any definite combination of special sense experiences, and we have to leave them unanalysed as "lower sense complexes."

There is a biological reason for the immediacy that arises out of these more intimate senses. They are so old racially that they are most fundamentally related to the welfare of the organism. It is not alone man's conscious intellection that has become refined through all the generations of evolution, but these "trailing

_____
[1] *Journal*, p. 363.   [2] Ibid., p. 363.

clouds of glory " have moulded him effectively as well. Dr. Starbuck says :

" There has been a progressive refinement of the mechanism of affection, which has kept pace with that of cognition. The latter has been refined through the agency of the cerebrum and the logical functions. The former has developed through the instrumentality of the sympathetic nervous system and its connections with the special senses, the glands, intestines, and the circulatory system, as the mechanism for the immediate evaluation of higher experiences as wholesome or unwholesome, good or bad, right or wrong." [1]

Hegel says : " Beauty is merely the spiritual making itself known sensuously." Mr. Mudge, a former student of Dr. Starbuck, has summed it up as follows :

" The highest values we have, æsthetic, ethical and religious, find their fundamental setting in and through the lower senses and the feelings related to them. . . . The essential values are usually modest. Like the Kingdom of Heaven, they do not come with observation." [2]

Fox never analysed how his values came. To his religious mind these values, which have come so immediately, with no insistence as to their means of approach, can have but one source. It is the Lord who speaks, and from whom wisdom comes as well as knowledge. The way of the intimate senses for the analytic psychologist was for the mystic the Way of the Spirit.

[1] E. D. Starbuck : " Intuitionalism," in Hastings' *Encyclopædia of Religion and Ethics*, vol. vii. (1915), p. 400.
[2] E. L. Mudge : *The Lower-Sense Complexes in the God Experience* (University of Iowa Doctorate Thesis), Iowa City, 1916.

V

" OPENINGS "

ONE of the most characteristic mystical experiences of Fox was that for which he uses the expression " opened." These openings seem to him to be direct revelations that burst into his consciousness. He attributed them to a divine source: " The Lord opened to me." [1] Often he uses the word to describe the gaining of some truth which he might easily have gained from the Scriptures or from the religious leaders of his day. " My desire after the Lord grew stronger, and zeal in the pure knowledge of God, and of Christ alone, without the help of any man, book, or writing. For though I read the Scriptures that spoke of Christ and of God, yet I knew Him not, but by revelation as He who hath the key did open, and as the Father of Life drew me to His Son by His Spirit." [2]

The truth involved was no longer a mere statement of fact. It was a *living principle in his life*. I believe that these openings are a betrayal of the working of his mind in accord with normal mental procedure. This does not mean that the experience was less divine than Fox assumed, or that it was less a revelation of truth. It only means that we are trying to find out how the procedure may be explained.

[1] *Journal*, p. 74.   [2] Ibid., p. 82.

Driven by a desire for peace of mind, his period of storm and stress was one of extreme tension. He was a seeker for the life of the spirit. The jovial and superficial social life of his community repelled him. He sought out the more serious-minded people in nearby and even distant towns. Still he found no relief. Out of this condition of affairs there arose a clear and definite answer to his need in a way that seemed to him a direct revelation from the Lord,—indeed, the very voice of the Lord speaking to him. He described the experience thus :

"But as I had forsaken the priests, so I left the separate preachers also, and those esteemed the most experienced people ; for I saw there was none among them all that could speak to my condition. When all my hopes in them and in all men were gone, so that I had nothing outwardly to help me, nor could I tell what to do, then, oh, then, I heard a voice which said, ' There is one, even Christ Jesus, that can speak to thy condition ' ; and when I heard it my heart did leap for joy. [1]

"Then the Lord let me see why there was none upon the earth that could speak to my condition, namely, that I might give Him all the glory. For all are concluded under sin, and shut up in unbelief, as I had been ; that Jesus Christ might have the preeminence, who enlightens, and gives grace, and faith and power." [1]

These openings were not unique with Fox. Loyola and others had similar experiences. But they were so frequent in Fox, especially in his early manhood, that an understanding of them is essential to an understanding of Fox.

The first came to him during the night, after he had fled from his drinking companions at a fair :

"Thou seest how young people go together into vanity, and

[1] *Journal*, p. 82.

old people into the earth ; thou must forsake all, young and old,
keep out of all, and be as a stranger unto all." [1]

Other such auditory openings were that

". . . to be bred at Oxford or Cambridge was not enough
to make a man fit to be a minister of Christ " ; [2]

and the most dynamic one of his life :

" There is one, even Christ Jesus, that can speak to thy
condition." [3]

Others seemed to be not so definitely vocalized,
though formulated in words. Walking through the
country near Coventry, he was meditating on the
saying that " all Christians are believers, both
Protestants and Papists." The Lord then opened
to him that

" If all are believers, then they were all born of God, and
passed from death to life ; and that none were true believers but
such ; and though others said they were believers, yet they were
not." [4]

At another time it was opened in him that

" God, who made the world, did not dwell in temples made
with hands,"

but that

" His people were His temples, and He dwelt in them." [5]

[1] *Journal,* p. 68.　　[2] Ibid., p. 75.　　[3] Ibid., p. 82.
[4] Ibid., p. 74.　　[5] Ibid., p. 76.

He says of these openings :

"When I had openings they answered one another and answered the Scriptures, for I had great openings of the Scriptures." [1]

Others are described in visual rather than auditory terms. These were most often of a general illumination, such as the " ocean of light that flowed over the ocean of darkness," [2] or the " innumerable sparkles of fire " [3] indicative of the ripe souls in Scotland. Occasionally they took definitely imaged form, as in the " flaming sword " that stretched southward before the warring of Holland and the London fire, [4] or in the " people in white raiment by a river side " [5] in a valley which he later recognized as the Swarthmore country where his great following of the " First Publishers of Truth " arose.

There are three main points of approach for an understanding of such experiences. Fox's openings give evidence especially (1) that his senses were functioning at a maximum degree of efficiency. They also prove that (2) imperceptible differences were not only harvested and summed up to affect his general judgments generally, but that they were conserved and transformed through the absolutely normal exercise of mental procedure. (3) The Freudian Wish formulated the final result.

Wherever there is life-action there is to be found a high degree of potential energy that seeks to be set free. The tension becomes so great that the results enter consciousness in something like a burst. Fox's

---

[1] *Journal*, p. 78.   [2] Ibid., p. 87.   [3] Ibid., p. 316.
[4] Ibid., p. 97.   [5] Ibid., p. 150.

openings were of such an explosive character bursting
forth from his inner experience. They were generally
formulated in either visual or auditory imagery. We
label experience as visual or auditory, but to do so is
a relatively false distinction. As Mudge says, vision
is merely " the key that unlocks a roomful of things
more valuable than keys." As in that incident of his
life in which Fox " saw the new birth," the meaningful
element is not visual. In visual experiences that are
not the direct retinal response to external stimuli (as,
for instance, the visions that come to many an artist
in the realm of art or science or religion) the function
of vision is to objectify and focalize the more significant
fundamental and persistent lower sense elements in
consciousness. Fox saw " a waft of death " go over
Cromwell [1] because his own inner mechanism had
responded to the sagging nerves, the weakened vitality
of the Protector as he sat upon his horse in Hyde Park.
He saw the " glittering drawn sword stretched southward " [2] because his inmost being had responded to
the atmosphere of war and epidemics that hung over
the land. He " had seen from the Lord a considerable
time before that he should take Margaret Fell to be
his wife," for he had felt, even as she did when he spoke
to her of it, that inner rapture which he speaks of as
" the answer of Life from God thereunto." [3] This
inner, more intimate experience is objectified, exter-
nalized, made concrete by the imagery of vision, which
in life as in art is often but the " handmaid of deeper
meanings which it symbolizes " [4]—that complex mass

[1] *Journal,* p. 325.   [2] Ibid., p. 434.   [3] Ibid., p. 468.
[4] Mudge : *Sense-Feeling Complexes Conditioning the God Experience*
(Iowa City, 1916).

of bodily sensations which give it its warmth and vital affective aspects.

Biologically, audition is most closely related to quick action. The stag pauses with head and foot upraised at the slightest sound, and then bounds away. The rabbit telegraphs with quick taps on the earth's crust its signal to its fellows. The mother hen clucks and the chicks flock about her for their choicest food. The bluebird sings out his clear love-call, and his mate, a-quiver throughout her entire organism, awaits in intense expectation for his coming, or with a flash of colour darts to his side. Sight gives time for comparison and reasoning, but audition demands a more immediate organic response.

The mystic's inner experience is normally correlated with sound, and finds objectification and clarification in the formulated imaged sound of the voice of the Lord as did Fox in many of his openings. He found in such experiences dynamic suggestions that drove him forth into no less active a life than that of his youth. But its activities were centred about a particular task, and his life became purposeful and efficient.

While the higher senses objectify and externalize experiences, making them discrete and dynamic, it is the more intimate inner senses that add warmth and intimacy to even the higher sense complexes. It is they which internalize experiences and evaluate them, and apprehend meanings and relationships. Heraclitus said, " Eyes and ears are poor witnesses to those who have barbarian souls." [1] Religion is like art in that it bears in its expression the evidence of the constant play and interplay that these senses have exercised

[1] Heraclitus: Fragment No. 107 (Diels' numbering).

in the formation of the consciousness and judgment as well as in the more intuitive responses. " Higher value " is the modern phrase with which we describe the immediate inner life that finds its objectification in the sense of worth and well-being. This sense of worth and well-being in Fox did not remain a comfortable and diffuse feeling. It definitely took form in the openings and made his life concrete and practical. There is religious defeat as well as success in the use of the realm of the intimate senses. A false mysticism has led many a person of naturally strong religious bent to believe that the end of life is the individual enjoyment of such exaltation as comes at the periods of illumination. It has resulted in such subjective anomalies as are to be found among the soma-drinkers or the Holy Rollers or pathological mystics. Then the value is lost. That person has sold his soul to a false god. As the envisioned presence in Longfellow's Legend Beautiful puts it, " Hadst thou stayed I must have fled." The higher things always come at high cost.

Fox somehow found the middle way. He found his own inner integration only to win thereby his deliverance into a world of worth through subjective vision turned into objective service. Like the monk in his cell, he learned through the communion in his heart that inner feel of content and relationship that issued forth into life, and like that monk he had to go forth to the service of mankind. He never tells how the sense of worth comes to him, but we can somewhat analyse it and find the elements drawn from the intimate experiences which sum up into those immediate evaluations by which he apprehends the meanings and relationships in the events of his life. When he heard the " voice of the Lord " saying, " My love was always to thee and thou art in My love," [1] it was his inner ear that heard and his whole inner self that responded, " ravished with the sense of the love of God "; [2] and the experience reacted upon him by a great " strengthening of his inner man." [3]   Such inner and immediate evaluation determined his attitude to folks and things.

Sight and hearing are mediating functions, but they do not evaluate even those inner experiences which are objectified in a voice or a vision.   When Fox had a vision of " an ocean of darkness and death and an infinite ocean of light and love, which flowed over the ocean of darkness," it was with immediate interpretation and a feeling of evaluation that he saw in it the infinite love of God. [4]

So Fox, having it opened in him " that God who made the world did not dwell in temples made with hands," responded with an immediate valuation :

" This at first seemed a strange word, because both priests and people used to call their temples or churches—dreadful places—holy ground and the temples of God.   But the Lord showed me clearly that He did not dwell in these temples which men had commanded to be set up, but in people's hearts. . . . His people were His temples, and He dwelt in them." [5]

The back-lash from an experience becomes a stimulus, and having formulated such an opening, it rebounded to make Fox feel that his mission in life was to bring all men off from their false teachers to their one true Teacher in their own hearts.

[1] *Journal*, p. 116.   [2] Ibid., p. 116.   [3] Ibid., p. 116.
[4] Ibid., p. 87.   [5] Ibid., p. 76.

Fox's sudden revelations or openings are not the direct outcome of the activity of the intimate senses. They are the sudden burstings forth after prolonged periods of subconscious ripening in what Jastrow calls the " underground workshop of thought." William James says :

" The subliminal region, whatever else it may be, is at any rate a place now admitted by psychologists to exist for the accumulation of sensible experiences (whether attentively or inattentively registered) and for their elaboration according to ordinary psychological laws, into results that end by attaining such a ' tension ' that they may at times enter consciousness with something like a burst." [1]

Fox felt rightly that there was nothing unique in these experiences of his. They were the normal and rightful experience of all men of his day, even as prophetic spirits of Biblical days. Even as directly as to the apostles of old, the Lord speaks to His people Himself.

Modern psychology supports Fox in his belief in the normality of such inner development as found expression in these openings. That which James called " unconscious incubation," Morton Prince calls " conservation." He writes :

" A large mass of observations demonstrate that there are an enormous number of experiences belonging to both normal and abnormal mental life, which we are unable to voluntarily recall during any period of our lives, no matter how hard we try, or what aids to memory we employ. For these experiences there is lifelong amnesia. Nevertheless it is easy to demonstrate that, though the personal consciousness of everyday life

[1] William James : *Varieties of Religious Experience* (London, 1911), p. 236.

cannot recall them, they are not lost, properly speaking, but conserved." [1]

Under certain conditions of hypnosis, abstraction, dreaming and pathological states, " we can prove conservation when voluntary memory for experience is absolutely lost." [1]

Long-delayed responses in Fox's experience are evidence of this conservation. Events, people, ideas which had apparently been left behind as settled, kept pulling on his being. His mind kept mulling over problems long after they had been discarded. Only after he failed to find help from the many priests he sought out, it was opened to him that to be bred at Oxford or Cambridge was not enough to fit a man to be a minister of God. The pull of his family relationships kept working upon him in all the wanderings of his early stress period, but it was only after several months that he had " a regard upon his mind to his parents and relations lest he should grieve them." [2] In his pathological experience at Lichfield, was it not

---

[1] " Thus B. C. A., who suffers from an intense fear or phobia of cats, particularly white cats, can recall no experience in her life which could have given rise to it. Yet when automatic writing is resorted to, the hand writes a detailed account of a fright into which she was thrown when she was only five or six years of age by a white kitten which had a fit while she was playing with it. The writing also describes in minute details the furnishings of the room where the episode occurred, the pattern of the carpet, the decorative design of the window shade, the furniture, etc. . . . As to the accuracy of the ' automatic ' account and the possibility of fabrication, the description of the room has been corroborated by the independent and written statement of an older member of the family. It was not possible to confirm the incident of the kitten, as there were no witnesses . . . but I have never known a fabricated statement to be made in this subject's automatic script, and I have obtained from her a large number of statements of different kinds in the course of several years' observations " (Morton Prince : *The Unconscious* (New York, 1914), p. 12.)   [2] *Journal*, p. 70.

the lingering memories of his own boyhood life with sheep in the fields that caused him to stop and have some intercourse with the shepherds ? Was it not his boyhood habit of going into the fields barefoot that now made him feel the impulse (which he attributes to the " command of the Lord ") to take off his shoes and leave them with the shepherds as he went on, barefoot, into the town ?[1]

Kaplan writes :

" The hopes and aspirations, the regrets and fears, the doubts, the self-communings and wrestlings with self, the wishes, the loves, the hates, all that we are not willing to give out to the world, and all that we would forget and would strive not to admit to ourselves—all this belongs to our inner life, and is subject to the same law of conservation." [2]

Such conserved experiences are capable of undergoing elaborate remoulding and afterwards appearing in consciousness so thoroughly transformed as not to be superficially recognizable. Baldwin shows that the imagination plays a large creative part in the growth of such reality.[3]

Fox's life records rich evidence of such transformation. His early training was in an earnest religious home. The Bible was his constant companion. Dr Hodgkin suggests that probably the motto of the Purefoy family encrusted in the little church of the village of his boyhood, " Pure foy me joye," may have entered into the inmost woof of his boyish memories.[4]

[1] *Journal*, p. 132.
[2] Kaplan : *The Psychology of Prophecy*. J. H. Kaplan, Philadelphia, 1908.
[3] James Mark Baldwin : *A Genetic Theory o Reality* (New York, 1915), p. 141.
[4] Thomas Hodgkin : *George Fox* (London, 1897), p. 11.

He was urged to become a priest by many of his friends. Seeking aid for his troubled state of mind during his days of storm and stress, he turned constantly to the representatives of the Christian Church. So it is not strange that when the " call " came to him it should be to the labours of a " preacher of righteousness." [1] Nor is it strange that his conviction should head up in the form of Jesus Christ as the one alone who could speak to his condition.[2]

Freud [3] has made many studies of the inhibition of wishes or desires whereby he has proven to his own satisfaction that any such strong feeling, whether expressed or unexpressed, which does not find fulfilment at the time is sublimated or repressed. In the inmost centre of a man's being it is harvested, and somewhere, somehow makes itself known. It may be that a dream gives forth such a " Freudian wish " into the light of consciousness. It may be that the wish thus given forth had never been consciously entertained. Or it may be in some other form than that of a dream that it comes forth into the open. But one fact remains apparently true—that no such longing of the heart is ever lost. Fox denounced those who relied upon their dreams for evidence of wisdom, so he tells us nothing of his own dreams. But his openings are almost as productive of evidence of that which was occupying his mind and heart.

Fox found himself out of sympathy with his surroundings. He was disgusted with the frivolous ways of his elders and of youthful companions. People

---

[1] *Journal*, p. 366.   [2] Ibid., p. 82.
[3] S. Freud : *The Interpretation of Dreams* (London, 1916), pp. 136, 199, 440. Trans. by A. A. Brill. (George Allen & Unwin, Ltd.)

laughed at his peculiarities from the time that he was a boy. With his family and friends he found himself not in tune. He could not follow the lines of activity they suggested for him. They advised that he join the army, that he prepare for the priesthood, that he marry and settle down. None of these suggestions met his needs. He was " but a lad and must get wisdom." [1] He refused to go into the " trade of preaching." [2] Religiously inclined, he turned not to the schools, but to individuals, for help. He craved companionship, but all those to whom he went failed to give him that for which his soul longed. He gained a little from this one and a little from that. But as he did so his need became more insistent and consequently his longing more intense. The wish became father to the thought. The hiatus between his attainments and the object of his longing was bridged by the inrush of the opening, and his life became unified thereby. The great longing for deliverance from his troubles and anguish of mind had sunk so deep into his subliminal self that it aided in concentrating the activity of subconscious incubation into heading up into that form which could most fully satisfy all the needs of his life.

The chart of the " Evolution of an Opening " is an attempt to present in visual form the rôle of such an experience in the life of Fox. I have selected that one, already frequently referred to, which was most outstanding in its influence toward the unification of his inner nature. He had been born into a social atmosphere of religious interest and within a home of strict spiritual training under the guidance of parents rich in zeal for upright living. There he developed

[1] *Journal*, p. 70.　　　　　[2] Ibid., p. 228.

THE EVOLUTION OF AN OPENING

"There is one, even Christ Jesus, who can speak to thy condition."

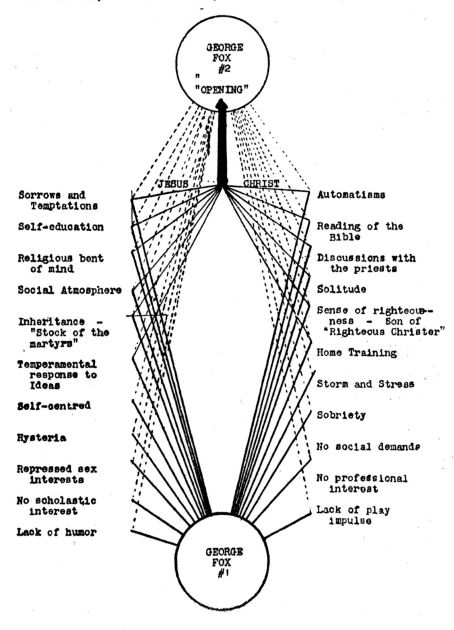

GEORGE
FOX
#2

"OPENING"

JESUS   CHRIST

Sorrows and
  Temptations

Self-education

Religious bent
  of mind

Social Atmosphere

Inheritance —
  "Stock of the
  martyrs"

Temperamental
  response to
  Ideas

Self-centred

Hysteria

Repressed sex
  interests

No scholastic
  interest

Lack of humor

Automatisms

Reading of the
  Bible

Discussions with
  the priests

Solitude

Sense of righteou-
  ness - Son of
  "Righteous Christer"

Home Training

Storm and Stress

Sobriety

No social demands

No professional
  interest

Lack of play
  impulse

GEORGE
FOX
#1

an inclination to sobriety that repressed whatever native impulse toward play or humour may have been his early endowment. Instincts cannot be destroyed. If repressed, there follows a period of instability through which the instinct is transformed and refined and conserved in some more exalted form. With neither professional nor scholastic interest to concentrate his attention, he turned away from all conventional demands. Love did not enter his life to unify it till later than the average age of such experience. When it did it was under circumstances that demanded the repression of sexual interests. His psychical nature was very delicately poised between hysteria and sanity. The Fox of this period of storm and stress (Fox 1 in the chart) was reaching out in all directions, undergoing sorrow and temptation, yet without having found any dominating force to unify his life. His energies were scattered. He apparently dissipated his power in useless discussions with priests, in self-centred reactions to all social suggestions, in desultory reading rather than in systematic study. The black lines of the figure are an attempt to suggest this scattering of his talents.

Some of these, however, found themselves drawn together by a common purpose. His sorrows and temptations drove him to seek some power beyond his own for help. His religious bent of mind turned him for such help to the religious leaders of his day. They seemed to give him no aid, but in truth his discussions with them clarified his own convictions. His inherited tendencies toward puritanic righteousness found time for fruition in his hours of meditative solitude. But most of all was it his familiarity with the Bible that led the bursting forth from the tension of subliminal transformation to formulate itself in the ideal of Christ Jesus, who alone could answer his personal and social needs. The lines focusing on the arrow therefore show how these experiences of family inheritance and the mystical atmosphere of his day found themselves focalized in a hot-spot built upon the ideal drawn out of his religious discussions, study and reading of the Bible. The prevalent Jesus Christ concept in Calvinistic England remained the ideal for Fox. It therefore gave form to his developing convictions. All the forces of his life headed into this thought, and it became the moving centre of the opening.

Automatisms were not new to his experience. It is no wonder, therefore, that the tension of this subliminal incubation should end by liberating an uprush centring in the ideal of Jesus Christ, which burst, clear and definite in outline, into the consciousness of Fox as the auditory opening : " There is one, even Christ Jesus, that can speak to thy condition." Into his enlarged and warmer personality (Fox 2) the opening (marked by the heavy arrow head) had rushed, not as separated from its genetic foundations, but, as it were, drawing with it the warmer and finer conservation of all the traits which the more crude Fox had possessed. In the chart these are represented by the dotted lines, which centre back into the more mature Fox.

When he heard the voice his " heart did leap with joy."[1] Such a voice makes an immediate appeal, and there is a focusing of energies for immediate expenditure in motor response. If it were only an auditory response that was involved, the still, small voice would never be noticed. But the heart tension, the quickened

[1] *Journal*, p. 82.

respiration, the trembling limbs, are all meaningful elements that demand expression in some action, and the stored energy finds kinæsthetic outpouring. Jesus said, " The Father worketh hitherto, and I work." So Fox added to his story of the joy in the " voice of the Lord " : " Thus when God doth work, who shall hinder it ? and *this I knew experimentally.*" [1]

[1] *Journal,* p. 82.

VI

"SPEAKING TO CONDITIONS"

AFTER the first few years of his public career Fox seldom speaks of openings, though there is evidence that such bursts of illumination continued. A much more persistent expression with him was the " discerning of spirits." If the experience is objectively referred, it is described as " speaking to conditions." When, however, it remains a subjective experience, he calls it the Guidance of the Lord or of the Spirit.

Repeatedly does Fox testify to the faculty with which he felt that he had been endowed. He felt it not alone in the meeting—though there also—but in direct individual personal contacts. He says :

" The Lord had given me a spirit of discerning, by which I many times saw the states and conditions of people, and could try their spirits. For not long before, as I was going to a meeting, I saw some women in a field, and I discerned an evil spirit in them ; and I was moved to go out of my way into the field to them, and declare unto them their conditions. At another time there came one into Swarthmore Hall in the meeting time, and I was moved to speak sharply to her, and told her she was under the power of an evil spirit ; and the people said afterwards she was generally accounted so. There came also at another time another woman, and stood at a distance from me, and I cast mine eye upon her, and said, ' Thou hast been an harlot ' ; for I perfectly saw the condition and life of the woman. The woman answered and said that many could tell her of her outward sins, but none could tell her of her inward. Then I told her that her heart was not right before the Lord, and that from the inward came the outward. This woman came afterwards to be convinced of God's truth, and became a Friend." [1]

Of a trooper who came to him in prison he writes : " I spake to his condition, and his understanding was opened." [2] Thomas Lower, as Fox tells us in the Journal, gave testimony that Fox was not wrong in supposing that he was indeed able to speak to conditions. The record runs thus :

" I spoke particularly to him ; and he afterwards said my words were as a flash of lightning, they ran so through him. He said he had never met with such men in his life, for they knew the thoughts of his heart ; and were as the wise master-builders of the assemblies that fastened their words like nails." [3]

Though Fox was most censorious in much of his attitude, all of his discerning was not searching out the evil in people. In describing his journeys in America especially, page after page mentions the people " of accord " whom he met and recognized at once. The power, however, was not infallible. Though he read aright that James Nayler " had run out into imaginations," Fox did not speak to his condition. When Nayler would have approached him in love, he turned from him, and would show him neither the love nor the friendliness that he needed to save him from his downfall. Neither could Fox understand or have any sympathy with Cromwell's method of tactful compromise to reach his ends.

[1] *Journal*, p. 185.   [2] Ibid., p. 127.   [3] Ibid., p. 265.

In general, however, the Guidance of the Spirit, the voice of the Lord, found Fox a worthy tool for the accomplishment of its aims. His mysticism became, therefore, no mere self-effacing ecstatic revelling in the presence of the Lord, but an upright, noble reaction to the intuitive reading of the wisdom that seems somehow bound up in all the harvesting of sensational deposits and of instinctive endowments, changed, refined, co-ordinated into a noble personality.

The delicate reading of environment comes through the channels of which we have already spoken :—through the keen awareness of the special senses, through the conservation and summation of perceptions even so slight as to be imperceptible to the consciousness, through the whole wealth of intimate sense experiences, and through the ripening and refining of the instincts. The delicate reading through these many channels gives an evaluating quality to consciousness that enables it not only to judge conditions, but to guide the organism " in the direction of the accentuation of the *valuable* reactions and away from those that bode ill." When this takes the form of a feeling for adjustment we might call it " cosmæsthesia," as Dr. Starbuck suggests, or " telæsthesia " if it takes the form of " a feeling after the consequences of a reaction before it has completed itself, a dim awareness of ends about to be attained." " The developed equivalent of these two endowments of consciousness, cosmæsthesia and telæsthesia, which designate the essential nature of the wisdom of instinct, is the higher wisdom of the heart, much of which cannot be cognized." [1]

[1] E. D. Starbuck : " Intuitionalism," in Hastings' *Encyclopædia of Religion and Ethics* (New York, 1915), vol. vii, p. 399.

In Fox there was that divine discontent that marks the pull of an untried situation. He was " God's fool " with an inner initiative that drove him untutored along untried pathways. The compulsion of the spirit in him gave full emphasis to his natural racially-old responsiveness and immediacy of feelings. There can be, I believe, no line drawn *in kind* between the intuitive direction of the bird on the wing and the Guidance of the Spirit in Fox. He expressed a fact that is in accord with modern scientific study when he records of the truths into which he was led :

"I did not see by the help of men nor by the letter (though they are written in the letter), but I saw them by the Light of the Lord Jesus Christ, and by His immediate Spirit and power." [1]

Surely intuition is the very heart of the wisdom that lurks in the mystical life.

None of the glory of any of these accomplishments did Fox take to himself. Always he abased himself as the agent through whom such deeds were done. And yet in contrast his self-regard was so insistent that in his youth he would take advice from no man, placing his own judgment as superior to that of parents, relatives, friends, or even those strangers whom he had sought out for the ostensible purpose of gaining guidance. Through the years, however, it became so ingrained with higher objectives that with the same assurance, though with entire self-negligence, he could feel that he was the direct representative of the Lord, and so spoke with authority to high and low, priest or layman, magistrate or citizen, Pope or King.

[1] *Journal of George Fox* (8th edition, London, 1901), vol. i, p. 101.

VII

FOX'S REASONABLE PRACTICALITY

Fox writes of his first year or so of experience in preaching :

"The Lord said unto me that if but one man or woman were raised by His power to stand and live in the same Spirit that the prophets and apostles were in who gave forth the Scriptures, that man or woman should shake the country in their profession for ten miles round." [1]

Meditating thus, he came to Pendle Hill, in the North of England, and although it was " very steep and high," he climbed to the top of it to be rewarded with a vision. From thence " the Lord let him see in what places He had a great people to be gathered." That night the vision was elaborated, and " the Lord let him see . . . a great people in white raiment by a river side, coming to the Lord." [2]

Thus his campaign opened out before him. He was to be, not a priest, not a craftsman in a trade which he had learned as an apprentice at Oxford or Cambridge,[3] but, as he later described himself, " a preacher of righteousness." [4] There was a great people to be gathered, and he had identified the country, which *he*

[1] *Journal*, p. 149. [2] Ibid., p. 151.
[3] Ibid., p. 228. [4] Ibid., p. 366.

was to " shake for ten miles round," as Westmorland, " in and about Wensleydale and Sedbergh." [1]

With most remarkable success he carried out this enterprise. He won the loyal support and friendship of the family of Judge Fell. Although the Judge himself never became a convert to Fox's doctrines, he was most friendly and his home became the headquarters of the new fellowship. A group of young preachers gathered about Fox as " Publishers of Truth." Many of these were almost as gifted as he. Francis Howgill and John Audland [2] left their parishes to proclaim the truth as Fox interpreted it. Edward Burrough [3] became known as " son of thunder and consolation," and later died, a Quaker martyr, in prison in London. James Parnell, " a little lad about sixteen years of age, . . . was convinced. The Lord quickly made him a powerful minister of the Word of life, and many were turned to Christ by him, though he lived not long." [4] He too was imprisoned, and " very cruel they were to him, . . . and in that jail they did destroy him." [5] He was but a lad of twenty when he died. The group that Fox drew about him was a group of vigorous young men in the very prime of life. By 1654 Fox records :

" Above sixty ministers had the Lord raised up, and did now send abroad out of the north country. The sense of their service was very weighty upon me." [6]

Rufus M. Jones says of them :

" They so completely caught the idea of Fox that they all spoke the same religious language." [7]

[1] *Journal*, p. 151.   [2] Ibid., p. 154.   [3] Ibid., p. 157.
[4] Ibid., p. 191.   [5] Ibid., p. 225.   [6] Ibid., p. 201.
[7] Ibid., p. 201 (footnote).

If Fox had not thought through things till his own convictions were clear and definite and convincing, he could not have gathered and inspired such a group of young vigorous men and women, ready for service and undaunted by danger, difficulty or persecution. Without reasonableness and rationality he could not have won the courteous friendship of Oliver Cromwell, he could not have drawn to *his* truth the scholarly Robert Barclay, the practical and far-seeing William Penn. In fact, William Penn wrote of him :

"He had an extraordinary gift in opening the Scriptures. He would go to the marrow of things, and show the mind, harmony and fulfilling of them with much plainness, and to great comfort and edifying." [1]

"I have been surprised at his questions and answers in natural things, that whilst he was ignorant of useless and sophistical science, he had in him the foundation of useful and commendable knowledge, and cherished it everywhere." [2]

"And though the side of his understanding which lay next to the world, and especially the expression of it, might sound uncouth and unfashionable to nice ears, his matter was nevertheless very profound, and would not only bear to be often considered, but the more it was so, the more weighty and instructing it appeared." [3]

"Many times hath my soul bowed in an humble thankfulness to the Lord, that He did not choose any of the wise and learned of this world to be the first messenger in our age of His blessed truth to men ; but that He took one that was not of high degree, or elegant speech, or learned after the way of this world, that his message and work He sent him to do might come with less suspicion or jealousy of human wisdom and interest, and with more force and clearness upon the consciences of those that sincerely sought the way of truth in the love of it. I say, behold-

---

[1] William Penn : Preface to *Journal*, p. 53.
[2] Ibid., p. 59.   [3] Ibid., p. 51.

ing with the eye of my mind, the marks of God's finger and hand visibly in this testimony from the clearness of the principle, the power and efficacy of it which shined in his and their life and testimony that God employed in this work, it greatly confirmed me that it was of God." [1]

Fox seemed to have failed with men only when his jealousies or prejudices got the upper hand with him. At their first meeting Cromwell had said, with tears in his eyes :

"Come again to my house, for if thou and I were but an hour of a day together, we should be nearer one to the other." [2]

But the more often they met, the more distrustful did Fox become of Cromwell and his methods of government that resulted in persecution rather than religious liberty. He kept the personal friendship of the Protector, but he never won him to the truth as he saw it. The priest of his home town he never forgave for using in his sermons on Sunday that which Fox had said to him in discussion on weekdays. This man, whom Fox so thoroughly disliked, was never won to his truth, but became Fox's " great persecutor." [3]   The priest of the church at Ulverston where the Fell family had attended may have deserved the severe denunciation which Fox gave him, but it may also have been that Fox's prejudices and jealousy for Margaret Fell overpowered his sweet reasonableness.

Although Fox had not intended to start a new sect nor to organize a new church, the persecutions of the day drove the Quaker sufferers into closer fellowship

[1] William Penn : Preface to *Journal*, p. 52.
[2] *Journal*, p. 214.   [3] Ibid., p. 72.

one with another. For their mutual protection and assistance an informal democratic organization soon sprang up. It was modelled on Paul's conception of a universal church held together by the living presence of Christ. It recognized the freedom of the individual —a freedom which must be exercised for the well-being of the organism as a whole. Fox records :

" I was moved of the Lord to recommend the setting up of five monthly meetings of men and women in the city of London (besides the women's meetings and the quarterly meetings), to take care of God's glory, and to admonish and exhort such as walked disorderly or carelessly, and not according to truth. For whereas Friends had had only quarterly meetings, now Truth was spread, and Friends were grown more numerous, I was moved to recommend the setting up of monthly meetings throughout the nation. And the Lord opened to me what I must do, and how the men's and women's monthly and quarterly meetings should be ordered and established in this and in other nations ; and that I should write to those where I did not come to do the same." [1]

[1] *Journal*, p. 459. The organization which Fox perfected consists of local groups which are organized into Preparative Meetings, whose business is to attend to all matters of local concern and to prepare more general business for the Monthly Meeting. A Monthly Meeting may consist of two or more Preparative Meetings. Monthly Meetings in turn report to and are responsible to a Quarterly Meeting which is generally established on a geographical basis to cover a district that is not too scattered. It is frequently a county. Quarterly Meetings meet, as the name suggests, four times a year, and they in turn report to the General or Yearly Meeting, which includes the entire membership. It meets by adjournment, for about one week out of the year. The Meeting for Sufferings is a representative body from all the Quarterly Meetings, which forms the delegated part of the Yearly Meeting and which acts by the authority and on behalf of the Yearly Meeting on all matters of general business during the part of the year when the Yearly Meeting is not in session. Its name arose from the work it had to do in the first days of bitter persecutions. In America it now generally bears the name of Representative Committee.

The remaining twenty-four years of his life were spent in the work of organization, though his ministry did not slacken.

The children were not neglected by him. In fact, they were a very active part of the organization. (When every adult member of the Quaker group at Bristol was in prison the children maintained the meeting there by regularly going to the meeting-place and holding the Meeting for Worship.) So Fox advised the setting up of a school for boys at Waltham, and of a " woman's school " at Shacklewell " for instructing girls and young maidens in whatsoever things were civil and useful in creation." [1]

In all of this work he insisted upon the development of individual responsibility, so that all might have a concern and care that the God in whose honour they professed to serve should not be blasphemed, and that all who professed the Truth might " walk in the Truth in righteousness and holiness," and might " order their conversation aright." [2] Because of the consistency and reasonableness of such a demand and its application in the organization which he effected, the Meeting for Sufferings which he instigated has had an unbroken history for two and a half centuries.

Fox always speaks as if he had had no personal share in formulating his aims and as if he were but a tool in the hands of the Lord, who showed him what to do and how it was to be done.

In his youth he had led a lonely and largely solitary life. To his parents and friends he must have seemed most unreasonable in his refusal to accept any of their suggestions as to the profession he should enter and

[1] *Journal*, p. 461.   [2] Ibid., p. 462.

in his wandering, unsystematic and apparently aimless young manhood. It is most doubtful if he had ever reasoned out in his own mind the basis of his refusal. When, however, he had gone into public preaching, he writes :

"The Lord opened to me three things relating to those three great professions in the world,—law, physic, and divinity (so called). . . . I saw they were all out of the wisdom, out of the faith, out of the equity and perfect law of God." [1]

He spent the years, when he might have been in college studying for a profession, going now here, now there with no apparent definite purpose. He says he was seeking wisdom and getting knowledge from the Lord. He learned through experience to organize, intensify and clarify the facts of the objective world so that he drew therefrom direct judgments of immediate value. While not irrational, his procedure appears much more intuitive than rationally argued out. He felt his way along in much the same way that animals have found their way through perseverance on to higher deliverances.

The purpose of Fox, as of all mystics, seems to have been " Seek ye first the Kingdom of Heaven, and all things shall be added unto you." That wisdom can be so gained, Fox knew, not through logical processes, but experimentally. He based his life unwittingly upon the fact which Dr. Starbuck says

"amounts to a turning-point in the history of thought—that the proof is forthcoming that even our clear conscious judgments are based upon evidence that must be felt out rather than cognized." [2]

[1] *Journal*, p. 98.
[2] Starbuck : " Intuitionalism," in Hastings' *Encyclopædia of Religion and Morals*, p. 399.

For any ethical or religious judgment there is always necessary a conflict of ends. In Fox this conflict was intense, and it took years for him to achieve experimentally his higher self as a religious leader. He had refused to become an ordained priest. He preached because he felt driven by the inner need to give forth his message and draw people to the Truth. It was only after years that he formulated and clarified this mission, so that when asked his profession he replied that he was a preacher of righteousness. He seems ever too practical and too active a person to stop for purely analytical abstract reasoning. His writings are never philosophical treatises. They are of the common stuff of which the homely life of his England was made. They are earnest appeals for a life of righteousness, ponderous, full of repetitions and crude involved thinking, and without perspective. He was successful because of the very strength of his convictions and the skill which he had developed for the mastery of people. In the ultimate decisions of life it is the inarticulate intuition, mere faith in the guidance of the feeling mass, that arises out of the conflicts of experience, that can save mankind. This seems to have been Fox's way. It does not mean, however, that he was irrational. Bergson says :

" Intelligence and instinct, having originally been interpenetrating, retain something of their common origin. Neither is ever found in a pure state. . . . They haunt each other continually ; everywhere we find them mingled ; it. is the proportion that differs." [1]

[1] Bergson : *Creative Evolution* (New York, 1911), p. 135. (See Figure (p. 102) : Forms of Intelligence.)

FORMS OF INTELLIGENCE IN THE ORDERS OF NATURE

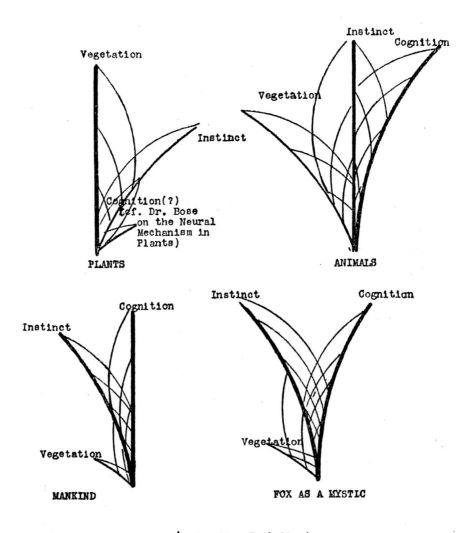

(Suggested by Bergson's Creative Evolution)

It seems to me that while we cannot dichotomize Fox's mental procedure to show forth clearly these two elements, he did exemplify in his life that his insight is both intuitive and rational—or at least not irrational—at one and the same time, and that his truth arose from the interweaving of the two together.

His conscious perceptions seem to feed themselves upon all those consciously available, though logically indescribable biases, prejudices, organic and kinæsthetic sensations arising out of the bodily processes in which he was so rich. His evaluation of situations arises not so much from clear logical reasoning about them as from those delicate powers of discrimination and association for which we believe we have found evidence in Fox. His judgments seem to come from the total awareness of the whole man in harmony with the forces of life that played through him—that which Plato describes as the harmony of the entire man. Fox felt rather than thought his way into the situations he had to meet. Dr. Starbuck says :

" It is likely that most of life will remain below and above the reach of accurate description and formulation, and that mankind will continue to derive much of its truth or value from the ' recesses of feeling, the darker, blinder strata of character,' which ' are the only place in the world in which we catch real facts in the making, and directly perceive how events happen and how work is actually done.' " [1]

While reason may aid in the task of organization, intensification and clarification of the truth that arises out of the sensitive inner life in Fox, it cannot be readily

[1] Starbuck : " Intuitionalism," in Hastings' *Encyclopædia of Religion and Ethics*, p. 400.

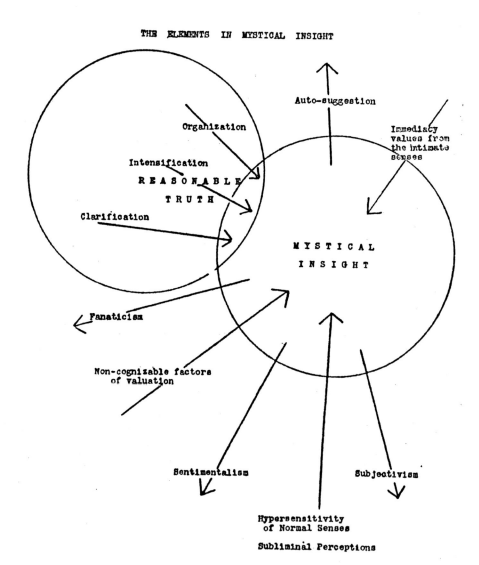

THE ELEMENTS IN MYSTICAL INSIGHT

caught in the act. The trend of Fox's life as a whole, however, is not irrational. It was practical and efficient in carrying out constructively and consistently to the end the mission to which he had felt called.

His mystical insight, then, arises out of the hyperæsthesia of his normal senses and their subliminal ramifications, out of the immediacy values from the intimate senses, out of the non-cognizable factors of valuation, though probably with the aid of the clarifying effects of the reason. It was of value because it tore itself away from all control by the elements of autosuggestion or fanaticism, of sentimentalism and subjectivism. (See Figure : The Elements in Mystical Insight.)

VIII

FOX'S ENDOWMENT OF ENERGY

IT is the natural endowment of energy which he had at his disposal, and which he used, that contributed, I believe, to Fox's superior living and brought to him a wealth of truth value. George Fox throughout his life was one of the most energetic of men. From his early manhood till his last imprisonment—through forty years of mature life—he was constantly wandering from place to place in his preaching. He was exposed to the hardships of the weather and of travel in days when transportation was only by coach, horseback or on foot, not alone in England, but for two years through the wilderness of America. He slept frequently out of doors. He suffered physical abuse and persecutions among the laymen as well as in the horrible conditions of the jails in which he was imprisoned. The later years of his life, when his broken health forbade much travel, found him still working indefatigably, even as he had while confined in prison. He wrote the record of his life that " all may know the dealings of the Lord with me," [1] and also treatises, epistles, replies to theological books of other denominations, messages to statesmen and potentates, all of which have been collected into eight stout volumes. In his more vigorous years

[1] *Journal*, p. 65.

he had been accustomed to dictate such writings as he rode through the country. Apparently he always carried books with him. Preaching almost daily, and often for hours at a time, sensing the social and political needs of the times, perfecting the organization of a large and scattered group of followers, restraining unwise and fanatical outcroppings, Fox yet showed no evidence that he had recourse to any special source of energy.

Few men are active to the limit of their energies. Some few do rise, as Fox did, above the mediocre, semi-alert condition of the average man. Every crisis in the history of the world has found its hero ready to step into the breach. "When Duty whispers low, ' Thou must,' the youth replies, ' I can ' " ; and he does ! Life ever had gotten on and found new and richer expression through the interaction or release of energy which has been captured and stored.[1] Few realize their reserve and use it consciously. But when the emergency comes in the individual life one finds himself possessed of power undreamed.[2]

So in the life of Fox one finds him constantly having at his disposal stores of energy rich in import to his life. His habits of eating and sleeping were both irregular. During a period of special anxiety he fasted for ten days. The habit of sleeping out of doors—often from necessity, not choice—continued during most of his active life, until a report was raised that he would not lie on a bed.[3] In over twenty years of strenuous living, several years were spent in horrible, unsanitary jails with insufficient food and protection.

[1] Cf. H. F. Osborne: *The Origin and Evolution of Life* (New York, 1917), p. 16 ff.
[2] Cf. W. James: *Energies of Men.*   [3] *Journal*, p. 144.

Only three months after his marriage persecutions among Friends were most severe, and his wife was among those imprisoned. Throughout that winter he had a very severe illness, largely psychic in its immediate cause. The attack came suddenly as he was walking down the hill one day. He continued to grow weaker until at last he had to remain at a Friend's house, where he lost both sight and hearing.[1] Thus he lay for several weeks, till few thought that he could recover, and it was reported in London and in the country that he was already dead. But when they who were with him gave up all hope, he reacted by immediately desiring his clothing to be brought to him and a carriage to be furnished that he might go to visit another Friend who also lay ill about twelve miles away. Against the wishes of his friends he went. Weak as they had thought him, his store of energy proved sufficient. He even regained a glimmering of sight. For several months he thus moved on from place to place, visiting and encouraging those who were ill. As the heat of the violent persecutions was allayed, he came " from under the travail and sufferings that had lain with such weight " upon him, and he quickly recovered. His wife being released from prison at that time, he started almost at once for two years of missionary work and the visiting of groups of Friends in America. There he would travel for days, at times seeing no man or woman or dwelling-house,[2] sleeping under the stars at nights when water froze beside the camp-fire and the wolves howled in the forests about.[3]

[1] *Journal*, pp. 476–481.
[2] Ibid., p. 501 (cf. also pp. 499, 509, 518, 521, 525, 531).
[3] Ibid., p. 530.

So abundant was his store of energy that if motor activity were inhibited the energy that should have been expended was stored up till it burst forth in some intense form, at times pathological to a greater or less extent. Once he had decided to speak to the justices to entreat them not to oppress the servants in their wages. He was deterred by finding the inn where they held court so full of fiddlers that he thought to have a more serious time with them in the morning. But in the morning they had gone to another town eight miles away. The sudden inhibition to the nervous system, closing it to its contemplated type of action, caused its delicate mechanism to find other outlet for the energy focused for immediate action. The energy from the speech centres passed over and effected the temporary paralysation of the visual centres, so that he "was struck even blind." [1] As this accumulated energy was gradually expended in the physical strain of running the eight miles, his sight returned. Reaching the court, the originally contemplated exhortation to the judges became amplified to include another to the servants that they also might serve justly and honestly.[2]

Even more pathological, though indicative of the excessive energy at the immediate disposal of the man, was the release of summed-up inhibited energy at Lichfield.[3] " In response to an adequate stimulus the nervous system is integrated for a specific purpose," says Dr. Crile, and " an unexpressed smouldering emotion is measurably relieved by action." [4] However,

[1] *Journal*, p. 95. [2] Ibid., p. 96.
[3] Ibid., pp. 132-133.
[4] G. W. Crile : *The Origin and Nature of the Emotions* (Philadelphia, 1915), p. 33.

if action is inhibited almost totally, the summation becomes extreme. Fox had served a year's imprisonment at Derby, half of which had been in an unspeakably vile prison, crowded in with a mixed company of common offenders of the law. This had followed several years spent in very active life out of doors, or mingling with others who, like himself, found their chief interest in religious matters. Ordinarily the youthful criminal, upon release, finds his energy, no longer under mechanical restraint, expressing itself in some vicious excess. Fox, also young and normally of a motor temperament, found his unexpended energy of a year so smouldered and accumulated that it exploded in an outburst that is less abnormal than might at first appear, as Royce says.[1] Fox was at that time in no condition to test such automatisms or openings as his previous experience had taught him to trust. So when the steeples of Lichfield, towering over the fields, caught his eye, he had a restless sense that something must be done, something vigorous, intense, significant. His imprisonment had been due to his reaction against Church practices and teaching, though it had been on a technical charge of blasphemy. It is therefore no wonder that, in his highly integrated nervous condition and weakened health from confinement, the mere sight of three church spires should set loose in him the impulse to go at once. Secretly evading his companions, he went over hedge and ditch till within a mile of the town. Leaving his shoes with shepherds there, he went barefoot into the town, crying through the streets, "Woe to the bloody city of Lichfield!"

[1] Royce: "George Fox as a Mystic," in *Harvard Theological Review*, January 1917.

His imprisonment on the charge of blasphemy had been extended six months, due to the illegal action of enraged commissioners whose offer to make him a captain in the army had been met with the reply that he " lived in the virtue of that life and power which took away the occasion of all wars." [1] Their insistent flattery he had put aside with the remark that " if that was their love and kindness he trampled it under his feet." [2] Was it the lurking effect of these warlike suggestions and images that led him to see " a channel of blood running down the streets and the market-place like a pool of blood " ? [3]

Fox has recorded, as we have noted, that on a few occasions he " was struck even blind," at times when he was stirred by deep emotion. Mosso has shown that the effect of emotion upon the circulatory system is that it centres the blood in the brain.[4] Fox's delicate circulatory system responded with such force of energy that he was not only blinded thus, but by such concentration in emotion the blood was driven away from the surface capillaries of his body, so that when a priest sought to aid his troubled mind, not by giving the spiritual aid he sought but by letting blood, they could get no drop of blood from him. [5]

Cannon, even more definitely, has proven the delicacy of response to the most vital of all stimuli, emotions and ideas. He has told a clear story of the speeding-up of the action of the bodily mechanism through the chemical action of the adrenal, the thyroid and other

[1] *Journal*, p. 128.   [2] Ibid., p. 128.
[3] Ibid., p. 133.
[4] A. Mosso : *Fear* (London, 1896), p. 30.
[5] *Journal*, p. 73.

internal secretory glands.[1]   As we have already seen, Fox was gifted with a body so heavily endowed with energy that it could resist thirty years of exposure, abuse and irregularity of habit, and yet so sensitive that its special organs were keenly aware of all the stimuli that bombarded them, and so gentle and delicate in its interactions that the sufferings of his friends and loved ones, or the tribulations of his nation, could throw him into weeks of serious illness.   The work of Cannon helps us to understand the reasons and the way of this response.

Some students have claimed that such superior activity is due to the ability of the organism to tap some supernatural stores of reserve energy.   But it seems to me that such scientists as Cannon and Crile are telling a story more of compensation in the use of energy than of the release of additional energy.   Though one lives more vitally under increased stimulation, it is apparently at the expense of the normal functioning of other parts of the bodily organism as soon as it goes beyond the point of metabolic equilibrium.

Frederick H. Smith, studying the energy of Jesus, concludes :

" It is quite clear that He lived and energized in a level of consciousness above the ordinary. . . . His continuous labour of teaching, preaching, healing, and doing wonderful things was interrupted only by His short periods of retirement, when He would seek seclusion for prayer, meditation, recuperation.   It can hardly cause wonderment that at the crisis of His life the strenuosity thereof should have exhausted His physical powers, for His energies had been consumed by His wonderful energizing.

[1] Cannon : *Bodily Changes in Pain, Hunger, Fear and Rage* (New York, 1915), pp. 92, 119–123, 275–279, etc.

GEORGE FOX

. . . He was physically weakened. Unable to bear His cross, He fell and had to be helped. On the cross He expired sooner than is usually the case." [1]

In Fox there is no evidence either of a special spiritual sense, nor of some equally mysterious store of spiritual energy. He lived merely a normal life on the higher levels of its developed efficiency, using his energies in his work and not dissipating them into channels out of harmony with his life-work or lacking in value to it. It is in this more refined normal living, I believe, that we shall find one of the main sources of truth in his mysticism. A more alert awareness, a livelier functioning of his senses, a fuller consciousness, gave him a grasp on eternal truth that, though potentially possible to his fellow-men, they generally fail to secure for themselves.

[1] Frederick H. Smith : *The Higher Powers of Men* (Lamorie, Iowa, 1918), p. 193.

IX

REJECTIONS

Much of the history of mysticism is not alone a record of joyous accounts of souls lost in wondrous admiration of the Divinity with which they believe themselves to have become united. It is also a record of darkly unpleasant experiences when the mystic (so called) has sunk into pathetic if not disgusting pathologies. George Fox, so delicately poised between all sorts of conflicting traits, both good and evil, was fortunate in that he succeeded in thwarting his evil tendencies and strengthening his finer ones. The experience at Lichfield is but one example which shows how easily he might have passed over into an abnormal fanaticism. The strength of his mysticism, therefore, lies not alone in the sources from which it drew its various elements, but fully as much in the freedom which it attained from certain characteristics that were native to him. His personal idiosyncrasy of dress and appearance might easily have assumed a place of unwarranted importance. Although a leather suit was not very unusual at the time and was probably chosen for its durability, it is hard to understand why he needed to persist in wearing it until it became a symbol of his denunciation of the " earthly and airy spirit " in which both priests and professors " held their profession of religion and worship, so that it was a dreadful thing to them when it was told them, ' The man in leathern breeches is come.' " [1] The leathern suit was perhaps, indeed, a hindrance, and prevented him from being able to accomplish all that might otherwise have been possible. Once when he went to see Cromwell, the officers were so rude to him because of his clothes that he did not get to the Protector. " And sometimes," he says, " they would turne uppe my coate & see for my leather briches & then they woulde be in a rage." [2]

Even though he tells that he took no pride in his long hair with its curly lock behind, for " it was not of his own putting on," he still persisted in wearing it so, even " though it frequently gave offence to many." [3]

Ridiculous as these personal idiosyncrasies seem, the attitude which they represent came to have its constructive side in his practical mystical life. Putting no value on such non-essentials, it left him free to turn his attention and energies to more constructive things. Instead of accepting the fashions and standards of his time, he learned to weigh them at their true value and to seek for use only those that were consistent with a full expression of the truths which had been revealed in him. So simplicity—of apparel, of house-furnishings, of meeting-houses, of manner and of speech—became a tenet of the Society which he founded.

If all men have " that of God " in them, then the only inequalities of any value are those of riches of spirit. Why, then, should one strive to excel another

---

[1] *Journal*, p. 139.
[2] *Journal of George Fox* (Cambridge edition, 1911), p. 170.
[3] *Journal*, p. 239.

in richness of apparel, and follow the changes of vogue in fashion for no other reason than that ? Why should one address a man of higher social rank as " you," and one of inferior rank as " thee," when true rank is a matter of worth rather than of wealth or of birth ? And yet some of the severest persecutions came to Fox and his followers because of their persistent use of " thou " and " thee " to all, no matter what their degree. If " the Lord teaches His people Himself," [1] why should one man be placed high up in a pulpit above the rest of the congregation to lay down the law to them ? The Friends' Meeting for Worship was started by Fox with no such division, but as a group in which any or all may in turn be the leader.

Conventionality was, then, one of the first rejections in Fox's life. He was thereby free to weigh, and to choose for worth, and for worth alone, dress, manners, convictions, principles, truths. Sensitive in the extreme to social environment, he became, therefore, not its slave but its master.

The victim—or the guardian—of an unbounded self-assurance, he always felt himself capable of meeting any situation. But the conceit of the child who judged himself so much more righteous than his companions and elders became in the man a living dynamic faith. With a consciousness of the presence of the Divine which was central as a feature in that which he called " Light," a consciousness that he " was born of God " and had " become a son of God," he was ready for any emergency because it was not he who was able to say and do the things he did, but the " power of the Lord " working through him. So to the Lord he

[1] *Journal*, p. 76.

gave all the honour and glory ; and the praise of his fellow-men did not puff him up nor their adverse criticism depress him. Had he not been carried through to this higher and finer attitude, he too might have run off into such fanaticism—" imaginations "[1] he calls it—as did James Nayler. Nayler also believed in the Indwelling Christ in man, but he failed to draw the line of good judgment, and allowed a fanatical group of some seven admirers, men and women, to give him a Triumphal Entry into Bristol, as an incarnation of the Christ returned in the flesh. In reality Nayler did not accept this honour, if such it could be called, as a personal matter. He tolerated it only because he felt himself to be typical of all men in that all possess the Spirit of God in their hearts. Fox never in any way came so near to such fanaticism. When one woman threw herself at his feet, kneeling to do him honour, he reprimanded her severely and turned in disgust from such actions.

Instead of going off into vain dreamings and fanatical preaching, his preaching and his work were all intensely practical, humane, consistent, and generally free from all the extravagances for which the social state of England of that time was a rich field. Full of sectarian fanaticism, controversy, persecutions and changing faiths and governments, it was dangerously rife with temptations. But Fox, with clear vision, urged upon magistrates, rulers and potentates that they rule wisely and justly and turn to the Lord for their guidance ; upon tradesmen that they be scrupulously honest in all their dealings ; upon servants that they serve cheerfully and honestly. All that he preached he put into effect in

[1] *Journal*, p. 269.

his own life. So we find fanaticism discarded in Fox and an intensely practical religion replacing it. He became a thoroughly consistent expounder and exemplar of the ideal of a spiritual unity in all mankind.

This practical type of his religion led him to cast aside all petty sentimentality, and instead of a cheap and easy reliance on the Lord's power, attributing a Divine origin to every whim and fancy that appealed to his attention, this restless soul waited in deep reverence until his deepest intuitions assured him that the lighter imaginings of his mind were in complete harmony with the Inner Guidance of his life. He could wait to be sure that his aim was correct before striking. Once assured of the righteousness of his cause and the justification of his means to serve that cause, nothing could hinder or divert him.

He did not rely on his own assurance of guidance, but he demanded the accordance with the group guidance before he was willing to proceed. His marriage with Margaret Fell is a typical example of his seeking the corporate guidance of his group. Having obtained her consent, he sends for and consults with all her children and their respective husbands and wives. When no slightest opposition arises there, he lays the proposal before the meeting, and wins its approval of the union before he is free to continue. Thus he avoids any danger that might arise from auto-suggestion being confused with real inner guidance.

The plan of the Meeting for Worship as it developed among the group also was typical of the testing of an individual self-assertiveness. If one confused his own auto-suggestion with a real call to the ministry, no convention of outward formality compelled the group to abide inert through a false ministering. So quickly does a speech that *breaks into the silence* of the meeting instead of *out of it* show a lack of harmony that it would take the most obtuse person not to be aware of it. Though the freedom of the meeting was given to all who chose to enter, in the belief that each one, even the humblest, may become a true minister of the Lord, a radical case of fanaticism like that of Nayler stands out alone as a dark cloud in the history of those early days. Nearly three hundred years of Quaker history bear testimony to the fact that so long as the spirit of worship is maintained, the liberty of voluntary conformity to the ideal of the spiritual unity of all men is never mistaken for license. Undoubtedly Fox builded better than he knew. He had had no plan for the organization of a new church. But in discarding the ceremonies and ritual of the established churches, the simpler and more direct forms into which he and his followers drifted naturally were founded on such true psychological principles that they resulted in a social and group leadership that could not but succeed whenever it was unhampered by individualistic self-dependence and self-assertion. Fox's discarding of auto-suggestibility naturally carried him into such a social and group leadership.

Meetings for the conduct of business as well as for worship were maintained on the same basis of group guidance rather than of parliamentary law. One spoke out of the consciousness that arises in the group and expressed the thought that represented the spirit of the group. Again, years of historical evidence confirm the fact that it is no auto-suggestion but a real reading of the group consciousness that is to be found in such a spokesman. The result is not a mere addition of the thoughts and wills of many individuals. It is somehow a sort of multiplied composite in which each is affected and changed by all those about him. A person in such a gathering may enter with his mind and heart filled with a certain idea, thought or problem, and in the silence of the gathering may feel stealing over him an ordering, a clarification, a changing of tone that leaves him with the idea or thought intensified or changed and the problem solved in ways which alone he had never accomplished. Just as two colours placed side by side are changed and altered and become more luminous by the contact, so personalities gathered thus take unto themselves irradiations that perhaps change the whole tenor of their lives.

George Fox, in the gatherings of seeking souls of his day, was like platinum, which scientists have learned is a catalyzer whose mere presence sets loose energy in a chemical process and hastens the reaction. The Friends learned in personal terms that which scientists to-day are learning in chemical terms, that " where two or three are gathered together " there is in the midst a Divine Catalyzer which sets free in them forces and powers which raise them to a higher level of spiritual selfhood than can ever be attained alone.

It is no pathological auto-suggestion that marks Fox's developed mystical attitude, but a reliance on the spiritual guidance to be developed in an earnest group which finds at once its strength and its outlet in a Friends' Meeting for Worship such as he first founded. The marvel is that it should have taken seventeen centuries for any leader or group to discover the power that is possible to be found in such corporate communion, such " watching together for an hour " as Jesus sought to have in the Garden of Gethsemane. Has the world also been sleeping, and not able to watch for one hour *with* another soul in united prayer, even to learn therefrom the marvellous increase in power attained ?

In writing of George Fox as a mystic, Royce says of him :

"Other mystics have written words that people treasure for their own sake as pure literature, or as spiritual illumination, or as emotional inspiration ; but what Fox wrote was meant to guide his followers in their tasks and in the problems of their generation, and was bare of all adornments save that which its fervent practical spirit inevitably produced. . . . In his youth Fox knew a good deal about what spiritual solitude meant ; but he never revelled in such solitude for its own sake as the typical mystics do. On the contrary, until he found the way out of it he was ill at ease. He was perfectly capable of meeting God 'in the bush,' and was always very sure that God dwells not in temples made with hands ; but he had no wish to avoid 'the mart and the crowded street,' provided only that he could utter his testimony in the presence of his fellows ; and he obviously preferred to look for God in the meeting side by side with his brethren. The religion of Fox was, then, a very insistently social religion, in which solitude was an incident, not a goal. Contemplation was compatible with work ; and the Light was still with him in the company of his friends." [1]

In his earlier years his seeking of solitude seemed to indicate a subjectivism interested only in the welfare of his own soul. But when he was under great stress and temptation to despair, he made no elaborate problem out of his sufferings. He had few fears and no deep

[1] J. Royce: "George Fox as a Mystic," in *Harvard Theological Review*, January 1913, p. 38 f.

sense of guilt. In fact, he had so little that he was tempted to commit some evil act in order that he might justly be oppressed in spirit! "His enemy is, as Royce says, "always outside of him, in the evil of the world, in the common foe of mankind."[1] The lack of insight in the priests, the lack of righteousness in professors, is a real sorrow to him, as is also the lack of justice and equity in magistrates and rulers. Always there is for him an objective reference even in his most personal moments of illumination. Into his tension of soul comes an opening that "it was needful I should have a sense of all conditions; how else could I speak to all conditions?"[2] His experiences in the mystical realm were thus swiftly translated into terms of humane activity. So in replacing a rejected subjectivism he develops a type of mysticism so sane in its objective reference that it can appeal to men and women of all classes and ranks in society as the true way of life.

Fox was fortunate in that he rejected many of those traits which might have carried him, as so many mystics have been carried, into the ways of pathology instead of along the path of sane and sound religious experience. Thus his discarding of conventionality of manner of worship left him free to find his way into constructive forms of worship and a practical type of religion which had a strong social reference. His disregard of personal conventions, of dress and speech, enabled him to turn his emphasis upon essentials, and it gave him a hold upon people as a spiritual leader that one less insistently centred on spiritual values would have been unable to attain. Having his childish conceit refined into a consciousness of Divine Guidance enabled him to avoid

---

[1] Royce: Op. cit., p. 87.   [2] *Journal*, p. 87.

the evil effects of flattery and to steer clear of fanaticism. Sentimentality and subjectivism were overcome by an insistence upon a noble respect for the Indwelling Spirit in the hearts of all men that required of him the same attitude of reliance upon the judgment of others led like him, as upon his own. In this way he developed a type of group guidance in worship and in business that was more consistent with primitive Christianity than with other seventeenth-century church organizations.

Conventionality, fanaticism, auto-suggestion, sentimentalism and subjectivism were, therefore, all discarded out of his program of a victorious life. His mysticism became a sane and practically consistent social religion based upon a deep personal and corporate Inner Guidance that found its source in a direct consciousness of the presence of divinity in human affairs. It found its expression in the Friends' Meeting for Worship and in a type of social life and organization that comes most nearly being a perfect example of pure democracy. It was indeed a " holy experiment " in the art of living, not as a communistic settlement wherein each individuality is sacrificed to the group, but as a democracy wherein each individual is raised, or should be, to his greatest height of power to be and to serve.

PART THREE

THE EMANCIPATION OF A HIGHER
SPIRITUAL SELFHOOD IN FOX

X

CONFLICTING TRAITS

LIKE all great natures, Fox was able to harmonize conflicting traits of character and temperament, until having found not only a dominant centre, but a spiritualized centre that controlled his every action, he could throw himself into the maelstrom of life with the perfect ease and confidence with which an experienced swimmer allows himself to rest upon the buoyant waves of the ocean. No easy rose-strewn pathway, though, was that which Fox trod in reaching his higher selfhood. That which Tagore says of mankind in general is true of Fox in particular :

" Man's mistakes and failures have by no means been trifling or small, they have strewn his path with colossal ruins ; his sufferings have been immense, like birthpangs for a giant child ; they are the prelude of a fulfilment whose scope is infinite. Man has gone through and is still undergoing martyrdom in various ways, and his institutions are the altars he has built whereto he brings his daily sacrifices, marvellous in kind and stupendous in quantity. All this would be absolutely unmeaning and unbearable if all along he did not feel that deepest joy of the soul within him which tries its divine strength by suffering and proves its exhaustless riches by renunciation. . . . For a man who has realized his soul there is a determinate centre of the universe around which all else can find its proper place, and from thence only can he draw and enjoy the blessedness of a harmonious life." [1]

[1] Tagore : *Sadhana*, p. 34.

It was out of a nature rife with antitheses and antagonisms, and through years of temptations, loneliness, sorrows, persecutions, that Fox forged for himself a personality strong as tempered steel. Because of it, he gave his life in service to lead his fellow-men into a true worship of a God, well known and immanent. No altar " to an unknown God "[1] is the Society of Friends, wherein he laboured with marvellous and stupendous abandon.

A new-born child consists, according to Dr. Crile, " of plastic clay, from which the real man is created." Fox was no exception to the fact that the human body is like a living dictograph, upon which are played the many tunes of life. Registered within it in symbolic language are the records of its evolution. The plastic clay of native endowments is the background on which the events of life play. It becomes mellow and rich in its response to a master voice till it can record and give forth harmonies to which it had no ability of response at first. " The brain patterns that dominate at the close of the adolescent and at the beginning of the adult period fix and determine until death the life reactions of the individual. The action patterns thus formed in the plastic brain constitute the personality of the individual, and make the reactions of the human mechanism as inevitable and as true as are the reactions of a man-made machine."[2]

George Fox's personality was integrated by the selective development of certain of his manifold endowments until at maturity he had achieved a set

[1] Acts xvii. 23.
[2] Crile : *A Mechanistic View of Peace and War* (New York, 1915), p. 100.

CONFLICTING TRAITS

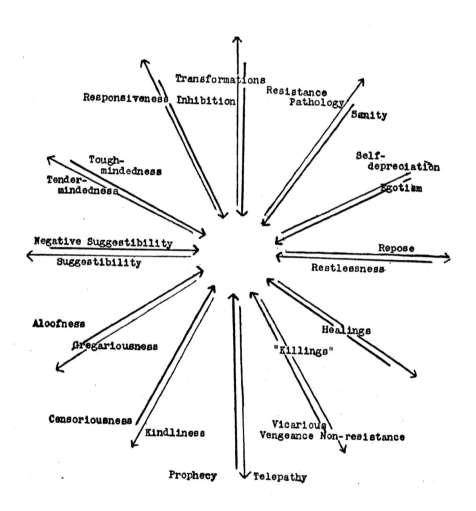

9

of "action patterns" that were so unified that his entire life became the harmonious realization of his highest self—a life trod unfalteringly in a joyous, conscious, constant, immediate companionship with the Divine.

Rich in native endowments was this child of the seventeenth century. He was robust and vigorous, or he could not have endured the persecutions, the imprisonments, and the irregular habits of food and sleep. Yet he was withal so responsive that his body was many times violently affected by sympathetic interplay with psychic reactions. He was keenly sensitive in all the windows of his body to the sensible world about him, as well as to conditions and the character of peoples and movements. Yet he held himself aloof from them. He was suggestible so that he became the foremost prophet of his age, voicing out the currents in the spiritual atmosphere of his day. Yet he was so negatively suggestible that he did not follow the established paths but led his age into new spiritual fields which were true deliverance from the dogmatism, and superficiality, and insincerity of the Church at that time. He was censorious of persons, of the Church, and of the State, with antipathies and antagonisms toward those who assailed *his* truth or affected *his* loves. Yet he was so gentle and winning that he drew to him not only a large religious following, but a large group of close personal friends who were ready to offer their lives that he might be free and live. He was egoistic to the point of making everybody serve his ends. Yet he had real freedom from any disposition to self-aggrandizement. With a natural vehemence of speech, he was entirely uncomplaining as to his personal griefs. A stern controversialist, all his hostilities were curbed and controlled by the principles of his Quaker faith. After years of persecution and suffering, the victim of broken health, he was untiring in his diligence of labour to the end. Active, restless, with a motor type of personality, he had the power to possess the peace that passeth all understanding in the very midst of his activity. He was capable of an extravagant mystical rapture, as is evident from a contemporary portrait.[1] Yet he carried on his work with great skill and calm objectivity. He was a good leader of men, and an effective manager of a complex organization, scrupulously honest and efficient in the management of worldly affairs. He showed marked abnormality in his psychic illnesses and automatisms, or openings as he calls them. But he was so constituted that he was able to retain essential self-control and sanity where a weaker brain might have tended toward a systematizing of delusions. He was withal able to accomplish great results.

With so much of tension between conflicting traits, this man shows in mature life a personality so unified that one feels him as set aside from his fellows. It is as if there were a chasm between the outer shell of his social contacts and the mighty inwardness of his soul's life of constant companionship with his God. The chasm was bridged, however, by an habitually consistent type of immediate response, that had been developed during those adolescent years of seeking and turmoil. The crude character of the native endowments of the rough-hewn youthful Fox had been refined till they fitted together perfectly into the beautiful mosaic of his mature brain pattern.

[1] Portrait by Gerard Honthorst. Frontispiece to *Journal*, Vol. I.

Resistance and Transformations.

In tracing the sources of his mysticism, we have seen that physically Fox was a man of striking endowments, with a body so strong that it could resist thirty years of exposure, abuse and irregularity of habit. At the same time he was so sensitive that its special organs were keenly aware of all the stimuli that bombarded them, and so gentle and delicate in its interactions that the sufferings of his friends and best beloved, or the tribulations of his nation, would throw him into weeks of illness.

Responsiveness and Inhibition.

Psychically he was as sensitive as he was physically. He developed an attitude of mind and heart wherein he could hold himself apart from all outward response to personal criticism of himself. But one finds the man just as sensitive to the report that a good man in America had " spoken highly of the truth, and more highly of him than he felt it fit for him to mention or take notice of," [1] as the lad, with his " gravity and stayedness of mind and spirit not usual in children," [2] had been sensitive to the hurt when rude fellows laughed at him.   His anger was quickly aroused at the priests, who turned needy beggars away unaided,[3] or at the stable-boys who robbed his horse of its food.[4]   He was alert to detect, and earnest to try to correct, wrong social conditions.   In short, it was his sensitivity to all social and national affairs that helped to mould his religion and the Society, which grew up from it into a new type of social and practical brotherhood.

[1] *Journal,* p. 507.   [2] Ibid., p. 66.
[3] Ibid., p. 157.   [4] Ibid., p. 290.

CONFLICTING TRAITS.

RESISTANCE.

" I was scarcely able to move or stand by reason of the ill-usage I had received ; yet with considerable effort I got about a mile from the town, and then I met with some people who gave me something to comfort me, because I was inwardly bruised ; but the Lord's power soon healed me again" (p. 114).

" I leaped my horse into the boat, thinking John's horse would follow when he had seen mine go in before him. But the water being pretty deep, John could not get his horse into the boat. Therefore I leaped out again on horseback into the water, and stayed with John on that side till the boat returned. There we tarried, from the eleventh hour of the forenoon to the second in the afternoon, before the boat came to fetch us ; and then we had forty-two miles to ride that evening ; and by the time we had paid our passage, we had but one groat left between us in money. We rode about sixteen miles, and then got a little hay for our horses. Setting forward again, we came in the night to a little alehouse, where we thought to have stayed and baited. But, finding we could have neither oats nor hay there, we travelled all night ; and about the fifth hour in the morning got to a place within six miles of Wrexham, where that day we met with many Friends, and had a glorious meeting " (p. 292).

TRANSFORMATIONS.

" I went to another. . . . He would needs give me some physic, and I was to have been let blood ; but they could not get one drop of blood from me, either in arms or head (though they endeavoured to do so), my body being, as it were, dried up with sorrows, griefs and troubles, which were so great upon me that I could have wished I had never been born " (p. 73).

" There was one Brown, who had great prophecies and sights upon his death-bed of me. . . . When this man was buried a great work of the Lord fell upon me, to the admiration of many, who thought I had been dead, and many came to see me for about fourteen days. I was very much altered in countenance and person, as if my body had been new moulded or changed . . ." (p. 87).

" It was upon me from the Lord to go and speak to the justices, that they should not oppress the servants in their wages. . . . But finding a company of fiddlers there, I did not go in, but thought to come in the morning, when I might have a more serious opportunity to discourse with them. But when I came in the morning, they were gone, and I was struck even blind, that I could not see. I inquired of the innkeeper where

" I had travelled through every county in Wales, preaching the everlasting gospel of Christ " (p. 293).

" In the meeting they threw at me coals, clods, stones, and water; yet the Lord's power bore me up over them that they could not strike me down. At last, when they saw they could not prevail by throwing water, stones, and dirt at me, they went and informed the justices in the sessions, who thereupon sent officers to fetch me before them " (p. 294).

" I was put into a tower where the smoke of the other prisoners came up so thick it stood as dew upon the walls, and sometimes it was so thick that I could hardly see the candle when it burned; and I being locked under three locks, the under-jailer, when the smoke was great, would hardly be persuaded to come up to unlock one of the uppermost doors for fear of the smoke, so that I was almost smothered. Besides, it rained in upon my bed, and many times, when I went to stop out the rain in the cold winter-season, my shirt was as wet as muck with the rain that came in upon me while I was labouring to stop it out. And the place being high and open to the wind, sometimes as fast as I stopped it the wind blew it out again. In this manner I lay all that long, cold winter till the next assize, in which time I was so starved, and so frozen with cold and wet with the rain that my body was greatly swelled and my limbs much be-numbed " (p. 430).

the justices were to sit that day; and he told me, at a town eight miles off. My sight began to come to me again; and I went and ran thitherward as fast as I could " (p. 95).

" She told him that the last Sabbath-day (as she called it) there came an angel or spirit into the church at Beverley, and spoke the wonderful things of God, to the astonishment of all that were there; and when it had done, it passed away, and they did not know whence it came, nor whither it went; but it astonished all,— priests, professors, and magistrates of the town. This relation Justice Hotham gave me afterwards, and then I gave him an account of how I had been that day at Bever-ley steeple-house, and had declared truth to .the priest and people there " (p. 136).

" The clerk up with his Bible, as I was speaking, and struck me on the face with it, so that my face gushed out with blood; and I bled exceedingly in the steeple-. house " (p. 146).

" After this I returned into Westmorland, and spoke through Kendal on a market-day. So dreadful was the power of God upon me, that people flew like chaff before me into their houses " (p. 166).

" They removed me into a worse room, where I had neither chimney nor fire-hearth. This being towards the sea-side and lying much open, the wind drove in the rain forcibly so that the water came over my bed, and ran so about the room that I was fain to skim it up with a platter. When my clothes were wet, I had no fire to dry them; so that my body was benumbed with cold, and my fingers swelled so that one was grown as big as two. Besides, they would suffer few Friends to come to me, and many times not any; no, not so much as to bring me a little food. . . . Commonly a threepenny loaf served me three weeks, and sometimes longer, and most of my drink was water with wormwood steeped or bruised in it " (p. 440).

" I was so exceedingly weak, I was hardly able to get on or off my horse's back; but my spirit being earnestly engaged in the work the Lord had concerned me in and sent me forth about, I travelled on therein, notwithstanding the weakness of my body, having confidence in the Lord, that He would carry me through, as He did by His power " (p. 461).

" We got on shore as soon as we could and I with some others walked to the house of a Friend, above a quarter of a mile from the bridge. But being very ill and weak, I was so tired, that I was in a manner spent by the time I got thither. There I abode very ill several days, and though they several times gave me things

" I spoke among them the Word of the Lord, which was as a hammer, and as a fire amongst them. . . . The mighty power of the Lord was over all; and so wonderful was the appearance thereof, that priest Bennett said the church shook, insomuch that he was afraid and trembled " (p. 167).

" Whereupon I set my eyes upon him, and spoke sharply to him in the power of the Lord: and he cried, ' Do not pierce me so with thy eyes; keep thy eyes off me ' " (p. 187).

" When I was come to Lancaster, the spirits of the people being mightily up, I stood and looked earnestly upon them, and they cried, ' Look at his eyes ! ' " (p. 344).

" Before I left I went to visit one Galeenus Abrahams, a teacher of chief note among the Mennonites, or Baptists. I had been with him when I was in Holland about seven years before and William Penn and George Keith had disputed with him. He was then very high and shy, so that he would not let me touch him, nor look upon him (by his good will) but bid me ' Keep my eyes off him, for,' he said, ' they pierced him.' But now he was very loving

to make me sweat, they could not effect it. What they gave me did rather parch and dry up my body, and made me probably worse than otherwise I might have been. Thus I continued about three weeks after I landed, having much pain in my bones, joints, and whole body, so that I could hardly get any rest; yet I was pretty cheery, and my spirit kept above it all. Neither did my illness take me off from the service of Truth; but both while I was at sea, and after I came to Barbadoes, before I was able to travel about, I gave forth several papers (having a Friend to write for me), some of which I sent by the first conveyance for England to be printed" (p. 488).

"We went some of the way by land, the rest by water, and, a storm arising, our boat was run aground, in danger of being beaten to pieces, and the water came in upon us. I was in a great sweat, having come very hot out of a meeting before, and now was wet with the water besides; yet, having faith in the divine power, I was preserved from taking hurt, blessed be the Lord!" (p. 499).

"About this time I had a fit of sickness, which brought me very low and weak in my body; and I continued so a pretty while, insomuch that some Friends began to doubt of my recovery. . . . One night as I was lying awake upon my bed in the glory of the Lord which was over all, it was said unto me that the Lord had a great deal more work for me to

and tender, and confessed in some measure to truth" (p. 556, note).

"I went to Reading, where I was under great exercises and suffering and in great travail of spirit for about ten weeks" (p. 363).

"'I will not be afraid of thee, George Fox; thou speakest so loud thy voice drowns mine and the court's; I must call for three or four criers to drown thy voice; thou hast good lungs'" (p. 415).

"As I was walking down a hill, a great weight and oppression fell upon my spirit. I got on my horse again, but the weight remained so that I was hardly able to ride. . . . We came to Hornchurch, where there was a meeting on First-day. After it I rode with great uneasiness to Stratford, to a Friend's house. Here I lay exceedingly weak, and at last lost both hearing and sight. . . . In this condition I continued some time. Several came about me; and though I could not see their person I felt and discerned their spirits, who were honest-hearted, and who were not. . . . Under great sufferings and travails, sorrows and oppression I lay for several weeks, whereby I was brought so low and weak in body that few thought I could live. Some that were with me went away, saying they would not see me die. . .

do for Him before He took me to Himself" (p. 540).

"The illness I got in my imprisonment at Worcester had so much weakened me that it was long before I recovered my natural strength again " (p. 544).

"Though I rode not very far in a day, yet through weakness of body, continual travelling was hard to me. Besides, I had not much rest at night to refresh nature; for I often sat up late with Friends, where I lodged, to inform and advise them in things wherein they were wanting; and when I was in bed I was often hindered of sleep by great pains in my head and teeth, occasioned, as I thought, from cold taken by riding often in the rain. But the Lord's power was over all, and carried me through all, to His praise " (p. 546).

When they that were about me had given me up to die, I spoke to them to get a coach to carry me to Gerrard Roberts's . . . for I found it was my place to go thither. I had now recovered a little glimmering of sight, so that I could discern the people and fields as I went, and that was all. . . . I lay all that winter, warring in spirit with the evil spirits of the world, that warred against Truth and Friends. . . . After some time it pleased the Lord to allay the heat of this violent persecution. . . . As the persecution ceased I came from under the travails and sufferings that had lain with such weight upon me; so that towards the spring I began to recover and to walk up and down, beyond the expectation of many, who did not think I could ever have gone abroad again " (p. 476 ff.).

In sharp contrast to his sympathetic outreach into the life about him, we find him apparently entirely heartless in the manner in which he could withdraw in his stress period from all companionship with his family, relatives and friends. Considering the lightning-like responsiveness of his body, one is surprised even when one finds that his heartlessness is only apparent, and is but an example of delayed response. Events, people, ideas which apparently had been left behind as settled, kept pulling on his being. His mind kept mulling over a problem long after it had apparently been discarded. Months after he had left his parents, the ties of family affection, which had been so thoroughly inhibited, forced their way out, and "I had a regard upon my mind lest I should grieve them, for I understood they were troubled at my absence." [1] In his youth he "could not sing," for he "was not in a state to sing." [2] However, some five years later, when being cruelly treated by his jailer in prison, the inhibited impulse rushes up in him, and he is "moved in the Lord's power to sing." [3] When invited to weddings he would not go, but a few days later the tension between his natural sympathy and his inhibition would break. Then he would feel drawn to go to visit the new home in order to take the young people a gift of money, especially if they were poor. [4]

The successive and progressive character of his openings during the early years show that even the intuitional insight evident in them comes only after long periods of incubation of inhibited tendencies,

[1] *Journal*, p. 70. [2] Ibid., p. 72.
[3] Ibid., p. 191. [4] Ibid., p. 74.

with their attendant tension and struggle. During two years these periods of struggle and searching alternated with times of illuminating vision. Then the uprushings from what Jastrow calls "the underground workshop of thought," had forged a pathway that required no longer the intermission of intense despair. His delayed reactions were overcome by an habitually consistent type of immediate response.

It seems as if Fox must have had both receptor and motor nerves of extremely delicate sensitivity and responsiveness, and yet as if there were difficulty in getting the circuit between them closed. The energy from inhibited actions seemed to be summed up until with a snap the interwoven synapses sprang into conjunction and the energy burst through into some intense form of activity. At times the activity became pathological to a greater or less extent. This is particularly evident in the episode at Lichfield. While the synapses at first did not close readily, they were very sure. Problems worked at him even after he had apparently ceased to work at them, and eventually they found their solution.

Perhaps it was this lack of naturally swift co-ordination causing what appears to be a chasm between the sensitivity of his inner being and the reticence toward outward response that made possible in him so many of the characteristics which seem mutually exclusive.

Tough-mindedness and Tender-mindedness.

William James has described two classes of people, tough-minded and tender-minded. But George Fox was both of these. He described himself as a tender youth and it grieved him when friends and

CONFLICTING TRAITS.

INHIBITION.	RESPONSIVENESS.
" When boys and rude persons would laugh at me, I let them alone and went my way " (p. 67).	" I was fearful, having a regard upon my mind to my parents and relations, lest I should grieve them, for I understood they were troubled at my absence " (p. 70).
" I had an uncle there, one Pickering, a Baptist ; the Baptists were tender then ; yet I could not impart my mind to him, nor join with them " (p. 70).	" This I spoke, being at that time sensible of Christ's sufferings " (p. 71).
	" I was fearful of being drawn out by them ; yet I was made to speak, and open things to them " (p. 87).
" It grieved me that I should have opened my mind to such a one. I saw that they were all miserable comforters, and this increased my troubles upon me " (p. 72).	" A report went abroad of me, that I was a young man that had a discerning spirit " (p. 88).
	" The priest said to her, ' I permit not a woman to speak in the church.' . . . Whereupon I was wrapped up, as in a rapture " (p. 92).
" I fasted much, walked abroad in solitary places many days, and often took my Bible, and sat in hollow trees and lonesome places till night came on, and frequently in the night walked mournfully about by myself " (p. 79).	" It was a great grief to my soul and spirit when I heard him talk so lightly ; so that I told him he was too light to talk of the things of God " (p. 217).
	" As I rode up the street, a justice of the peace came out to me, asked me to alight, and desired that I would stay at his house, which I did " (p. 285).
" I was afraid of all company. . . . I had not fellowship with any people. . . . When I myself was in the deep, shut up under all, I could not believe that I should ever overcome " (p. 83).	" While he struck me, I was moved in the Lord's power to sing, which made him rage the

" I left my relations, and broke off all familiarity or fellowship with young or old " (p. 69).

" He bade me take tobacco and sing psalms. Tobacco was a thing I did not love, and psalms I was not in a state to sing ; I could not sing " (p. 72).

more. Then he fetched a fiddler, and set him to play, thinking to vex me. But while he played, I was moved in the everlasting power of the Lord God to sing ; and my voice drowned the noise of the fiddle, struck and confounded them, and made them give over fiddling and go their way " (p. 191).

relatives gave him worldly advice.[1] So tender did he feel his spirit to be that he was " afraid both of professor and profane," lest he " be hurt by conversing with either." [2] He was naturally of a deeply religious nature, with his supreme interest in religion and in that alone. Yet he was so tough-minded that he refused to join any religious group. He would not join with the priests of the Established Church, nor with any of the dissenting bodies so numerous in his day. He saw that " to be a true believer was another thing than they looked upon it to be." [3] Neither did he have fellowship with any people outside the churches, for he was " afraid of all carnal talk and talkers," [4] in whom he could see nothing but corruptions. He was so tough-minded that he found no good in any to whom he went to seek for help, finding only that " none could speak to his condition." [5] He was, on the other hand, so tender that, turning his spirit inward, he learned " to rely on the Lord alone, seeking heavenly wisdom and getting knowledge from the Lord." [6] Fellowship he found with Christ, who " opened the door of Light and Life " [7] to him. Thus he " knew experimentally " [8] that God indeed speaks immediately to the hearts of men. He could speak to God so directly that his public prayer was marked with such intensity that " the house seemed to be shaken," and people exclaimed that it had become again even as in the days of the apostles.[9] When, however, they requested that he should appear in prayer again, his repellent attitude was at once dominant,

---

[1] *Journal*, p. 71. [2] Ibid., p. 80. [3] Ibid., p. 75.
[4] Ibid., p. 83. [5] Ibid., p. 82. [6] Ibid., p. 80.
[7] Ibid., p. 83. [8] Ibid., p. 82. [9] Ibid., p. 90.

and he replied that he "could not pray in man's will." [1]

So tender was his spirit to criticism that words of praise were as a thistle to him.[2] Yet he could harden himself until the good report and bad report of others were as nothing to him.[3] His soul grieved at the drunkenness of an acquaintance who professed Christianity, and he refused to go into any house in that village.[4] He "had sore exercise and travail of spirit over the wickedness of the town"[5] in which he suffered imprisonment. But when Oliver Cromwell gave orders to his followers that Fox be taken to dinner at Whitehall, Fox curtly refused, and bade them tell the Protector that he would "not eat of his meat nor drink of his drink."[6] When the King would have pardoned Fox and set him free from prison, he refused to accept any "pardon," knowing himself to be innocent, and therefore unjustly imprisoned.[7]

He was very gentle and loving in the care of those "tender plants,"[8] his spiritual children in the Truth. "Travail of spirit"[9] did he feel for the meeting which he was about to attend. But when one of these "tender plants" fell by the wayside, Fox was unrelenting in turning from him. James Nayler, a man of a keen delicacy of feeling, but of less rigour than Fox, had been a brilliant follower of his teaching. With none of Fox's fearless censoriousness of others, and with trust in their good judgment, there came a time when Nayler seemed unable to withstand the strain of the early days of Quakerism. He lost grip by a

[1] *Journal,* p. 90. [2] Ibid., p. 184. [3] Ibid., p. 131.
[4] Ibid., p. 231. [5] Ibid., p. 131. [6] Ibid., p. 215.
[7] Ibid., p. 541. [8] Ibid., p. 297. [9] Ibid., p. 507.

silly, if not entirely pathological, expression of the teaching of the Indwelling Christ. When he would have come to Fox in affection and have kissed him, Fox would not receive " his show of kindness." Fox records, " The Lord moved me to slight him." [1] Many others he healed of their mental and physical ills, but this most brilliant and sweet-spirited of his followers, of whose downfall he had even a premonition, he does not prevent from going astray. When the fanatic deed is done, he thrusts him aside and " admonishes him and his company." [2] What James Nayler needed was spiritual guidance at the right time, and, failing that, mental treatment later. But Fox was jealous for his beloved Society and the Truth for which it stood, and tough-minded toward all that rose against it. So he left Nayler for Parliament to wreak upon him the harshest punishment it could devise. Pilloried, whipped through the streets, branded, and with his tongue bored by a red-hot iron, he was cast into solitary confinement with hard labour. Was Fox's hard attitude toward Nayler due partly to the fact that he resented the personal criticism of himself that came from Nayler in a letter to Margaret Fell ? Nayler questions if Fox be not jealous of his brilliant preaching of the Truth.

In no way perhaps was Fox's tough-mindedness more evident than in his persistence in wearing his hat, or in refusing to take oaths. His allegiance to his country he shows not by taking oaths,[3] and by blindly obeying the laws which a changing government made and unmade. His patriotism is shown by being at all times scrupulously honest,[4] by appearing

[1] *Journal*, p. 271. [2] Ibid., p. 271.
[3] Ibid., p. 427. [4] Ibid., p. 414.

in court when ordered to do so, by willingly and cheerfully suffering imprisonment for the breaking of those
laws which he finds incompatible with that which he
sees as truth, by travelling without surveillance and
surrendering himself at the prison to which he had
been condemned,[1] by refusing to take advantage of
the privilege of walking a mile from the prison until
the authorities had measured that mile, lest he should
overstep the limit,[2] by refusing to be released from his
last unjust imprisonment by a King's pardon.[3] His
respect for the magistrates and officers of the law he
did not show by what was to him the silly convention
of " hat honour," [4] even though his refusal led to much
persecution for him.

Positive and Negative Suggestibility.

His positive and negative suggestibility were just
as conflicting traits as were his tender- and tough-
mindedness. Mystical ideas had filtered into English
life from many sources until they permeated the common
life of the middle of the seventeenth century. George
Fox, therefore, was born not only into a home of
religious attitude, but also into a general environment
full of mystical ideas to which he was suggestibly
sensitive.

In England in the fourteenth century Wyclif seems
the first to break the bondage of the nation to the
Church. As his followers there arose a group of itinerant
preachers, " evangelical men " he calls them. Through
them the people of England were influenced until
his views triumphed in the Reformation. This lay

[1] *Journal,* p. 356. [2] Ibid., p. 125.
[3] Ibid., p. 541. [4] Ibid., p. 246-248.

CONFLICTING TRAITS.

TOUGH-MINDEDNESS.[1]	TENDER-MINDEDNESS.
" When I saw old men behave lightly and wantonly towards each other, I had a dislike thereof raised in my heart, and said within myself, ' If ever I come to be a man, surely I shall not do so, nor be so wanton " (p. 66).	" I durst not stay long in a place, being afraid both of professor and profane, lest, being a tender young man, I should be hurt by conversing much with either " (p. 79).
" When we had drunk a glass apiece, they began to drink healths, and called for more drink, agreeing together that he who would not drink should pay all. I was grieved that any who made a profession of religion should offer to do so. They grieved me very much, having never had such a thing put to me before by any sort of people. Wherefore I rose up, and, putting my hand in my pocket, took out a groat, and laid it upon the table, saying, ' If it be so, I will leave you ' " (p. 68).	" I was afraid of all company. . . . I was afraid of all carnal talk and talkers, for I could see nothing but corruptions " (p. 83).
	" I was fearful, and returned homeward into Leicestershire, having a regard upon my mind to my parents and relations, lest I should grieve them, for I understood they were troubled at my absence " (p. 70).
" I left my relations, and broke off all familiarity or fellowship with young or old " (p. 68).	" I met with a very tender people, and a very tender woman, whose name was Elizabeth Hooten" (p. 78).
" I went to many a priest to look for comfort, but found no comfort from them " (p. 70).	
" I saw they were all miserable comforters " (p. 72).	" I was grieved that they offered such things to me, being a tender youth " (p. 71).
" My relations would have had me married ; . . . others would have had me join the auxiliary band among the soldiery, but I refused " (p. 71).	" But the next day, or soon after, I would go and visit them, and if they were poor I gave them some money " (p. 74).

[1] References are to the Journal as edited by R. M. Jones : *George Fox: An Autobiography.*

" When I was invited to marriages (as I sometimes was), I went to none at all " (p. 74).

" During all this time I was never joined in profession of religion with any, but gave up myself to the Lord, having forsaken all evil company, taken leave of father and mother, and all other relations, and travelled up and down as a stranger in the earth " (p. 79).

" As I had forsaken the priests, so I left the separate preachers also, and those esteemed the most experienced people ; for I saw there was none among them all that could speak to my condition " (p. 82).

" I was moved to pray ; and the Lord's power was so great that the house seemed to be shaken. . . . He came to me, and desired that I would pray again ; but I could not pray in man's will " (p. 90).

" There was another great meeting of professors. . . . They were discoursing of the blood of Christ. . . . And I cried out among them, and said, ' Do you not see the blood of Christ ? See it in your hearts ' " (p. 91).

" Towards Nottingham . . . I espied the great steeple-house. . . . When I came there . . . the priest . . . took for his text . . . words of Peter. . . . And he told the people that this was the Scriptures, by which they were to try all doctrines, religions, and opinions. Now the Lord's power was so

" When the time called Christmas came, while others were feasting and sporting themselves, I looked out poor widows from house to house, and gave them some money " (p. 73).

" I found there were two thirsts in me—the one after the creatures, to get help and strength there, and the other after the Lord, the Creator, and His Son Jesus Christ " (p. 84).

" A strong temptation to despair came upon me " (p. 69).

" I was a man of sorrows in the time of the first workings of the Lord in me " (p. 79).

" I heard a voice which said, ' There is one, even Christ Jesus, that can speak to thy condition ' ; and when I heard it, my heart did leap for joy " (p. 82).

" When God doth work, who shall hinder it ? and this I knew experimentally " (p. 82).

" A report went abroad of me, that I was a young man that had a discerning spirit " (p. 88).

" I saw the harvest white, and the seed of God lying thick in the ground, as ever did wheat mighty upon me that I could not hold, but was made to cry out and say, ' Oh, no ; it is not the Scriptures ! ' and I told them what it was, namely, the Holy Spirit, . . . whereby opinions, religions, and judgments were to be tried " (p. 109).

At York Cathedral : " When the priest had done, I told them I had something from the Lord God to speak to the priest and people. 'Then say on quickly,' said a professor. . . . Then I told them that this was the Word of the Lord God unto them,—that they lived in words, but God Almighty looked for fruits amongst them " (p. 138).

" Captain Drury brought me before the Protector himself at Whitehall. . . . Many . . . words I had with him. . . . Then I went out. . . . Then I was brought into a great hall, where the Protector's men were to dine. I asked them what they brought me thither for. They said it was by the Protector's orders, that I might dine with them. I bid them let the Protector know that I would not eat of his bread, nor drink of his drink. When he heard this he said, ' Now I see there is a people risen that I cannot win with gifts or honours, offices or places ; but all other sects and peoples I can ' " (pp. 212– 215).

" The jailer was cruel, and the under-jailer very abusive both to me and to Friends that came to see me. . . . Once he came in a

that was sown outwardly, and none to gather it " (p. 88).

" This I spoke, being at that time in a measure sensible of Christ's sufferings " (p. 71).

" We had a meeting at Providence, which was very large, consisting of many sorts of people. I had a great travail upon my spirit, that it might be preserved quiet, and that Truth might be brought over the people "(p. 507.)

" As I walked upon a bank by the house, there came several poor travellers, asking relief, who I saw were in necessity ; and they gave them nothing, but said they were cheats. It grieved me to see such hard-heartedness amongst professors ; whereupon, when they were gone in to their breakfast, I ran after the poor people about a quarter of a mile, and gave them some money " (p. 157).

" Great was the exercise and travail in spirit that I underwent during my imprisonment there, because of the wickedness that was in this town " (p. 131).

" Judge Fell . . . was out of the country all this time that I was thus cruelly abused. . . . When he came home . . . he asked me to give him a relation of my persecution ; but I told him they could not do otherwise in the

great rage and beat me with his cudgel. . . . While he struck me, I was moved in the Lord's power to sing, which made him rage the more. Then he fetched a fiddler, and he set him to play, thinking to vex me. But while he played, I was moved in the Lord's power to sing ; and my voice drowned the noise of the fiddle, struck and confounded them, and made them give over fiddling and go their way " (p. 191).

" ' Why do you not put off your hats ? ' said the Judge to us. We said nothing.

" ' Put off your hats,' said the Judge again. Still we said nothing. Then said the Judge, ' The Court commands you to put off your hats.'

" 'Then I spoke and said, ' Where did ever any magistrate, king, or judge, from Moses to Daniel, command any to put off their hats, when they came before him in his court, either amongst the Jews, the people of God, or amongst the heathen ? and if the law of England doth command any such thing, show me that law either written or printed.'

" Then the Judge grew very angry, and said, ' I do not carry my law-books on my back.' ' But,' said I, ' tell me where it is printed in any statute-book, that I may read it.' . . . ' Come,' said he, ' where had they any hats, from Moses to Daniel ? come, answer me ; I have you fast now.'

" I replied, ' Thou mayest read in the third of Daniel, that the three children were cast into the fiery furnace by Nebuchadnezzar's

spirit wherein they were, and that they manifested the fruits of their priest's ministry, and their profession and religion to be wrong " (p. 174).

" And Friends, be careful how ye set your feet among the tender plants, that are springing up out of God's earth ; lest ye tread upon them, hurt, bruise, or crush them in God's vineyard " (Postscript to Epistle to Friends) (p. 297).

" I went to another ancient priest and reasoned with him about the ground of despair and temptations. But he was ignorant of my condition ; he bade me take tobacco and sing psalms. Tobacco was a thing I did not love, and psalms I was not in a state to sing ; I could not sing " (p. 72).

" After the meeting there came a woman to me whose husband was one of the judges of that country, and a member of the assembly there. She told me that her husband was sick, not likely to live, and desired me to go home with her to see him. It was three miles to her house, and I being just come hot out of the meeting, it was hard for me then to go ; yet considering the service, I got a horse, went with her, visited her husband, and spoke to him what the Lord gave me. The man was much refreshed, and finely raised up by the power of the Lord ; and afterwards came to our meetings " (p. 519).

command, with their coats, their hose, and their hats on.' . . .

"The Judge fell upon us about our hats again, bidding the jailer take them off; which he did, and gave them to us; and we put them on again" (pp. 246–248).

"If I would have been freed by a pardon, I need not have lain so long, for the King was willing to give me pardon long before, and told Thomas Moore that I need not scruple being released by a pardon, for many a man that was as innocent as a child had had a pardon granted him; yet I would not consent to have one. For I would rather have lain in prison all my days, than have come out in any way dishonourable to Truth; and therefore I chose to have the validity of my indictment tried before the judges" (p. 541).

"Being thus made prisoners . . . we got some Friends to accompany my wife and her daughter into the north, and so were conveyed to Worcester. Thence by the time I thought my wife would reach home, I wrote her the following letter :

"Dear Heart:

"Thou seemedst to be a little grieved when I was speaking of prisons, and when I was taken. Be content with the will of the Lord God. For when I was at John Rous's, at Kingston, I had a sight of my being taken prisoner ; and when I was at Bray Doily's, . . . as I sat at supper, I saw I was taken, and I saw I had a suffering to undergo. But the Lord's power is over all; blessed be His holy name for ever !

"G. F."

(p. 539).

CONFLICTING TRAITS.

NEGATIVE SUGGESTIBILITY.

" Now there were great threatenings given forth in Cumberland that if ever I came there they would take away my life. When I heard it I was drawn to go into Cumberland " (p. 181).

" The innkeeper's wife came and told me that the governor and magistrates were sending for me, to commit me to prison also. . . . Soon after came other friendly people, and told me that if I went into the street, the governor and magistrates would imprison me also ; therefore they desired me to keep within the inn. Upon this I was moved to go and walk up and down in the streets " (p. 290).

" My relations would have had me married ; but I told them I was but a lad, and must get wisdom. Others would have had me join the auxiliary band among the soldiery, but I refused, and was grieved that they offered such things to me, being a tender youth " (p. 70).

" At Evesham I heard that the magistrates had cast several Friends into divers prisons, and that, hearing of my coming, they had made a pair of high stocks. I sent for Edward Pittaway, a Friend that lived near Evesham, and asked him the truth of the thing. He

SUGGESTIBILITY.

" One Brown . . . had great prophecies and sights upon his death-bed of me. He spoke only of what I should be made instrumental by the Lord to bring forth. . . . When this man was buried a great work of the Lord fell upon me, to the admiration of many, who thought I had been dead, and many came to see me for about fourteen days. . . . The same eternal power of God, which brought me through these things, was that which afterwards shook the nations, priests, professors and people. . . . I saw the harvest white, and the seed of God lying thick in the ground, as ever did wheat that was sown outwardly, and none to gather it ; for this I mourned with tears " (p. 88).

" I was in a great sweat, having come very hot out of a meeting before, and now was wet with the water besides ; yet, having faith in the divine power, I was preserved from taking hurt " (p. 499).

" I heard over night of their meeting and of the warrant, and could have gone out of their reach if I would, for I had not appointed any meeting at that time, and I had cleared myself of the north, and the Lord's power was over all. But I considered that there being a noise of a plot in the north, if I should go away, they might fall upon Friends ; but if I gave myself up to be taken, it

said it was so. I went that night with him to Evesham " (p. 229).

" We returned to our inn, where were two desperate fellows fighting so furiously that none durst come nigh to part them. But I was moved, in the Lord's power, to go to them ; and when I had loosed their hands, I held one of them by one hand and the other by the other, showed them the evil of their doings, and reconciled them " (p. 233).

might prevent them, and Friends should escape the better. So I gave myself up to be taken, and prepared for their coming " (p. 405).

" Soon after there was another great meeting of professors. . . . They were discoursing of the blood of Christ, and as they were discoursing of it, I saw, through the immediate opening of the invisible Spirit, the blood of Christ " (p. 91).

religion and Quakerism have much in common. In fact, George Fox himself was of this " stock of martyrs," [1] through his maternal ancestry. He and his followers, consciously or unconsciously, " were the genuine apostolic successors of Wyclif's evangelical men." [2]

From the middle of the reign of Elizabeth, Green says :

"England became the people of a book, and that book was the Bible. . . . Elizabeth might silence or tune the pulpits, but it was impossible for her to silence or tune the great preachers of justice and mercy and truth who spoke from the book which she had again opened to her people. . . . The great problems of life and death . . . pressed for an answer not only from noble and scholar, but from farmer and shopkeeper as well." [3]

True religious toleration was not even substantially achieved till 1689. In the intervening period of struggle and bitter persecutions Quakerism arose. Before the time of this religious liberty, ten years before the death of Fox in 1691, Quakerism numbered sixty-six thousand people.[4]

Throughout the Middle Ages, when formal ecclesiasticism ruled the religious life and scholasticism moulded the minds of men, there were some brave men who could not be content with a life of ritualism and dogmatism. They reached out individually, or in groups, for the great adventure of a personal knowledge of a God " nearer to them than breathing, closer

[1] *Journal*, p. 66.

[2] Rufus M. Jones : *Studies in Mystical Religion* (London, 1909), p. 366.

[3] Green : *History of the English People*, chap. viii.

[4] Isaac Sharpless : " Society of Friends," in *Schaff-Herzog Encyclopædia*, vol. iv, p. 393.

than hands or feet." These mystics were, as such ever are, explorers in the spiritual realm.

Probably of all these groups, the teachings of the Family of Love had as much to do with creating the general mystical atmosphere into which Fox came, as any one influence. In many ways Fox resembled its founder, Henry Nicholas, born in Westphalia in the sixteenth century. The House of Love brought into public notice many doctrines and practices generally supposed to have originated with the Quakers. It was its founder's purpose " to raise the entire membership ' to full-grown men in Christ,' so that each member should attain to the experience of a ' begodded person.' " [1] The central idea is " insistence on real righteousness and actual holiness as contrasted with the fiction of a merely imputed righteousness and a forensic holiness. . . . This righteousness, this new life, comes from a spiritual incorporation of the person into God's life, so that the person, once a mere man, becomes ' godded ' or made conformable to Christ, who was an absolutely begodded man." [2] An equally lofty conception of the moral life in its daily walk and conversation is the concomitant of this spiritual exaltation. Nicholas called his followers away from oaths and war and capital punishment. Even as George Fox did later, he emphasized the silent waiting upon the Lord. " Grow up in stillness," he advises, " and singleness of heart, praying for a right sight in the truth, for that shall make you free." [3]

[1] Jones: *Studies in Mystical Religion* (London, 1909), p. 433.
[2] Ibid., p. 433.
[3] Henry Nicholas: Introduction to *Glass of Righteousness*, chap. xviii, p. 25.

His attitude toward the Scriptures and toward outward ordinances and ceremonies—"God services" he calls them—is almost the same as that later adopted by Friends.

The writings of the great Teutonic mystic, Jacob Boehme, however, may have had a more direct influence upon Fox and his followers. They were translated into English just at the time that Fox was growing into manhood. A contemporary writer records that these were more bought by the followers of Fox than any other books.[1] Undoubtedly Fox read them. It was his custom to read many books, and to carry other books than the Bible with him as he travelled through the country.

The times were rife with religious interests, and there were numerous persons, both inside and outside the Quaker group, who, quite independently, had the inner experience and arrived at the insight that religion to be true and spiritual must "be well grounded in the witness of the indwelling Spirit."[2] These others, as well as Fox, were undoubtedly conditioned by, if not to some extent the product of, the peculiar social and spiritual conditions of the time. The small mystical sects and the current mystical literature filled the time with a suggestiveness to which such people were so constituted as to be peculiarly responsive.

In the midst of the efforts then being made to rescue the Church from the corruptions which had grown up around it, there were men who felt that Luther and Cranmer had not gone far enough. They felt that there was much sacerdotalism to be purged away

[1] Muggleton : *Looking-Glass for George Fox* (2nd edition), p. 10.
[2] Ibid.

before the original simplicity of Christianity could be restored. Such men found a leader in George Fox, who, though not at all the discoverer of a new approach to God, is nevertheless the genuine prophet of the Indwelling Spirit. He " drew together into one unified movement aspects of truth which were powerless while in abstraction." [1]

Fox was suggestible not alone to the mystical ideas of his time which met the needs of his own soul. He was tenderly responsive to the needs of others, and could have a vision of " a great people to be gathered" [2] " Being in the way the Lord led " [3] him. He had that " prepared soul of a prophet which is by temperament and experience saturated with the mental elements that combine into the vision." [4] It is because of " the delicate adjustment of a human mind for catching the distant vibrations or ' overtones ' of the universe " [5] that such a call can come. It resulted in Fox in one of those moments on the high level of experience which have made men of all ages name it the voice of God speaking, and it comes out of an experience of such profundity and immediateness that one is stirred below the level of the conscious self, and feels what Lowell has described as " that perfect disenthralment which is God." [6]

Such a moment came to Fox not as the result of the vague indefinite general suggestiveness of the mystical atmosphere of his land. No doubt he had

[1] Jones: Introduction to Braithwaite: *Beginnings of Quakerism,* p. xxviii.
[2] *Journal,* p. 150.   [3] Genesis xxiv. 27.
[4] Kaplan: *Psychology of Prophecy.* Philadelphia, 1908.
[5] Ibid.
[6] Lowell: *The Cathedral.*

a spirit ripe because of it. It was, however, directly called forth by the death-bed prophecy of " one Brown," who predicted great things of Fox. So sensitively was Fox prepared for such a suggestion, that when it came in this form it threw him into the first of these great sweeping psychical and physical changes that are to be found scattered through his life. No doubt the boy in his wanderings had dreamed incoherently of some such mission, but to have it voiced by another under such circumstances was putting the tender plant under forcing conditions too severe for it at the time. Fox describes the experience thus :

" When the man was buried a great work of the Lord fell upon me, to the admiration of many, who thought I had been dead and many came to see me for about fourteen days. I was very much altered in countenance and person, as if my body had been new moulded or changed. My sorrows and troubles began to wear off, and tears of joy dropped from me, so that I could have wept night and day with tears of joy to the Lord, in humility and brokenness of heart. . . . The same eternal power of God, which brought me through these things, was that which after-wards shook the nations, priests, professors and people. . . . I saw the harvest white, and the seed of God lying thick on the ground, as ever did wheat that was sown outwardly, and none to gather it ; for this I mourned with tears." [1]

This indirect suggestion from the dying man he had responded to positively. But he had repeatedly spurned the direct suggestions of those who had tried to aid him in finding his way out of indecisions into a life procedure. He had been urged to become a priest in the Established Church, but he had refused.[2] Later in life he announced his profession as that of

[1] *Journal,* p. 88. ·   [2] *Ibid.,* p. 67.

a " preacher of righteousness." [1]   People sought to
be kindly to him, but he judged them empty of that
which they professed and held himself apart from
them.[2]   Each thing they suggested, he rebelled against.[2]
When his relatives urged him to marry, he told them
he was "but a lad, and must get wisdom." He
refused to become a soldier in the Civil War then
raging, in accordance with the advice of others.[3]   In
each priest he sought out with the ostensible purpose
of obtaining aid and advice, his unrecognized tough,
negative, critical attitude could find only fault and
emptiness.   He "disliked" Stephens because he
would preach on Sundays thoughts expressed by Fox
during the week.[4]   The priest at Mancetter "grieved"
him by telling Fox's troubles to his servants and advising
him to take tobacco and sing psalms ; but "tobacco
was a thing he did not love, and psalms he was not
in a state to sing."[5]   He travelled seven miles to
Tamworth, and found the priest "like an empty hollow
cask."[6]   Against each he reacted with scorn and
criticism.   Never would he accept unquestioned the
standards of others.   However, no doubt there was a
harvesting of all the impress of the kindnesses people
attempted to lavish upon him, and the kindlier side of
his nature helped them to ripen and to formulate his
own kindly attitude to all people.   Then could he
love even his enemies and persecutors.[7]

The festivities of Christmas he would not celebrate
with others, nor in their conventional ways.[8]   He was
ever rebellious against fixed customs and the cere-

[1] *Journal,* p. 366.   [2] Ibid., p. 69.   [3] Ibid., p. 70.
[4] Ibid., p. 71.   [5] Ibid., p. 72.   [6] Ibid., p. 72.
[7] Ibid., p. 348.   [8] Ibid., p. 73.

monies of others. Still he could not resist the appeal of the season, and he went from house to house looking out poor widows and giving them gifts of money.

One wonders if his insistence upon the equality of women with men in all matters of life and religion may not have arisen not only out of the sense of the superior worth of his own noble mother, but also in revolt against the general attitude of the curious sect of his day who claimed that "women have no souls, no more than a goose." [1] It may have arisen in part, too, from the intensity with which he gallantly protested against the rudeness of the priest to the woman who had asked a question in a public meeting for discussion at Leicester. [2] That which was evidently intense anger at the priest to whom, as to all of his class, Fox was very ready to take a negative attitude, he describes as "being wrapped up as in a rapture"! So he stepped forward and reprimanded the priest publicly. "For," says Fox in telling of it, "the woman asking a question, he ought to have answered it, having given liberty for any to speak."

His mission, as he conceived it, was "to bring people off" from all their present associations. Not even an admixture of goodness did he seem able to see in any of them. He was to "bring people off" from "all their own ways," from "their churches," from "the world's teachers made by man," from "the world's worships," from "the world's religions," from "the world's fellowships and prayings and singings," from "Jewish ceremonies and heathen fables,"

[1] *Journal,* p. 77.   [2] Ibid., p. 92.

from " men's inventions and worldly doctrines," and from " all their beggarly rudiments with their schools and colleges for making ministers of Christ." [1]

Not alone was he unconventional in his attitude toward social customs. He was negatively opposed to them. He felt it his duty to bear witness against the social inequality of his day by addressing all as " thee," and " thou " without respect to their wealth or social standing.[2] He also refused to take off his hat to any, high or low, or to " bow or scrape with his leg to any." [3] He went to the courts to cry against injustice, to public-houses of entertainment to warn them to let none have more drink than would do them good, to fairs and markets " to declare against their deceitful merchandise, cheating, and cozening," to school masters and mistresses " warning them to teach children sobriety in the fear of the Lord," and to masters and mistresses, fathers and mothers in private families, to " take care that their children and servants might be trained up in the fear of the Lord." He testified " against wakes, feasts, May-games, sports, plays and shows," "against all sorts of music, and against the mountebanks playing tricks on their stages." [4]

Church bells and steeples also had a negative effect upon him. The bells " struck at his life," [5] and the sight of a steeple-house across the fields brought to him the Lord's voice, saying, " Thou must go cry against yonder great idol, and against the worshippers therein." [6] So obsessed was he with his reaction against the whole Church life of his day (though he describes it as " the

---

[1] *Journal,* p. 105. [2] Ibid., p. 105. [3] Ibid., p. 106.
[4] Ibid., p. 107. [5] Ibid., p. 107. [6] Ibid., p. 109.

Lord's power" which was " so mighty and so strong " in him), that entering the church he could not refrain until the priest had finished his sermon. He cried out in the midst of it, contradicting the preacher, and declaring the " Truth " directly to the congregation.

Reports of danger ahead were as much a red flag to draw Fox on as was a sense of a need which he could fulfil. At Evesham there was made a pair of stocks preparatory to his coming. He investigated the report of this and found it true. Against the advice of his friends he " went that night to Evesham," held a meeting there, and the next morning visited Friends in both prisons before leaving.[1] At Warwick the people were very rude, threw stones at him and his companions, even broke his horse's bridle. But having gone quite out of the town, Fox felt impelled to turn back, and did so, going through the market-place preaching and " showing the people their unworthiness to claim the name of Christian." [2] At an inn at Kingsbridge he went among the people who were drinking and reprimanded them for doing so. The next morning he also reprimanded the innkeeper for " his incivility " in having forced upon Fox his candle the night before and having told him to go to his own room.[3] At Baldock he found two desperate men fighting, and, being warned not to go near them, Fox went fearlessly straight to them and " loosed their hands." [4]

At Beaumaris the innkeeper's wife came to Fox and warned him that the governor and magistrates were sending to imprison him.[5] Other friendly people

[1] *Journal*, p. 229. [2] Ibid., p. 231. [3] Ibid., p. 237.
[4] Ibid., p. 233. [5] Ibid., p. 290.

warned him not to go into the street. Whereupon Fox was moved to go and walk up and down in the street, telling people what an uncivil, unchristian thing they had done to cast his friend into prison. So the friend was soon set free, and Fox was not attacked.

Persecutions but strengthened the man in his ways and his preaching. Even when the mob dragged him till he was unconscious and left him on the wet common, he soon regained not only consciousness, but strength to stand up and cry with a loud voice, " Strike again ; here are my arms, my head and my cheeks." When one rude fellow did strike his hand with a staff so hard that they thought it had " been spoiled for ever," Fox merely " looked at it in the love of God," and in a moment its strength returned.[1]

" Hugh Peters, one of the Protector's chaplains, told him they could not do Fox a greater service for the spreading of his principles in Cornwall than to imprison him there," Fox writes in his Journal.[2] And indeed, so it proved to be. Many came from most parts of the nation to visit the prisoner, and many were moved to go to the steeple-houses, and several went to the prisons to preach, " and a great convincement began in the country."

His strongest personal reaction against any one person seems to have been against Lampitt, the priest at Ulverston church which Margaret Fell and her family attended. This antagonism held into his later period, when he seemed to have left all other personal animosity behind.[3] Was this man Lampitt really more foul than others whom Fox was meeting that he

[1] *Journal*, p. 171. [2] Ibid., p. 259.
[3] Ibid., pp. 160, 169.

needs to denounce him most scathingly, or was it not rather that his revulsion of feeling was intensified by the fact that he apparently held the confidence and friendship of Margaret Fell, whom Fox undoubtedly loved from his first acquaintance with her, even though he tells a friend at the time of his marriage, years later, that the thought of it had been in his mind but six months?[1]

Even a suggestion of approaching death was enough to drive Fox back into robust health. During his illness of 1670, while Margaret Fell, now Margaret Fox, was imprisoned, Friends left his bedside because they "would not see him die." They thought him past hope of recovery. In fact, reports had circulated that he was already dead. To the tough-minded, negatively-suggestible Fox such influences resulted only naturally in the beginning of his recovery. If it was expected that he would die, even though he had apparently lost both sight and hearing, he would feel the atmosphere of those about him, and his inmost being would send forth refreshing strength. A glimmering of sight returned at once, and demanding his clothing and a coach to take him, he went twelve miles to the home of a friend who was also ill. This apparently almost fatal illness seems to have been but the physical reaction to his psychical state. It had been induced by his tender sensitivity to the persecutions of his wife and friends. When these persecutions ceased, and it was safe for his wife to be released, his health returned, and he recovered " beyond the expectation of many."[2]

When, however, the time of his death drew near,

[1] *Journal of George Fox* (Cambridge edition, 1911), vol. ii, p. 154.
[2] *Journal*, pp. 476–481.

his sensitive mind felt the truth, and in peace he met the end with the words, " Now I am clear, I am fully clear." [1]

Aloofness and Gregariousness.

Another pair of characteristics, as opposite in type as those we have already noted, were his sympathetic gregariousness and his aloofness. Perhaps, indeed, his very aloofness was developed from his intense awareness of others. It is probable that as a child his sensitive nature had been so attacked by intense experiences in his contact with people that he fled in self-defence to the gentler influences of the out-of-doors. As a child he was, as William Penn tells us, " of another frame of mind than the rest of his brethren ; being more religious, inward, still, solid, and observing, beyond his years." [2] He himself tells us that he had " a gravity and stayedness of mind and spirit not usual in children." [3] His attention was already being directed to spiritual things, and away from the more direct sense experiences of which he was unusually observant.

His mother, wise and sympathetic, understood the lad and humoured his eccentricities. His father, " righteous Christer," was probably more stern and unsympathetic ; he never accepted his son's spiritual leadership. In George the inheritances from the two warred against each other, making the chasm between his warm inner loving, sympathetic self and his cold outer, censorious aloof self, which was the shell of his

---

[1] *Journal*, pp. 578.
[2] William Penn : Preface to *Journal*, p. 46.
[3] *Journal*, p. 66.

CONFLICTING TRAITS.

ALOOFNESS.

" In my very young years I had a gravity and stayedness of mind and spirit not usual in children " (p. 66).

" When boys and rude persons would laugh at me, I let them alone and went my way " (p. 67).

" I left my relations, and broke off all familiarity or fellowship with young or old " (p. 69).

" When the time called Christmas came, *while others were feasting and sporting themselves* I looked out poor widows from house to house, and gave them some money " (p. 73).

" During all this time I was never joined in profession of religion with any, but gave up myself to the Lord, having forsaken all evil company, taken leave of father and mother, and all other relations, and travelled up and down as a stranger in the earth, which way the Lord inclined my heart; taking a chamber to myself in the town where I came, and tarrying, sometimes more, sometimes less in a place. For I durst not stay long in a place, being afraid both of professor and profane, lest, being a tender young man, I should be hurt by conversing much with either. For

GREGARIOUSNESS.

" When I came towards nineteen years of age, being upon business at a fair, one of my cousins, whose name was Bradford, having another professor with him, came and asked me to drink part of a jug of beer with them. I, being thirsty, went in with them, for I loved any who had a sense of good, or that sought after the Lord " (p. 68).

" I went to many a priest to look for comfort " (p. 70).

" When the time called Christmas came, while other were feasting and sporting themselves *I looked out poor widows* from house to house, and gave them some money " (p. 73).

" Travelling through some parts of Leicestershire, and into Nottinghamshire, I met with a tender people, and a very tender woman, whose name was Elizabeth Hooten. With these I had some meetings and discourses " (p. 78).

" Then I heard of a great meeting to be at Leicester . . . and thither I was moved by the Lord God to go, and be amongst them " (p. 92).

" Returning into Nottinghamshire, I found there a company of shattered Baptists, and others. The Lord's power wrought mightily, and gathered many of them " (p. 94).

this reason I kept much as a stranger, seeking heavenly wisdom and getting knowledge from the Lord, and was brought off from outward things to rely on the Lord alone " (p. 79).

" I was afraid of all company. . . . I had not fellowship with any people, priests or professors, or any sort of separated people, but with Christ, who hath the key, and opened the door of Light and Life unto me. I was afraid of all carnal talk and talkers, for I could see nothing but corruptions, and the life lay under the burthen of corruptions " (p. 83).

" While others were gone to dinner, I went to a brook, got a little water, and then came and sat down on the top of a rock hard by the chapel " (p. 155).

" Supper being provided for the priest and the rest of the company, I had not freedom to eat with them " (p. 157).

" There being many new soldiers raised, the commissioners would have made me captain over them ; and the soldiers cried out that they would have none but me. . . . I told them I knew whence all wars arose, even from the lusts, according to James' doctrine ; and that I lived in the virtue of that life and power that took away the occasion of all wars.

" Yet they courted me to accept

" I found that there were two thirsts in me—the one after the creatures, to get help and strength there, and the other after the Lord, the Creator, and His Son Jesus Christ " (p. 84).

" In the morning, . . . as I walked upon a bank by the house, there came several poor travellers, asking relief, who I saw were in necessity ; and they gave them nothing, but said they were cheats. It grieved me to see such hardheartedness amongst professors ; whereupon, when they were gone in to their breakfast, I ran after the poor people about a quarter of a mile, and gave them some money " (p. 157).

" About this time did the Lord move upon the spirits of many whom He had raised up and sent forth to labour in His vineyard, to travel southwards, and spread themselves in the service of the gospel to the eastern, southern, and western parts of the nation . . . for above sixty ministers had the Lord raised up, and did now send abroad out of the north country. The sense of their service was very weighty upon me " (p. 201).

" But inasmuch as they kept me so very strait, not giving liberty for Friends to come to me, I spoke to the keepers of the Castle to this effect : ' I did not know till I was removed from Lancaster Castle, and brought prisoner to this Castle of Scarborough, that I was convicted of a præmunire ; for the Judge did not give sentence upon me at the

of their offer, and thought that I did but compliment them. But I told them I was come into the covenant of peace, which was before wars and strifes were. They said they offered it in love and kindness to me because of my virtue; and such-like flattering words they used. But I told them, if that was their love and kindness, I trampled it under my feet " (p. 128).

" The Lord let me see why there was none upon the earth that could speak to my condition " (p. 82).

assizes in open court. But seeing I am now a prisoner here, if I may not have my liberty, let my friends and acquaintances have their liberty to come and visit me, as Paul's friends had among the Romans, who were not Christians, but heathen. For Paul's friends had their liberty ; all that would might come to him, and he had his liberty to preach to them in his hired house. But I cannot have liberty to go into the town, nor for my friends to come to me here. So you that go under the name of Christians, are worse in this respect than those heathen were ' " (p. 441).

social contacts. The inhibitions that controlled his nerve mechanism needed to be broken down before the chasm could be bridged, and he could take his place in the social group with ease. Boys and rude persons might laugh at his oddities in his boyhood,[1] and continue to do so throughout his life, but his earnestness, his innocency, his honesty, won people so that they " had generally a love for him." [2] " Thousands can truly say," says William Penn, " he was of an excellent spirit and savour among them, and because thereof the most excellent spirits loved him with an unfeigned and unfading love." [3]

To gain the more unified co-ordinated selfhood, where the two no longer conflicted, in the late years of his adolescence he pulled himself apart from all close associations with his family when they continued to urge upon him either marriage or professions which he did not care to follow. Though he frequently felt compunctions, and questioned lest he might have done harm to them by leaving them, he still held himself apart from all close family relationships. He formed none until in his late marriage with Margaret Fell he found a union of rich spiritual harmony, wherein her children became the close friends and loving companions he might otherwise have found in children of his own.

The same spirit of aloofness that as a child made him criticize his elders, as a youth led him to criticize his companions for their actions and leave them to their drinking. In the solitude of the night he interpreted his reaction as " the voice of the Lord "

[1] *Journal*, p. 67.   [2] Ibid., p. 67.
[3] Ibid., Preface by William Penn, p. 54.

commanding that he " should forsake all, young and old, . . . and be as a stranger unto all." [1]

With that inherent chasm between himself and others, he naturally found cause for continued disagreement with all those to whom he turned for aid in his period of storm and stress. Those who endeavoured to be kind to him, he judged to be empty of all that they professed. He found, first among the priests and later among the laymen of the different groups, therefore, none who could meet his needs. Yet his sympathetic gregarious nature would not let him rest. It would not let him live the life of a recluse or an ascetic hermit. He must find his way in the midst of the busy world. At last, into the breach, came that experience which bridged over the chasm between his inmost self and the world about him : the knowledge of " that of God " which he felt to be not only in himself, but in all men. This common element took for him the personal form which his home and social environment had trained him to believe of most value—that " one, even Christ Jesus," could speak to his condition.[2] It brought into his life a sense of unity with his fellow-men which sends him out, no longer socially solitary and aloof, but seeking and drawing about him a circle of close and loving friends as well as a large and more general spiritual following. The two thirsts " warring within him, one after the creatures and the other after the Lord " [3]—these outer and inner appeals of his life— were blended into one, for he starts into his public life convinced of the " primary fact that there is no necessary dualism between man and God, between

[1] *Journal*, p. 68.   [2] Ibid., p. 82.   [3] Ibid., p. 84.

the Divine Spirit and human spirits. Their natures are not foreign and unrelated—God and the human spirit belong together in as real a sense as the light and the eye do, or beauty and the artist's soul, or harmony and the musician's ear."[1]

Other mystics have reached the same conclusion. Pascal's famous words, " Thou wouldst not seek me if Thou hadst not already found me," confess to the same conception. St. Augustine expresses the same too : " Thou hast made us for Thyself, and our hearts are restless until they find rest in Thee." The spirit of the teachings of Jesus carries the idea of the immanence of God still farther than this conjunct life of God and the human heart. It is summed up in that newly found " saying " of Jesus : " Lift the stone and thou shalt find Me, cleave the wood and I am there."

In Fox the pathway of association could be permanently built that closed automatically the chasm between himself and his fellow-men. The characteristic of aloofness continued, however, even to the highest level of his experience. The automatic gates of each canal lock of his experience closed to keep his life on the higher level. They opened only when some other influence became more dominant than the affective affirmation of his oneness with God and with his fellow-men. The priest always remained such an influence. In him Fox never could find anything except his foulness of spirit, and from him he drew himself and those he loved apart.

Just as effective in disintegrating his later dominant attitude of oneness with mankind, as the threatened harm to his love, was the assailing of his Truth. In

[1] Rufus M. Jones ; *A Dynamic Faith*, p. 15 f.

James Nayler's fall, Fox's Truth was being assailed by the danger of fanaticism. Unhesitatingly he was moved to do what seems to us unjustifiably harsh. One feels that Fox might have saved the situation if he had not held aloof at the critical time when he had had a foreboding of trouble ahead.[1] But Nayler bears no grudge for his severity. Having recovered his health after tortures and imprisonment, in great beauty and humility of spirit James Nayler wrote :

"DEAR BRETHREN,

"My heart is broken this day for the offence that I have occasioned to God's truth and people, and especially to you, who in dear love followed me, seeking me in faithfulness to God . . . and I beseech you, forgive wherein I evilly requited your love in that day. God knows my sorrow for it, since I see it, that ever I should offend that of God in any, or reject His counsel."

Usually Fox's eager sympathy and his gregarious nature would not have let him turn harshly from a brilliant follower like Nayler. He was usually seeking out strategic persons in each group to which he spoke. He had a keen eye for " people of account." He felt himself the equal of any, no matter what the rank. He sought out not only the rulers of his own land, as he sought Oliver Cromwell, but he travelled to Barbadoes, to America, to Holland, and to Germany, recording everywhere the meeting of people of prominence and power, whether they were Indian chiefs or the head of the Mennonite Church of Holland. He inspired others to go to Rome to counsel with the Pope, to Constantinople to advise the Sultan of the Turks, to Alexandria, and to attempt to cross Asia even to China.

[1] *Journal*, pp. 234, 269.

William Penn writes of him :

" I write my knowledge and not report, and my witness is true, having been with him for weeks and months together on divers occasions, and those of the nearest and most exercising nature, and that by night and day, by sea and by land, in this and in foreign countries, and I can say I never saw him out of place, or not a match for every service or occasion." [1]

His aloofness and his gregariousness combined at times into an apparent indifference. He seeks out the " people of account " who may be instrumental in serving his cause. But when he meets a member of the nobility he speaks of her as " a lady (so called)." [2] If all men are indeed endowed with divinity, then the only measure of their rank is their faithfulness to its direction in their lives, and he will address all alike with the more intimate terms of Thee and Thou. Thereby he angered many petty officers and priests, who, though they thought it no dishonour to so speak to God and Christ, " could not endure to have it said to themselves." [3]

But neither his aloofness nor his gregariousness was ever lost or destroyed. Both were carried up into his more highly integrated self, and found expression in the type of religion and life which he and his followers developed. It is essentially in every respect a social religion based on such individual development as makes it almost ideally democratic. And yet it is a religion and a life that accepts neither the world's standards of the ritual of worship nor of the conventions of social intercourse. Each was valued in so far as it was consistent with the underlying principles of truth

[1] *Journal*, pp. 59, 494, 498, 503, etc.
[2] *Journal*, p. 445. [3] Ibid., p. 382.

which were the basis of union in the group. Though not drawn out of the world, they did not conform to it. They have thus ever been a " peculiar people." From all ranks they came. James Nayler left his plough in the field to join in the service of the Lord. William Penn was expelled from Oxford because of his refusal to remove his hat in chapel in accordance with the standard of his day.

Their gregariousness made a Society of Friends who so loved each other that their homes were opened wide to any of the fellowship in generous hospitality.[1] At a general meeting in Rhode Island they had become " so knit and united together, that they spent two days in taking leave one of another." [2] They would offer in entire sincerity that they might replace those suffering in prison, and if need be give their lives that others might live.[3] Their aloofness resulted in a solidarity for the group that has been its strength as well as its weakness. At the end of six years of ministry, sixty ministers had been gathered to the work with Fox. Around this nucleus gathered the first large group of many thousands. Hammered and tested in the fires of abuse and persecution, they were welded so solidly that they passed through the reaction time of traditionalism,[4] that followed—perhaps inevitably—the first constructive period, and were kept intact for future development and growth. A peculiar people they have ever remained, perpetuating, in principle and theory at least, most of the virtues, and perhaps some of the vices, of their founder.

[1] *Journal*, p. 197.   [2] Ibid., p. 505.   [3] Ibid., pp. 405, 267.
[4] It was during this traditional and Quietistic period that the Wesleyan movement arose.

Censoriousness and Loving-kindness.

Perhaps no vice is more noticeable in Fox, even from childhood, than his unwavering censoriousness. Yet this, too, was everywhere balanced and counteracted by its opposite of winsome love. He was uncompromisingly censorious, not only of customs and conventions, but of people as well. During the wanderings of his adolescent years, he found something lacking in even the most tender of people. He felt, rather than expressed, his condemnation till after he had tried his wings in his first spontaneous outbreak. One Sunday in 1648 he had interrupted a church service to protest against the teaching of the priest. This brought on his first imprisonment in a " nasty, stinking prison, the smell whereof got so into my nose and throat that it very much annoyed me." [1] No doubt this result had helped to deepen the impression of the experience. Perhaps it led, too, to the habit of challenging ministers before their congregations, though afterwards he restrained himself until the minister had finished his sermon. It was the custom of the times, and not illegal, for any to speak who wished after the regular sermon had been finished. One priest, whom Fox had angered by his censorious condemnation of the doctrines taught, told him that he should not judge so. Turning to the congregation, he said : " But neighbours, this is the business ; George Fox is come to the light of the sun, and now he thinks to put out my starlight." [2] Another said : " There never was such a plant bred in England " as George Fox.[3]

[1] *Journal*, p. 110.   [2] Ibid., p. 205.   [3] Ibid., p. 211.

CONFLICTING TRAITS.

Censoriousness.

" At Mansfield ... I was moved to go and speak to one of the most wicked men in the country, one who was a common drunkard, a noted whore-master, and a rhyme-maker; and I reproved him in the dread of the mighty God, for his evil courses " (p. 96).

" For of all the sects in Christendom (so called) that I discoursed with, I found none who could bear to be told that any should come to Adam's perfection—into that image of God, that righteousness and holiness, that Adam was in before he fell; to be clean and pure without sin, as he was. Therefore how shall they be able to bear being told that any shall grow up to the measure of the stature of the fullness of Christ, when they cannot bear to hear that any shall come, whilst on earth, into the same power and spirit that the prophets and apostles were in ?—though it be a certain truth that none can understand their writings aright without the same Spirit by which they were written " (p. 101).

" I went into the steeple-house, and stayed till the priest had done. The words which he took for his text were these, ' Ho, every one that thirsteth, come ye to the waters; and he that hath no money, come ye, buy and eat, yea come buy wine and milk without money and without price.' Then I was moved of the Lord

Kindliness.

" I showed that it is Saul's nature that persecutes still, . . . that it was the nature of dogs to tear and devour the sheep; but that we suffered as sheep, and bite not again, for we were a peaceable people and loved them that persecuted us " (p. 471).

" Next morning, being First-day, we went to the meeting in the orchard, where the soldiers had lately been so rude. After I had declared the Truth some time in the meeting, there came in many rude soldiers and people, some with drawn swords . . . and stopped at those four Friends . . . (who should have gone to the colonel as I would have had them), and began jangling with them. . . . On the day following, the four Friends went and spoke with the colonel and he sent for the soldiers, and cut and slashed some of them before the Friends' faces. When I heard this I blamed the Friends for letting him do so, and also that they did not go on the Seventh-day, as I would have had them, which might have prevented this cutting of the soldiers, and the trouble they gave at our meeting " (p. 333).

" Then I returned to Patrington again, and visited those Friends

God to say unto him, ' Come down, thou deceiver; dost thou bid people come freely and take of the water of life freely, and yet thou takest three hundred pounds a year of them for preaching the Scriptures to them ? Mayest thou not blush for shame ? Did the prophet Isaiah and Christ do so, who spoke the words, and gave them forth freely ?   Did not Christ say to His ministers, whom He sent to preach, " Freely ye have received, freely give " ? ' " (p. 136).

" It came upon me about this time from the Lord to write a short paper and send it forth as an exhortation and warning to the Pope, and to all kings and rulers of Europe " (p. 222).

" About this time I was sorely exercised in going to their courts to cry for justice, in speaking and writing to judges and justices to do justly; in warning such as kept public houses for entertainment that they should not let people have more drink than would do them good; in testifying against wakes, feasts, May-games, sports, plays, and shows, which trained up people to vanity and looseness, and led them from the fear of God; and the days set forth for holidays were usually the times wherein they most dishonoured God by these things.

" In fairs, also, and in markets, I was made to declare against their deceitful merchandise, cheating, and cozening; warning all to deal justly, to speak the truth, to let their yea be yea, and their nay

that were convinced there; by whom I understood that a tailor, and some wild blades in that town, had occasioned my being carried before the justice. The tailor came to ask my forgiveness, fearing I would complain of him. The constables were also afraid, lest I should trouble them. But I forgave them all, and warned them to turn to the Lord, and to amend their lives " (p. 145).

" This Justice Hotham had asked me before whether any people had meddled with me, or abused me; but I was not at liberty to tell him anything of that kind, but was to forgive all " (p. 146).

" After I had declared the Truth to them for some hours, the chief constable and some other professors fell to reasoning with me in the chapel yard. Whereupon I took a Bible and opened the Scriptures, and dealt tenderly with them, as one would do with a child. They that were in the Light of Christ and Spirit of God knew when I spake Scripture, though I did not mention chapter and verse after the priest's form to them " (p. 158).

" But the Lord's power was

they would have others do unto them; forewarning them of the great and terrible day of the Lord, which would come upon them all.

"I was moved, also, to cry against all sorts of music, and against the mountebanks playing tricks on their stages; for they burthened the pure life, and stirred up people's minds to vanity. I was much exercised, too, with school-masters and school-mistresses, warning them to teach children sobriety in the fear of the Lord, that they might not be nursed and trained up in lightness, vanity, and wantonness. I was made to warn masters and mistresses, fathers and mothers in private families, to take care that their children and servants might be trained up in the fear of the Lord and that themselves should be therein examples and patterns of sobriety and virtue to them" (p. 106).

"Then Colonel Packer began to talk with a light, chaffy mind concerning God, and Christ, and the Scriptures. It was a great grief to my soul and spirit when I heard him talk so lightly, so that I told him he was too light to talk of the things of God, for he did not know the solidity of a man" (p. 217).

"Next morning one called a lady sent for me, who kept a preacher in her house. . . . In her lightness she came and asked if she could cut my hair; but I was moved to reprove her, and bade her cut down the corruptions in herself with the sword of the Spirit of God" (p. 293).

in heavenly patience, which can bear injuries for His name's sake, I felt dominion therein over the rough, rude, and unruly spirits; and left them to the Lord, who knew my innocency, and would plead my cause" (p. 559).

"Very glorious meetings we had, wherein the Lord's powerful presence was very largely felt; and the affairs of Truth were sweetly carried on in the unity of the Spirit, to the satisfaction and comfort of the right-hearted" (p. 547).

"We rode to Bristol that night, where Friends received us with great joy" (p. 535).

"There being a ship ready, and the wind serving, we took our leave of Friends; parting in much tenderness and brokenness, in the sense of the heavenly life and power manifested amongst us. Having put our horses and necessaries on board in the morning, we went ourselves in the afternoon,

12

" There was a captain of horse in the town, who sent to me, and would fain have had me stay longer. . . . This captain was the fattest, merriest, cheerfullest man, and the most given to laughter, that ever I met with : insomuch that I was several times moved to speak in the dreadful power of the Lord to him ; yet it was become so customary to him that he would presently laugh at anything that he saw. But I still admonished him to come to sobriety, and the fear of the Lord and sincerity. We lay at an inn that night, and the next morning I was moved to speak to him again, when he parted from us. The next time I saw him he told me that when I spoke to him at parting the power of the Lord so struck him that before he got home he was serious enough, and discontinued his laughing. He afterwards was convinced, and became a serious and good man, and died in the Truth " (p. 236).

" I went . . . to Swarthmore . . . whither came up one Lampitt, a priest, who was a high notionist. With him I had much reasoning. He made as though he knew all things. But I told him that death reigned from Adam to Moses ; that he was under death and knew not Moses, for Moses saw the paradise of God ; but he knew neither Moses nor the prophets nor John ; for that crooked and rough nature stood in him, and the mountain of sin and corruption ; and the way was not prepared in him for the Lord. He confessed he had been under a cross in things

many Friends accompanying us to the ship ; and divers Friends and Friendly people followed us in boats when we were near a league at sea, their love drawing them, though not without danger " (p. 468).

" Upon this he was moved, and, looking angrily at me, said, ' Sirrah, will you swear ? '

" I told him I was none of his Sirrahs ; I was a Christian ; and for him, an old man and a judge, to sit there and give nicknames to prisoners did not become either his grey hairs or his office.

" ' Well,' said he, ' I am a Christian, too.'

" ' Then do Christian works,' said I.

" ' Sirrah ! ' said he, ' thou thinkest to frighten me with thy words.' Then, catching himself, and looking aside, he said, ' Hark ! I am using the word Sirrah again ; ' and so checked himself.

" I said, ' I spoke to thee in love ; for that language did not become thee, a judge. Thou oughtest to instruct a prisoner in the law, if he were ignorant and out of the way.'

" ' And I speak in love to thee, too,' said he.

" ' But,' said I, ' love gives no nicknames ' " (p. 415).

but now he could sing psalms, and could do anything. I told him that now he could see a thief, and join hand in hand with him; but he could not preach Moses, nor the prophets, nor John, nor Christ, except he were in the same Spirit that they were in " (p. 159).

" I showed them their unworthiness to claim the name of Christians, and the unworthiness of their teachers, that had not brought them into more sobriety; and what a shame they were to Christianity " (p. 231).

" The chairman . . . asked wherein I showed my respect to magistrates if I did not put off my hat. I replied, ' In coming when they called me ' " (p. 411).

" My allegiance doth not lie in swearing, but in truth and faithfulness, for I honour all men, much more the King " (p. 414).

He would argue fearlessly with governor, judge, justice or magistrate to show them the error of their ways. When John-ap-John, his companion in a ministerial trip into Wales, was imprisoned for standing with his hat on in church, Fox asked the Governor :

"Had not the priest two caps upon his head, a black one and a white one ? Cut off the brim of the hat, and then my friend would have but one : and the brims of the hat were but to defend him from the weather."

In the conversation that followed, the Governor flew into a rage at Fox's personal denunciation of him, and he threatened to imprison Fox too. But Fox, even in his censoriousness, had the power to hold the respect and win the goodwill of those whom he would serve by his criticism. So he asked the Governor " whether wrath, fury, rage and persecutions were not marks of reprobation." Whereupon the Governor fairly confessed he had too much wrath, haste and passion in him, invited Fox to dinner, and set his friend free.[1]

Colonel Packer was told that he was " too light to talk of the things of God, for he did not know the solidity of a man." [2] Another was advised that to " rejoice when he got evil against people was not a good mind in him." [3] Fox informed Judge Twisden, who had called him " Sirrah," that " for him, an old man and a judge, to sit there and give nicknames to prisoners did not become either his grey hairs or his office." But Fox added, " I spoke to thee in love ; for that language did not become thee, a judge." The judge, who had been angry, replied in the same spirit, " And I speak in love to thee, too." [4]

[1] *Journal*, p. 285 f.
[3] Ibid., p. 227.
[2] Ibid., p. 217.
[4] Ibid., p. 415.

In spite of his censoriousness, there was a gentleness and tenderness in his relation to his fellow-men that won for him their love and respect. Penn says of him :

"In all things he acquitted himself like a man, yea, a strong man, a new and heavenly-minded man. A divine and a naturalist, and all of God Almighty's making. . . . Civil beyond all forms of breeding in his behaviour. . . . He was a man that God endowed with a clear and wonderful depth, a discerner of others' spirits and very much a master of his own. . . . He was of an innocent life, no busybody, nor self-seeker, neither touchy, nor critical : what fell from him was very inoffensive, if not very edifying. So meek, contented, modest, easy, steady, tender, it was a pleasure to be in his company. He exercised no authority but over evil, and that everywhere and in all ; but with love, compassion and long-suffering. A most merciful man, as ready to forgive as unapt to take or give offence. . . . Indeed his very presence expressed a religious majesty, yet he never abused it." [1]

Even the cold official records of the Society of Friends bear testimony to this spirit of love which he inspired by speaking of him after his death as " dear George." But they did not wait till death to show the love he had inspired. To the surprise of Oliver Cromwell, one offered himself, " body for body, yea, life also " if necessary, to replace Fox in the prison. And Cromwell, turning to his attendants and council, asked, " Which of you would do so much for me if I were in the same condition ? " [2]

It was undoubtedly his ability to be very censorious only toward the evil deed, while very loving toward the doer, that gave him his enormous power. His

[1] William Penn : Preface to *Journal*, pp. 51, 54, 58, 59.
[2] *Journal*, p. 267.

aim was to save men from their evil deeds, even though those men be his very persecutors. For this end he was moved with others to petition Parliament to be allowed to replace those who were perishing in the jails, not so much to save their friends as, indeed, to save the jailers from being the cause of the death of these innocent ones.[1]

Prophecy and Telepathy.

A more extended illustration of his censoriousness and his kindliness is to be found in his prophetic and telepathic insight. He was keen in his judgment of character, or of circumstances, and ready to condemn any evil tendency. He could read immediately, unconscious of the process of reasoning involved, the tendencies of the times. He who watched every move of Parliament because of its effect upon his Truth, who had " great suffering and travail of spirit for the nation," [2] might readily forecast that it should be broken up within two weeks.[3] But his friends took this as a sign that he was indeed a true prophet. He could tell that with the death of Cromwell the Commonwealth would come to an end :

"A great stroke must come upon them in power; for they that had then got possession were so exceedingly high, and such great persecution was acted by them, who called themselves saints." [4]

His judgment had confirmed the previous prophecy of a woman that King Charles would then return to the throne. But his good common sense advised her

[1] *Journal*, p. 323.   [2] Ibid., p. 329.
[3] Ibid., p. 179.   [4] Ibid., p. 329.

to " wait upon the Lord and keep it to herself ; for if it were known that she went on such a message they would look upon it as treason." [1]

It was perhaps less likely that he could have foretold a plague upon London, or the Great Fire there, as well as the war in Holland. It was, however, exceedingly easy afterwards to refer to them as the fulfilment of a vision of " the angel of the Lord with a glittering sword stretched southward as though the court had been all on fire." [2]

His censoriousness is shown also in his predictions of the state of the weather, which are entirely naïve :

"It was observed that as far as Truth had spread in the north, there were pleasant showers and rain enough, while in the south, in many places, the fields were almost spoiled for want of rain." [3]

So in response to the Protector's proclamation for a fast throughout the nation for rain, Fox wrote to him that if he " had come to own God's Truth " he should have had rain ; and that the drought was a sign unto them of their barrenness and their want of the water of life. [4] He himself never delayed in his plans for travel, feeling certain that the elements would favour *his* journeyings. Were they not in accord with the will of the Lord ? If the weather ever was unfavourable to him, he forgets to record such instances save to show how the Lord protected him and helped him through even dire discomforts ! [5]

So quick was he to discern any censurable circum-

[1] *Journal*, p. 329.   [2] Ibid., p. 434.
[3] Ibid., p. 282.   [4] Ibid., p. 282.
[5] Ibid., pp. 496, 511, 521, 531–532.

CONFLICTING TRAITS.

PROPHECY.	TELEPATHY.

PROPHECY.

" Being one day in Swarthmore Hall, when Judge Fell and Justice Benson were talking of the news, and of the Parliament then sitting (called the Long Parliament), I was moved to tell them that before that day two weeks the Parliament should be broken up, and the Speaker plucked out of his chair. That day two weeks Justice Benson told Judge Fell that now he saw George was a true prophet; for Oliver had broken up the Parliament " (p. 179).

" Many such false prophets have risen up against me, but the Lord hath blasted them, and will blast all who rise against the blessed Seed, and me in that. My confidence is in the Lord; for I saw their end, and how the Lord would confound them, before He sent me forth " (p. 202).

" At night they had me before Colonel Hacker. . . . That night I was kept prisoner at Marshalsea; and the next morning by the sixth hour I was delivered to Captain Drury. I desired that he would let me speak with Colonel Hacker before I went; and he took me to his bedside. Colonel Hacker again admonished me to go home, and keep no more meetings. I told him I could not submit to that; but must have my liberty to serve God, and to go to meetings. ' Then,' said he, ' you must go before the Protector.' Thereupon I kneeled at his bedside, and

TELEPATHY.

" While I was here in prison divers professors came to discourse with me. I had a sense, before they spoke, that they came to plead for sin and imperfection " (p. 122).

" The justices gave leave that I should have liberty to walk a mile. I perceived their end, and told the jailer, that if they would set down to me how far a mile was, I might take the liberty of walking it sometimes. For I had a sense that they thought I would go away. And the jailer confessed afterwards that they did it with that intent, to have me go away, to ease them of their plague; but I told him I was not of that spirit " (p. 125).

" Here the Lord opened unto me, and let me see a great people in white raiment by a river side, coming to the Lord; and the place that I saw them in was about Wensleydale and Sedbergh. . . . The next day I went to a meeting at Justice Benson's, where I met a people that were separated from the public worship. This

besought the Lord to forgive him ;
for he was as Pilate, though he
would wash his hands ; and I
bade him remember, when the
day of his misery and trial should
come upon him, what I had said
to him. . . . Afterwards when
Colonel Hacker was imprisoned in
London, a day or two before his
execution, he was put in mind of
what he had done against the
innocent ; and he remembered it
and confessed it to Margaret Fell,
saying he knew well whom she
meant ; and he had trouble upon
him for it " (p. 210).

" I went out of town, leaving
James Nayler in the city. As I
passed from him I cast my eyes
upon him, and a fear struck me
concerning him ; but I went away.
. . . Soon after we came to Exeter,
where many Friends were in
prison ; and amongst the rest James
Nayler. . . . James had run out
into imaginations, and a company
with him, who raised a great
darkness in the nation. He came
to Bristol and made a great
disturbance there " (pp. 234,
269).

" I met him (Oliver Cromwell)
riding in Hampton Court Park,
and before I came to him . . . I
saw a waft [or apparition] of
death go forth against him ; and
when I came to him he looked
like a dead man. . . . So I passed
away, and never saw him more.
. . . (I) went into Essex, where I
had not been long before I heard
that the Protector was dead "
(p. 325).

was the place I had seen, where
a people came forth in white
raiment " (pp. 150, 153).

" About eleven at night, the
jailer, being half drunk, came and
told me that he had got a man
now to dispute with me : (this
was when we had leave to go a
little into the town). As soon as
he spoke these words I felt there
was mischief intended to my body.
All that night and the next day
I lay down on a grass-plot to
slumber, and felt something still
about my body : I started up,
and struck at it in the power of
the Lord, and still it was about
my body.
" Then I rose and walked into
the Castle-Green, and the under-
keeper came and told me that
there was a maid would speak with
me in the prison. I felt a snare
in his words, too, therefore I
went not into the prison, but to
the grate ; and looking in, I saw
a man that was lately brought to
prison for being a conjurer, who
had a naked knife in his hand. I
spoke to him, and he threatened
to cut my chaps ; but, being
within the jail he could not come
at me. This was the jailer's great
disputant " (p. 260).

" The innkeeper told me that
the Council had granted warrants
to apprehend me, because I was
not gone out of the nation (Scot-

" I wrote to Oliver several times, and let him know that while he was persecuting God's people, they whom he accounted his enemies were preparing to come upon him. . . . Besides, there came a woman to me, who had a prophecy concerning King Charles's coming in, three years before he came. . . . I saw her prophecy was true, and that a great stroke must come upon them in power " (p. 328).

" And I can say it is of the Lord that the King is come in, to bring down many unrighteously set up; of which I had a sight three years before he came in " (p. 349).

" There came to me several . . . who were going to be soldiers under Lambert, and would have bought my horse of me. Because I would not sell him, they were in a great rage against me, using many threatening words : but I told them that God would confound and scatter them; and within two or three days after they were scattered indeed " (p. 339).

In 1660 George Fox wrote from Lancaster prison in part thus :

" Inasmuch as I am ordered to be kept prisoner till I be delivered by order from the King or Parliament, therefore I have written these things to be laid before you, the King and Parliament, that ye may consider of them before ye act anything therein. . . . Much innocent blood hath been shed. Many have been persecuted to death by such as were in authority before you, whom God hath vomited

land). . . . The Baptists sent me a letter, by way of challenge, to discourse with me next day. . . . At the time appointed I went to the place . . . but none of them came. . . . Then we rode up the street to the market-place and by the main-guard, out at the gate by the third sentry, and so clear out into the suburbs ; and there we came to an inn and put up our horses, it being Seventh-day. I saw and felt that we had ridden as it were against the cannon's mouth or the sword's point ; but the Lord's power and immediate hand carried us over the heads of them all " (p. 313).

" We received account from New England that the government there had made a law to banish the Quakers out of their colonies, upon pain of death in case they returned ; that several of our Friends, having been so banished and returning, were thereupon taken and actually hanged, and that divers more were in prison, in danger of the like sentence being executed upon them. When those were put to death I was in prison at Lancaster, and had a perfect sense of their sufferings as though it had been myself, and as though the halter had been put about my own neck, though we had not at that time heard of it " (p. 373).

" He that was then mayor of Cork . . . sent four warrants to out because they turned against the just. Therefore consider your standing now that ye have the day, and receive this as a warning of love to you " (p. 351).

" While I was a prisoner in Lancaster Castle there was a great noise and talk of the Turk's overspreading Christendom, and great fears entered many. But one day as I was walking in my prison chamber I saw the Lord's power turn against him, and that he was turning back again. And I declared to some what the Lord had let me see, when there were such fears of his overrunning Christendom ; and within a month after, the news came that they had given him a defeat.

" Another time, as I was walking in my chamber, with my eye to the Lord, I saw the angel of the Lord with a glittering drawn sword stretched southward, as though the court had been all on fire. Not long after the wars broke out with Holland, the sickness broke forth, and afterwards the fire of London ; so the Lord's sword was drawn indeed " (p. 434).

" At this time there was a great drought ; and after this general meeting was ended, there fell so great a rain that Friends said they thought we could not travel, the waters would be so risen. But I believed the rain had not extended as far as they had come that day to the meeting. Next day in the afternoon, when we turned back into some parts of Wales again, the roads were dusty, and no rain had fallen there.

take me ; therefore Friends were desirous that I should not ride through Cork. But being at Bandon, there appeared to me in a vision a very ugly-visaged man, of a black and dark look. My spirit struck at him in the power of God, and it seemed to me that I rode over him with my horse, and my horse set his foot on the side of his face.

" When I came down in the morning, I told a Friend the command of the Lord to me was to ride through Cork; but I bade him tell no man. So we took horse, many Friends being with me.

" When we came near the town, Friends would have shown me a way through the back side of it ; but I told them my way was through the streets. Taking Paul Morrice to guide me through the town, I rode on.

" As we rode through the market-place, and by the mayor's door, he, seeing me, said, ' There goes George Fox '; but he had not the power to stop me. When we had passed the sentinels, and were come over the bridge, we went to a Friend's house and alighted. There the Friends told me what a rage was in the town, and how many warrants were granted to take me.

" While I was sitting there I felt the evil spirit at work in the town, stirring up mischief against me ; and I felt the power of the Lord strike at that evil spirit.

" By-and-by some other Friends coming in, told me it was over the town, and amongst the magistrates, that I was in the town. I said, ' Let the devil do his worst.'

" When Oliver Cromwell sent forth a proclamation for a fast throughout the nation, for rain, when there was a very great drought, it was observed that as far as Truth had spread in the north, there were pleasant showers and rain enough, while in the south in many places the fields were almost spoiled for want of rain. At that time I was moved to write an answer to the Protector's proclamation, wherein I told him that if he had come to own God's Truth, he should have had rain ; and that the drought was a sign unto them of their barrenness, and their want of the water of life " (p. 282).

From a letter written near the end of his winter of extreme illness, just after his marriage, is this :

" Be not amazed at the weather ; for always the just suffered by the unjust, but the just had the dominion " (p. 480).

After we had refreshed ourselves, I called for my horse, and having a Friend to guide me, we went on our way. Great was the rage that the mayor and others of Cork were in that they had missed me, and great pains they afterwards took to catch me, having their scouts abroad upon the roads, as I understood " (p. 465).

" As I was sitting at supper, I felt I was taken ; yet I said nothing then to any one of it. . . . Though there was no meeting when they came, yet I, who was the person they aimed at, being in the house, Harry Parker took me, and Thomas Lower for company with me ; and though he had nothing to lay to our charge, sent us both to Worcester jail, by a strange sort of mittimus " (p. 538).

stances, that the premonitions of danger in his pathway are most frequently but the clear reading of surrounding conditions. More difficult to explain—save through the closeness of corporate interaction which arises in such a group of spiritual companions knit together into closest union through love and kindliness—is the telepathic knowledge of the persecutions of Friends in New England. He had imaged kinæsthetically the feeling of a halter about his own neck at the time when several were hung upon Boston Common for their faithful adherence to Quaker testimonies.[1] Previously his prepared soul seems to have reached forward to meet experiences as in the vision from the top of Pendle Hill.

Even as in the realm of science, new spiritual truths are reached through a forward look of the imagination. Each of the five times in the history of mathematics, when there has been any great new discovery, it has come through the reaching forward of some great mind into the unknown, unexplored ideal for a formula in the likeness of which there is no thing in heaven or on earth, but whose truth is so unquestionable that all the science of mathematics has been based upon these great discoveries. The formulæ so grasped have proved to be workable tenets of thought. So it was that Fox's vision of the great people to be gathered in, the " people in white raiment by a river side," was prophetic of his work and the founding of the new society.[2] White indeed were the garments of the souls of these young, strong and vigorous Publishers of the Truth as they became Children of the Light.

[1] *Journal*, p. 373.　　　　　[2] Ibid., p. 150.

Vicarious Vengeance and Non-resistance.

But even so fine a spiritual nature as that of the mature Fox had drawn up into itself a form of revenge which is most amazing in its vehemence. But it, too, had taken on a finer and more hidden form. Fox could feel and say that he " lived in that spirit which takes away the occasion of all wars." [1] He could be so non-resistant that he could stand still and let himself be struck and stoned and bruised, and feel a love even then for those who persecuted him. [2] Yet he had a keen eye that watched for, and seldom missed, the vengeance that he felt sure would follow upon them for their evil deeds. But that vengeance did not need to come through his hands to satisfy him. He could stand aside and wait with patience for a vicarious vengeance more deadly than any he could have administered. He says, " Indeed I could not but take notice how the hand of the Lord turned against the persecutors." [3] When urged to make an example of some who had treated him badly, he replied he " should leave them to the Lord ; if the Lord forgave them I should not trouble myself with them." [4] His evident joy, however, in these judgments shows that he felt a very strong personal interest in them, and was by no means so non-resistant as he appears on the surface. He would not strike back with his own hands, but underneath all his kindly characteristics one feels the steel hand of revenge to all that wronged him or his truth, working as vigorously as in one who directly seeks revenge.

[1] *Journal*, p. 128.   [2] Ibid., p. 323.
[3] Ibid., p. 457.   [4] Ibid., p. 362.

CONFLICTING TRAITS.

VICARIOUS VENGEANCE.[1]

" After it was known that I was discharged, a company of envious, wicked spirits were troubled, and terror took hold of Justice Porter; for he was afraid I would take advantage of the law against him for my wrong imprisonment, and thereby undo him, his wife and children. And indeed I was pressed by some in authority to make him and the rest examples; but I said I would leave them to the Lord; if the Lord forgave them I should not trouble myself with them " (p. 362).

" Some of the soldiers, who had been convinced in their judgment, but had not come into obedience to the Truth, took Oliver Cromwell's oath; and, going afterwards into Scotland, and coming before a garrison there, the garrison, thinking they had been enemies, fired at them, and killed divers of them, which was a sad event " (p. 200).

" The keeper of the prison, being a high professor, was greatly enraged against me, and spoke very wickedly of me; but it pleased the Lord one day to strike him, so that he was in great trouble and under much terror of mind. . . . Towards the evening, he came into my chamber, and said to me, ' I have been as a lion against you; but now I come like a lamb.' . . .

NON-RESISTANCE.

" Captain Keat brought a kinsman of his, a rude, wicked man, and put him into the room; himself standing without. This evil-minded man walked huffing up and down the room; I bade him fear the Lord. Thereupon he ran upon me, struck me with both his hands, and clapping his leg behind me, would have thrown me down if he could; but he was not able, for I stood stiff and still, and let him strike " (p. 241).

" At Bootle . . . the people were exceedingly rude, and struck and beat me in the yard; one gave me a very great blow over my wrist, so that the people thought he had broken my hand to pieces. The constable was very desirous to keep the peace, and would have set some of them that struck me by the heels, if I would have given way to it " (p. 181).

" The people were quiet, and heard me gladly, till this Justice Sawrey (who was the first stirrer-up of cruel persecution in the north) incensed them against me, and set them on to hale, beat, and bruise me. But now on a sudden the people were in a rage, and fell upon me in the steeple-house before his face, knocked me down, kicked me, and trampled upon

---

[1] References to the Journal as edited by R. M. Jones: *George Fox : An Autobiography*.

And he desired that he might lodge with me. I told him he might do as he would; I was in his power. . . . Then he told me all his heart. . . . When morning came he rose and went to the justices, and told them that he and his house had been plagued for my sake. . . . One of the justices replied that the plagues were upon them, too, for keeping me " (p. 123).

" Great was the exercise and travail in spirit that I underwent during my imprisonment here, because of the wickedness that was in the town. . . . There was a great judgment upon the town, and the justices were uneasy about me. . . . At first they called me a deceiver, a seducer and a blasphemer. Afterwards when God had brought His plague upon them, they styled me an honest, virtuous man " (p. 131).

" Through the Lord's blessed power, Truth and Friends have increased, and do increase in the increase of God; and I, by the same power, have been and am preserved, and kept in the everlasting Seed, that never fell, nor changes. But Rice Jones took the oaths that were put to him, and so disobeyed the command of Christ. . . . But his and his company's prophecies came upon themselves; for soon after they fell to pieces, and many of his followers became Friends, and continued so. . . . Many such false prophets have risen up against me, but the Lord hath blasted them, and will blast all who rise against the blessed Seed, and me in that. My confi-

me. . . . At last he came and took me from the people, led me out of the steeple-house and put me into the hands of the constables bidding them whip me, and put me out of the town. They led me about a quarter of a mile, some taking hold by my collar, some by my arms and shoulders; and they shook and dragged me along. . . . When they had haled me to the common moss-side, a multitude following, the constables and other officers gave me some blows over my back with their willow rods, and thrust me among the rude multitude, who having furnished themselves with staves, hedge-stakes, holm or holly bushes, fell upon me, and beat me upon my head, arms and shoulders, till they had deprived me of sense; so that I fell down upon the wet common. When I recovered again, and saw myself lying in the watery common, and the people standing about me, I lay still a little while, and the power of the Lord sprang through me, and the eternal refreshings revived me; so that I stood up again in the strengthening power of the eternal God, and stretching out my arms toward them, I said, with a loud voice, ' Strike again; here are my arms, my head, and my cheeks.'

" There was in the company a mason, a professor, but a rude fellow, who with his walking rule-staff gave me a blow just over the back of my hand, as it was stretched out; with which blow my hand was so bruised, and my arm so benumbed, that I could not draw it to me again. Some

dence is in the Lord; for I saw their end, and how the Lord would confound them, before He sent me forth " (p. 202).

" Captain Drury . . . was an enemy to me and to Truth, and opposed it. When professors came to me, while I was under his custody, and he was by, he would scoff at trembling, and call us Quakers, as the Independents and Presbyterians had nicknamed us before. But afterwards he came and told me that as he was lying on his bed to rest himself in the daytime, a sudden trembling seized upon him; that his joints knocked together, and his body shook so that he could not rise from his bed. He was so shaken that he had not strength enough left to rise. But he felt the power of the Lord was upon him; and he tumbled off his bed, and cried to the Lord, and said he would never speak more against the Quakers, such as trembled at the word of God " (p. 215).

" The mayor of Launceston took up all he could, and cast them into prison. He would search substantial, grave women, their petticoats and their head-cloths. A young man coming to see me, I drew up all the gross, inhuman, and unchristian actions of the mayor, gave it to him, and bade him seal it up, and go out again the back way; and then come into town through the gates. He did so, and the watch took him up and carried him before the mayor; who presently searched his pockets and found the letter.

of the people cried, ' He hath spoiled his hand for ever having the use of it any more.' But I looked at it in the love of God (for I was in the love of God to all that persecuted me), and after awhile the Lord's power sprang through me again, and through my hand and arm, so that in a moment I recovered strength in my hand and arm in the sight of them all " (pp. 169–171).

" Justice Hotham had asked me before whether any people had meddled with me, or abused me; but I was not at liberty to tell him anything of that kind, but was to forgive all " (p. 146).

" He that had shed my blood was afraid of having his hand cut off for striking me in the church, as they called it; but I forgave him, and would not appear against him " (p. 147).

" I . . . came in the night to a little ale-house on a common, where there was a company of rude fellows drinking. Because I would not drink with them they struck me with their clubs; but I reproved them, and brought them to be somewhat cooler; and then I walked out of the house upon the common in the night " (p. 152).

" About this time I lost a very good book, being taken in the printer's hands. . . . Those who took it were so affected with it that they were loth to destroy it; but thinking to make a great advantage of it, they would have

13

Therein he saw all his actions characterized; which shamed him so that from that time he meddled little with the Lord's servants" (p. 263).

"Indeed I could not but take notice how the hand of the Lord turned against the persecutors who had been the cause of my imprisonment, or had been abusive or cruel to me in it. The officer that fetched me to Holker Hall wasted his estate, and soon after fled into Ireland. Most of the justices that were upon the bench at the sessions when I was sent to prison, died in a little while after. . . . Justice Fleming's wife died, and left him thirteen or fourteen motherless children. Colonel Kirby never prospered after. The chief constable, Richard Dodgson, died soon after, and Mount, the petty constable, and the wife of the other petty constable, John Ashburnham, who railed at me in her house, died soon after. William Knipe, the witness they brought against me, died soon after also. Hunter, the jailer of Lancaster, who was very wicked to me while I was his prisoner, was cut off in his young days; and the under-sheriff that carried me from Lancaster prison towards Scarborough, lived not long after. And Joblin, the jailer of Durham, who was prisoner with me in Scarborough Castle, and had often incensed the Governor and soldiers against me, though he got out of prison, yet the Lord cut him off in his wickedness soon after.

"When I came into that country again, most of those that dwelt in let us have it again, if we would have given them a great sum of money for it; which we were not free to do" (p. 379).

"I found the priest and most of the chief of the parish together in the chancel. I went up to them, and began to speak; but they immediately fell upon me; the clerk with his Bible, as I was speaking, and struck me on the face with it, so that my face gushed out with blood; and I bled exceedingly in the steeple-house. The people cried, 'Let us have him out of the church.' When they had got me out, they beat me exceedingly, threw me down, and turned me over a hedge. They afterwards dragged me through a house into the street, stoning and beating me as they dragged me along; so that I was all over besmeared with blood and dirt. They got my hat from me, which I never had again. Yet when I was got upon my legs, I declared the Word of life, showed them the fruits of their teacher, and how they dishonoured Christianity" (p. 146).

"When Friends were under cruel persecutions and sufferings in the Commonwealth's time, I was moved of the Lord to write to Friends to draw up accounts of their sufferings, and lay them before the justices at their sessions; and if they would not do justice, then to lay them before the judges at the assize; and if they would not do justice, then to lay them before the Parliament, the Protector, and his Council, that they might see

Lancaster were dead, and others ruined in their estates; so that, though I did not seek revenge upon them for their actings against me contrary to the law, the Lord had executed His judgments upon many of them " (p. 457 f.).

what was done under their government; and if they would not do justice, then to lay it before the Lord, who would hear the cries of the oppressed, and of the widows and fatherless whom they had made so " (p. 369).

At times, however, he does attend to a little matter himself, but then it has somewhat of a humorous tinge. For instance, while imprisoned at Launceston, the mayor became very arduous in casting Friends into jail. He would search them himself carefully first, " substantial, grave women " as well as men, and so thoroughly would he do it that he examined even their head-dresses and their petticoats. Fox was ever intense in his denunciation of discourtesy to a woman. Now he became very indignant, but he had no way to reach the mayor directly. So he wrote a letter describing all the indignities, gave it to a lad who visited him, advising him to go out of the jail the back way, then enter the city again by the main entrance. This the lad did. He was arrested and taken before the mayor, who, searching him, found the letter describing his own deeds. It had the desired effect. After that the mayor " meddled little with the Lord's servants." [1]

Keen and quick as he always was to see the Lord's hand in the judgments that came upon his enemies, he was just as keen and quick to see the more beautiful dealings of the Lord with himself and with those who were in the Truth. On the voyage to America in a leaky ship, " deliverances " were almost as numerous as were "judgments " in times of imprisonment and persecution. The winds and the seas were calmed by the Lord, who graciously heard their prayers ; a fresh gale arose when needed to speed them away from the Moorish pirate ship pursuing them.[2]

[1] *Journal*, p. 263.
[2] Ibid., pp. 485–488.

" Killings " and Healings.

The two opposing characteristics in Fox, his censoriousness and his loving-kindness, had each its striking effect on those with whom he came into contact. At times it seems almost uncanny and hypnotic, but it illustrates how closely humanity is bound together, and how little one person can live unto himself alone. Fox was physically endowed so that perhaps this objective reference of his personality was more powerful with him than it is with many people. We find the pages of his Journal interspersed with accounts of his healings and of the "judgments" to which we have just alluded.

William Penn's account of him, as well as his own words, give evidence of the general effect of his striking appearance at times. But less cultured men than Penn felt only an inexplicable terror in the presence of Fox, and superstition spread all sorts of reports of his witchcraft. James Lancaster's wife, persuaded that he had bewitched her husband, who was one of his devoted followers, attempted to kill him by pelting him with stones as he lay upon the ground stunned by the blows of an angry mob, while her husband protected him with his own body.[1]

His power as a preacher of righteousness so stirred the England of his day that people said they felt the very buildings shake, and feared the stones would crumble upon their heads.[2] He had a very loud voice, which rang out in no uncertain tones.[3] His piercing eyes seemed to penetrate into their very souls.[4] It is

[1] *Journal*, p. 173. [2] Ibid., p. 90.
[3] Ibid., pp. 110, 191, 415. [4] Ibid., pp. 187, 344, 557.

CONFLICTING TRAITS.

"KILLINGS."

"Captain Drury . . . told me that the Protector required that I should promise not to take up a carnal sword or weapon against him or the government, as it then was, and that I should write it in what words I saw good, and set my hand to it. . . . The next morning I was moved of the Lord to write a paper to the Protector, Oliver Cromwell; wherein I did, in the presence of the Lord God, declare that I denied the wearing or drawing of a carnal sword, or any other outward weapon, against him or any man; and that I was sent of God to stand a witness against all violence. . . . After some time Captain Drury brought me before the Protector himself at Whitehall. . . . When I came in I was moved to say, ' Peace be in this house'; and I exhorted him to keep in the fear of God, that he might receive wisdom from Him, that by it he might be directed, and order all things under his hand to God's glory. I spoke much to him of Truth, and much discourse I had with him about religion; wherein he carried himself very moderately. . . . As I spoke, he several times said, it was very good, and it was truth. . . . Many more words I had with him; but people coming in, I drew a little back. As I was turning, he caught me by the hand, and with tears in his eyes said, ' Come again to my house; for if thou and I were but an hour of a day together, we should

HEALINGS.

" I found there a distracted woman under a doctor's hand, with her hair loose about her ears. He was about to let her blood, she being first bound, and many people about her, holding her by violence; but he could get no blood from her. I desired them to unbind her and let her alone, for they could not touch the spirit in her by which she was tormented. So they did unbind her; and I was moved to speak to her, and in the name of the Lord to bid her be quiet; and she was so. The Lord's power settled her mind, and she mended. . . .

" Many great and wonderful things were wrought by the heavenly power in those days; for the Lord made bare His omnipotent arm, and manifested His power, to the astonishment of many, by the healing virtue whereby many have been delivered from great infirmities. And the devils were made subject through His name; of which particular instances might be given, beyond what this unbelieving age is able to receive or bear " (p. 112 f.).

" I went to a meeting . . . where was Richard Myer, who had been long lame of one of his arms. I was moved of the Lord to say unto him amongst all the people, ' Stand up upon thy legs,' for he was sitting down. And he stood up, and stretched out his arm that had been lame a long time, and said, ' Be it known unto you, be nearer one to the other'; adding that he wished me no more ill than he did to his own soul. I told him that if he did he wronged his own soul; and admonished him to hearken to God's voice, that he might stand in His counsel, and obey it; and if he did so, that would keep him from hardness of heart; but if he did not hear God's voice, his heart would be hardened. He said it was true. . . . Then I was brought into a great hall, where the Protector's gentlemen were to dine. I asked them what they brought me thither for. They said it was by the Protector's orders, that I might dine with them. I bid them let the Protector know that I would not eat of his bread, nor drink of his drink. When he heard this he said, 'Now I see there is a people risen that I cannot win with gifts or honours, offices or places; but all other sects and people I can.' It was told him again that we had forsaken our own possessions; and were not likely to look for such things from him.

.   .   .

" I went to Kingston, and thence to Hampton Court, to speak with the Protector about the sufferings of Friends. I met him riding in Hampton Court Park, and before I came to him, as he rode at the head of the life-guard, I saw and felt a waft [or apparition] of death go forth against him; and when I came to him he looked like a dead man.

" After I had laid the sufferings of Friends before him, and had

all people, that this day I am healed.' Yet his parents could hardly believe it; but after the meeting was done, they had him aside, took off his doublet, and then saw it was true. He soon after came to the Swarthmore meeting, and there declared how the Lord had healed him. Yet after this the Lord commanded him to go to York with a message from Him, which he disobeyed; and the Lord struck him again, so that he died about three-quarters of a year after " (p. 180).

" A Baptist woman . . . was sick. John Rush, of Bedfordshire, went with me to visit her. When we came in there were many tender people about her. They told me she was not a woman for this world, but that if I had anything that would comfort her concerning the world to come, I might speak to her. I was moved of the Lord God to speak to her; and the Lord raised her up again, to the astonishment of the town and country " (p. 233).

" John Jay . . . being to try a horse, got upon his back, and the horse fell a-running, cast him down upon his head, and broke his neck, as the people said. Those that were near him took him up as dead, carried him a good way, and laid him on a tree.

" I got to him as soon as I could; and feeling him, concluded he was dead. As I stood pitying him and his family, I took hold of his hair, and his head turned any way, his neck was so limber. Whereupon I took his head in both my warned him, according as I was moved to speak to him, he bade me come to his house. So I returned to Kingston, and next day went to Hampton Court, to speak further with him. But when I came he was sick, and — Harvey, who was one that waited on him, told me the doctors were not willing I should speak with him. So I passed away, and never saw him more. From Kingston I went to Isaac Penington's, in Buckinghamshire . . . and soon after went into Essex, where I had not been long before I heard that the Protector was dead" (pp. 212, 325).

"As I was sitting in a house full of people, declaring the Word of life unto them, I cast mine eye upon a woman, and discerned an unclean spirit in her. And I was moved of the Lord to speak sharply to her, and told her she was under the influence of an unclean spirit; whereupon she went out of the room" (p. 184).

hands, and setting my knees against the tree, I raised his head, and perceived that there was nothing out or broken that way.

"Then I put one hand under his chin and the other behind his head, and raised his head two or three times with all my strength, and brought it in. I soon perceived his neck began to grow stiff again, and then he began to rattle in his throat, and quickly after to breathe.

"The people were amazed; but I bade them have a good heart, be of good faith, and carry him into the house. They did so, and set him by the fire. I bade them get him something warm to drink, and put him to bed. After he had been in the house a while he began to speak; but did not know where he had been. . . . Many hundred miles did he travel with us after this" (p. 513).

"Nathaniel Batts, who had been Governor of Roanoke . . . asked me about a woman in Cumberland, who, he said he had been told, had been healed by our prayers, and by laying on of hands, after she had been long sick, and given over by the physicians; and he desired to know the certainty of it. I told him we did not glory in such things, but many such things had been done by the power of Christ" (p. 525).

Extracts from letter to Lady Claypole, afterwards used for the settling of several minds:

"Keep in the fear of the Lord God, that is the Word of the Lord unto thee. For all these things happen to thee for thy

"There was a young man of Barbadoes whose name was John Drakes, a person of some note in the world's account, but a common swearer and a bad man, who, when he was in London, had a mind to marry a Friend's daughter, left by her mother very young, with a considerable portion, to the care and government of several Friends, whereof I was one. He made application to me that he might have my consent to marry this young maid. I told him . . . I should betray the trust reposed in me if I should consent that he, who was out of the fear of God, should marry her; and this I would not do.

"When he saw that he could not obtain his desire, he returned to Barbadoes with great offence of mind against me, but without just cause. Afterwards, when he heard I was coming to Barbadoes, he swore desperately, and threatened that if he could possibly procure it, he would have me burned to death when I came there. . . . About ten days after he was struck with a violent, burning fever, of which he died; by which his body was so scorched that the people said it was as black as a coal; and three days before I landed his body was laid in the dust" (p. 489).

good, and for the good of those concerned for thee, to make you know yourselves and your own weakness that ye may know the Lord's strength and power and may trust in Him. . . . For God is a God at hand, and the Most High rules in the children of men. This is the word of the Lord God unto you all; what the Light doth make manifest and discover, as temptations, distractions, confusions, do not look at these temptations, confusions, corruptions, but at the Light which discovers them and makes them manifest; and with the same Light you may feel over them, to receive power to stand against them. The same Light which lets you see sin and transgression, will let you see the covenant of God, which blots out your sin and transgression, which gives victory and dominion over it, and brings into covenant with God. For looking down at sin, corruption, and distraction, ye are swallowed up in it; but looking at the Light, which discovers them, ye will see over them. That will give victory, and ye will find grace and strength. There is the first step to peace. That will bring salvation. . . . So in the name and power of the Lord Jesus Christ, God Almighty strengthen thee.

"G. F."

(p. 320).

perhaps no wonder that those whom he censured or opposed felt within themselves the disintegrating force of his burning scorn, and they lost the ability to cope with the world and its problems, and losing grip even on life itself, slipped into failure or death.

One hardly needs question what the effect must have been upon Oliver Cromwell of this striking man, "stiff as a tree and pure as a bell,"[1] who stamped himself indelibly upon his time. At the command of Captain Drury, in 1652 or 1653, Fox had written a statement giving his promise that he "would not take a carnal sword or weapon against" Cromwell or his Government.[2] But stronger, perhaps, than any carnal weapon was the denunciation of the injustice that arose during the Commonwealth, and the prophecies of the collapse of the Government if its oppressions continued, and the personal warnings to Cromwell lest he accept the crown as king, made by a man who had evidently made a great impression upon him. As Carlyle says in editing Cromwell's letters and speeches :

"Yes, George, this Protector has a sympathy with the Perennial ; and feels it across the Temporary ; no hulls, leathern or other, can entirely hide it from the sense of him." [3]

At the close of his first personal interview, Cromwell had said to Fox, " If thou and I were an hour of a day together we should be nearer one to the other." [4] Of Friends as a whole, exemplified in Fox, he said :

"Now I see there is a people risen that I cannot win with gifts or honours, offices or places ; but all other sects and peoples I can." [5]

[1] *Journal*, p. 454.   [2] Ibid., p. 212.
[3] Carlyle : *Oliver Cromwell's Letters and Speeches*, vol. iii, .p. 225.

Fox's directness and lack of regard for conventional customs allowed him to ride to the coach-side of the Protector as he drove in Hyde Park with a great concourse of people, and to speak directly to him of the persecutions of Friends. Nor did Cromwell resent the liberty. He told one of his wife's maids that he had " good news " for her, for " George Fox is come to town." [1] Though Cromwell's manner in conversation with Fox appeared light and somewhat flippant, he was in reality deeply moved, and told his wife and friends later that he " had never parted so from him before." [2] Cromwell's daughter, being " much troubled in mind " at this time, Fox wrote to her a letter which, when read to her, " stayed her mind for a time," and under its influence she improved in health temporarily, though she died not many months later.[3]

Again Fox went to Hampton Court to speak with the Protector of the sufferings of Friends. He records :

" I met him riding in Hampton Court Park, and before I came to him, as he rode at the head of his life-guard, I saw a waft [or apparition] of death go forth against him ; and when I came to him he looked like a dead man." [4]

Hearing his purpose, Cromwell bade Fox come to his home. But the next day he found Cromwell too ill for the doctors to allow him to see visitors. So Fox passed out of London and saw him no more, for within a few weeks he heard that Oliver the Protector was dead.[5]

[1] *Journal*, p. 275.   [2] Ibid., p. 276.
[3] Ibid., p. 320. Copies of this letter were used with similar curative effect by many Friends.
[4] *Journal of George Fox* (Cambridge edition, 1911), p. 328.
[5] Ibid., p. 324 f.

Had Fox's expressive face and manner shown to Cromwell, who had already been warned, " The Lord will suddenly smite thee," [1] something of Fox's thought of his approaching death ? Did it hasten the katabolism of his strained nerves and lessening strength ? Such questions can never be answered directly. But the work of such students as Cannon [2] and Crile [3] has shown the tremendous and amazing physical effects of the stimulation that comes through emotions and the force of ideas, which is of such far-reaching importance in our understanding of the interactions of one personality upon another in human relationships.

If his censoriousness could become so objectively effective that it could thus gnaw at the very life sources of others, no less did his loving-kindness carry with it drops of healing. In America the ex-governor of Roanoke inquired as to the truth of a report that a woman had been cured after a long illness by prayers and laying on of hands. To this Fox replied simply that they " did not glory in such things, but *many such things had been done* by the power of Christ." [4] To Fox they seemed miraculous and inexplicable, otherwise than supernaturally. No doubt they helped to develop in him that sense of surety in his call as a special instrument of the Lord.

To the student of psycho-analysis and of the power of suggestion with its interplay between the psychical and the physical, however, I believe that each one of

[1] Letter addressed to Cromwell a month before his death. Cf. *Journal*, p. 325 (note).
[2] Cannon : *Bodily Changes in Pain, Fear and Hunger.*
[3] Crile : *The Emotions : A Mechanistic View of Peace and War.*
[4] *Journal*, p. 526.

these cures can be explained naturally—though no less wondrously—as the result of Fox's hypersensitivity, of the guiding wisdom of his instincts, of his intuitional summing up of the situation into an ultra-rational judgment, and of his instantaneous motor response by doing with abundant common sense the right thing at the right time. Rufus Jones well says of him in regard to his influence over an hysterical woman :

" His commanding presence, his piercing eye, and the absolute assurance which his voice gave that he was equal to the occasion, were worth a thousand doctors with their lancets." [1]

Restlessness and Repose.

Conflicting traits which have frequently been referred to indirectly, and yet which are among the most striking in his personality, are his motor-mindedness and his " waiting on the Lord." He was bred and raised in the country, and as a lad he " walked many nights by himself," and " walked abroad in solitary places many days . . . and frequently in the night walked mournfully." [2] This restlessness we find characteristic of his entire life. He was never fond of long-continued unpractical contemplation. Royce says of his Journal that it is more like a soldier's record of a campaign than like the typical mystic's description of his wondrous journey Godward.[3] He felt that it was the command of the Lord which told him he must forsake all, young and old, and be as a stranger to all. In fact, it was the active unresting spirit within the man that forced him on relentlessly from place to place

[1] *Journal*, p. 113 (note).   [2] Ibid., p. 71, 79.
[3] Royce : " George Fox as a Mystic," in *Harvard Theological Review*, January 1913, p. 44.

so that he *could* not remain in any one place. Being at the same time serious-minded and deeply interested in religious problems, he learned to serve the Lord in the one way that his temperament permitted. His youthful tendency to an apparent vagrancy was not so much due to any painful emotion, any temptation to wild living, any crisis of conversion, any period of doubt or impiety, as to the mere necessity for movement and action. His readiness for brisk motor activity moulds his whole career. Royce says : " Were he an angel in heaven he would prefer a missionary expedition into the depths to an eternity of rest in the beatific vision." [1] His most common method of describing his sense of a mission in life was that " the Lord moved me." It was thus that he interpreted those motor strains and tensions which played such an exceedingly large part in the guidance which controlled his life. Yet even he, energetic, restless, untiring, found much occasion and much need for a stillness such as few men attain. Walking toward a jail to visit the prisoners, he " was ravished with the sense of the love of God, and greatly strengthened in his inner man." So he sat still, having his " spirit gathered into the love of God." [2]

It is upon this union of the human spirit with the love of God that Fox builds the type of worship which has been one of the distinguishing features of Quaker practice. It is one which to all outward appearance is that of entire quiet passivity. In an epistle to Friends he writes :

" This is the Word of the Lord to you all : Every one in the measure of life *wait*, that with it all your minds may be guided

[1] Royce: Op. cit., p. 44.   [2] *Journal*, p. 116.

CONFLICTING TRAITS.

RESTLESSNESS.

" At the command of God, the ninth of the Seventh month, 1643, I left my relations, and broke off all familiarity or fellowship with young or old. I passed to Lutter-worth, where I stayed some time. From thence I went to Northamp-ton, where also I made some stay ; then passed to Newport-Pagnel, whence, after I had stayed awhile, I went to Barnet, in the Fourth month, called June, in the year 1644. . . . I thus travelled through the country " (p. 69).

" Sometimes I kept myself re-tired to my chamber, and often walked solitary in the Chase to wait upon the Lord " (p. 69).

" I was *brought* to call to mind " (p. 69).

" I went to many a priest to look for comfort " (p. 70).

" This opened in me as I walked in the fields " (p. 76).

" I brought them Scriptures, and told them there was an anoint-ing within man to teach him, and that the Lord would teach His people Himself " (p. 76).

REPOSE.

" When I came into the jail where those prisoners were, a great power of darkness struck at me ; and I sat still, having my spirit gathered into the love of God " (p. 116).

" While others were gone to dinner, I went to a brook, got a little water, and then came and sat down on the top of a rock hard by the chapel. In the after-noon the people gathered about me, with several of their preachers. It was judged there were above a thousand people, to whom I declared God's everlasting truth and Word of life freely and largely for about the space of three hours " (p. 155).

" I directed them to the Divine Light of Christ, and His Spirit in their hearts, which would let them see all the evil thoughts, words, and actions that they had thought, spoken, and acted; by which Light they might see their sin, and also their Saviour Christ Jesus to save them from their sins. This I told them was their first step to peace, even to stand still in the Light " (p. 162).

" Before I went into the steeple-house, I sat a little upon the cross, and Friends with me ; but the Friends were moved to go into the steeple-house, and I went in after them " (p. 182).

" Great trouble and temptation came many times upon me " (p. 77).

Fox " travelled up and down as a stranger in the earth, which way the Lord inclined my heart " (p. 79).

" I durst not stay long in a place " (p. 79).

" I kept much as a stranger, seeking heavenly wisdom and getting knowledge from the Lord, and was brought off from outward things to rely on the Lord alone " (p. 80).

" I was taken up in the love of God " (p. 84).

" The Lord opened me. . . . My living faith was raised " (p. 84).

" My secret belief was stayed firm, and hope underneath held me, as an anchor in the bottom of the sea, and anchored my immortal soul to its Bishop, causing it to swim above the sea " (p. 85).

" Here I was moved to pray; and the Lord's power was so great that the house seemed to be shaken " (p. 90).

" I was moved to go after them " (p. 91).

" The next day we came into Cumberland again, where we had a general meeting of thousands of people on top of a hill near Langlands. A glorious and heavenly meeting it was; for the glory of the Lord did shine over all; and there were as many as one could well speak over, the multitude was so great. Their eyes were turned to Christ, their teacher; and they came to sit under their own vine; insomuch that Francis Howgill, coming afterwards to visit them, found they had no need of words; for they were sitting under their teacher Christ Jesus; in the sense whereof He sat down amongst them, without speaking anything " (p. 196).

From an Epistle to Friends:
" This is the Word of the Lord to you all: Every one in the measure of life wait, that with it all your minds may be guided up to the Father of life, the Father of spirits; to receive power from Him, and wisdom, that with it you may be ordered to His glory: to whom be all glory for ever! All keep in the Light and Life, that judgeth down that which is contrary to the Light and Life. So the Lord God Almighty be with you all. . . .
" All Friends that speak in public, see that it be in the life of God; for that begets to God; the fruits of that shall never wither. This sows to the Spirit which is in prison, and the Spirit reaps life; and the other sows to the flesh, and of the flesh reaps corruption. This you may see all the world over amongst these seedsmen. . . .

" Thither I was moved by the Lord God to go " (p. 92).

" I was wrapped up, as in a rapture " (p. 92).

" Great things did the Lord lead me into, and wonderful depths were opened unto me, beyond what can by words be declared " (p. 97).

" I felt that His power went forth over all, by which all might be reformed if they would receive and bow unto it " (p. 99).

" I was moved to cry against all sorts of music " (p. 107).

" When I heard the bell toll to call people together to the steeple-house, it struck at my life " (p. 107).

" Now the Lord's power was so mighty upon me, and so strong in me that I could not hold, but was made to cry out " (p. 109).

" Then was I commanded by the Lord to pull off my shoes " (p. 132).

" Immediately the Word of the

Therefore wait in the Spirit of the Lord, which cuts down and casts out all this, the root and branches of it. So in that wait to receive power, and the Lord God Almighty preserve you in it ; whereby you may come to feel the Light, that comprehends time and the world, and fathoms it : which, believed in, gives you victory over the world. Here the power of the Lord is received, which subdues all the contrary, and puts off the garments that will stain and pollute " (p. 203 note).

" I sat still, with my mind retired to the Lord. At last I felt the power and Spirit of God move in me ; and the Lord's power did so shake and shatter them that they wondered, though they did not live in it " (p. 216).

" When I was come to the orchard, I stood upon the stone that Friends used to stand on when they spoke ; and I was moved of the Lord to put off my hat, and to stand awhile, and let the people look at me ; for some thousands of people were there. . . . Then the Lord opened my mouth " (p. 273).

" When they were well gathered, I went into the meeting, and stood upon a chair about three hours. I stood a pretty while before I began to speak. After some time I felt the power of the Lord over the whole assembly : and His everlasting life and Truth shone on all. The Scriptures were opened to them, and the objections

14

Lord came to me that I must go thither " (p. 132).

" I was moved of the Lord God to speak to her " (p. 233).

" We declared the Truth as we went along the streets, till we came to the jail, the streets being full of people."

" When they that were about me had given me up to die, I spoke to them to get a coach to carry me to Gerrard Roberts's, about twelve miles off, for I found it was my place to go thither. . . . When I came to Gerrard's, he was very weak, and I was moved to speak to him, and encourage him. After I had stayed about three weeks there, it was with me to go to Enfield. Friends were afraid of my removing; but I told them I might safely go " (p. 478).

" Though by reason of my weakness I could not travel amongst Friends as I had been used to do, yet in the motion of life I sent the following lines as an encouraging testimony to them :—" (p. 479).

" The illness I got in my imprisonment at Worcester had so much weakened me that it was long before I recovered my natural strength again. For which reason,

they had in their minds answered " (p. 283).

" I passed to another town, where was another great meeting, the old priest being with me; and there came professors of several sorts to it. I sat on a haystack, and spoke nothing for some hours; for I was to famish them from words. The professors would ever and anon be speaking to the old priest, and asking him when I would begin, and when I would speak ? He bade them wait; and told them that the people waited upon Christ a long while before He spoke. At last I was moved of the Lord to speak; and they were struck by the Lord's power " (p. 141).

" After I had turned the people to the Spirit of God which led the holy men of God to give forth the Scriptures . . . perceiving the other Friends to be full of power and the Word of the Lord, I stepped down, giving way for them to declare what they had from the Lord to the people " (p. 315).

When followed by a pirate ship on the voyage to America :
" At night the master and others came into my cabin, and asked me what they should do. . . . I answered that it was a trial of faith, and therefore the Lord was to be waited on for counsel. So, retiring in spirit, the Lord showed me that His life and power were placed between us and the ship that pursued us. I told this to the master and the rest, and that

and as many things lay upon me to write, . . . I did not stir much abroad, . . . but when Friends were not with me, I spent much time in writing for Truth's service. . . . I gave several books to be printed " (p. 544).

the best way was to tack about and steer our right course. I desired them also to put out all their candles but the one they steered by, and to speak to all the passengers to be still and quiet " (p. 486).

up to the Father of life, the Father of spirits : to receive power from Him, and wisdom, that with it you may be ordered to His glory." [1]

Again he says of himself, " I sat still with my mind retired on the Lord." [2] How readily his followers learned the secret of this waiting on the Lord with their minds retired is evident in the power that developed in the silent meetings. He describes a glorious and heavenly meeting of thousands of people on top of a hill, at which he had spoken. Francis Howgill, coming afterwards to visit this group, " found they had no need of words, for they were sitting under their teacher Christ Jesus ; in the sense whereof he sat down amongst them, without speaking anything." [3]

At first one questions how it is possible for one who, like Fox, is so strenuously motor-minded, to pass over into such a stillness of spirit that he could sit upon a haystack in silence for hours while a multitude waited at his feet for him to speak to them.[4] Then one learns that this " waiting " of which he speaks is no quietistic inertness, but is rather an intense awareness, " when the soul is enlarged, when the senses are grown strong, when the mouth is opened wide " ready to pour forth the wisdom from the Lord.[5]

Margaret E. Washburn has shown that, having passed a stage of activity when motor response is strongly initiated and even tentative movements occur slowly and with some delay, stronger stimuli will produce a state when the motor response is so fully initiated and

---

[1] George Fox : Epistle to the sixty ministers who started out about 1652. Cf. *Journal*, p. 202 (note).
[2] *Journal*, p. 216.   [3] Ibid., p. 196.   [4] Ibid., p. 140.
[5] Isaac Penington : *Works*, vol. i, p. 537.

unopposed that it occurs without any delay, and therefore has none of the conflict that makes for consciousness.[1]   What therefore appears to be rest is really the intensest movement.   Such is the rest which the soul finds " in the powerful movings and operations of life."   Isaac Penington, cultured follower of Fox, writes from the religionist's point of view, and not at all as a psychologist :

" It does not find any stress of trouble, or hardship, or labour upon it, but sits still in the power, is at ease in the life, in the eternal virtue which lives and moves and is all in it ; and no pain, no trouble, no grievousness of any command is felt ; but to it all is easy, all is natural, all is purely pleasant ; the life performing all it calls for, even as fast as it calls for it.   And here not only a sabbath of days, but also a sabbath of weeks, yea, sometimes a sabbath of years is known and witnessed by such as have waited upon the Lord in singleness of heart.   There are degrees of the blessed estate : First there are desires, thirstings, and breathings, begotten after the life.   Secondly is a labouring in the service, by the virtue which springs from the life.   Thirdly, there is a rest, or sitting down at ease in the life.   Thus the spring stirring, the soul cannot but move towards its centre ; and as it entereth into and fixeth its centre, it partaketh of the rest." [2]

T. Carl Whitmer, in *The Way of My Mind*, says :

" I am enamoured of the touch and sure uncertainty of Beethoven and Rembrandt with their human lines.   Indeed, the absolute assimilation of technical meaning (the complete balance of thought and vehicle) never goes with the genuine reformer. That little mite of charming clumsiness, that thimblefull of relative unform is their fortune. . . . I would see a thesis on the ' Technical Awkwardness of the Eternally Great.' . . .

[1] Margaret E. Washburn : *Movement and Mental Imagery* (Boston, 1916), p. 36.
[2] Isaac Penington : *Works*, vol. i, p. 537.

Such men develop so rapidly and penetrate so deeply that what to the onlooker is heavy is really light ; what is unseen may have totally different proportions from what is seen. . . . Great souls do not rest content with the mere expression of their feelings, but so constantly reach into the Great Depths that what we know as balance of technique and idea is never completely attained. Their line has never quite the perfection of their thought. That fortune is reserved for those who do not cry out in the agony of their delivery." [1]

So perhaps to the casual observer the crude activities of Fox on the periphery of his busily revolving self show little of that intense, joyous, beautiful " rest in the Lord." The restlessness is there, but it is not an antithesis of activity. It is moral and spiritual activity raised to its height of intensest awareness, and co-operation with divine forces.

He who as a stranger enters a Friends' meeting will probably see little of the life there present until he realizes that no outward act marks the beginning of the service, but that the service begins, and ends, with the activity with which he and the others there worship the Lord intensely in the inmost recesses of their own souls. Most mystics, though they too have been active reformers and organizers, have tended to separate their outer and inner selves, their times of illumination and their periods of activity. While on the surface we see those traits of unceasing activity and of retirement at times as though they were separated, we never find the time of retirement lasting with any endurance. Even his enforced periods of solitude in times of imprisonment were filled with activity of mind and heart and pen. He himself knows nothing of any

[1] T. Carl Whitmer : *The Way of My Mind* (Pittsburg, 1917), p. 102.

division of spirit between the contemplation of God and the service of the world. His daily business is never a shadowy waste to him, but is radiant with the presence of the Lord in it.

"Contemplation was compatible with work, and the Light was still with him in the company of his Friends. . . . His God is not only an ocean of light, but also the counsellor of deeds. And even the Light, Fox praises not only for its purity, but for what it enables him to discern." [1]

Egotism and Self-depreciation.

Because he never could keep still, but must act somehow under all circumstances, he developed an initiative that gave him a self-assurance that seems to have in it very little of humility. But one finds that even his egotism is not without its contradictory characteristics.

He was conscious of his difference from others—he would have said his superiority to them—even as a child. He tells us himself that when he came to eleven years of age he knew pureness and righteousness! [2] While apprenticed to a man who was a shoemaker by trade and dealt in wool, he "never wronged man or woman in all that time"; [3] and though some rude persons did laugh at him, "people had generally a love to me for my innocence and honesty." [4] His assurance carried him to person after person for aid. He did not hesitate to go miles to see some one whose fame had come to him, but censorious and tough-minded, he placed his own opinion before that of men far older and supposedly wiser than he. Even

[1] Royce: Op. cit., p. 39.
[2] *Journal*, p. 66.   [3] Ibid., p. 67.   [4] Ibid., p. 67

CONFLICTING TRAITS.

Egotism.	Self-depreciation.
"When I came to eleven years of age I knew pureness and righteousness; for while a child I was taught how to walk to be kept pure" (p. 66).	"A strong temptation to despair came upon me. . . . Then I thought, because I had forsaken my relations I had done amiss against them. So I was brought to call to mind all my time that I had spent, and to consider whether I had wronged any" (p. 69).
"While I was with him he was blessed, but after I left him he broke and came to nothing" (p. 67).	
"I never wronged man or woman in all that time" (p. 67).	
"It was a common saying among those that knew me, 'If George says verily, there is no altering him'" (p. 67).	"As I cannot declare the misery I was in, it was so great and heavy upon me, so neither can I set forth the mercies of God unto me in all my misery. O the everlasting love of God to my soul, when I was in great distress! When my troubles and torments were great, then was His love exceeding great. . . . All honour and glory be to Thee, O Lord of Glory! The knowledge of Thee in the Spirit is life" (p. 80).
"People had generally a love to me for my innocency and honesty" (p. 67).	
"I went among the professors at Duckingfield and Manchester, where I stayed awhile, and declared truth among them. . . . But the professors were in a rage, all pleading for sin and imperfection, and could not endure to hear talk of perfection, and of a holy and sinless life" (p. 85).	"Christ, who had enlightened me, gave me His light to believe in; He gave me hope, which He Himself revealed in me, and He gave me His Spirit and grace, which I found sufficient in the deeps and in weakness" (p. 83).
"I knew nothing but pureness, and innocency, and righteousness; being renewed into the image of God by Christ Jesus, to the state of Adam, which he was in before he fell" (p. 97).	
"This I saw in the pure openings of the Light without the	"We had great meetings in those parts; for the power

help of any man ; neither did I then know where to find it in the Scriptures ; though afterwards, searching the Scriptures, I found it " (p. 102).

" I was glad that I was commanded to turn people to that inward Light, Spirit, and Grace . . . which I infallibly knew would never deceive any " (p. 103).

" As I spoke thus amongst them, the officers came and took me away. . . . But that day the Lord's power sounded so in their ears that they were amazed at the voice, and could not get it out of their ears for some time after, they were so reached by the Lord's power in the steeple-house " (p. 110).

" When I came, Lampitt was singing with his people ; but his spirit was so foul, and the matter they sung so unsuitable . . . I was moved to speak to him and his people. The word of the Lord to them was, ' He is not a Jew that is one outwardly, but he is a Jew that is one inwardly, whose praise is not of man, but of God ' " (p. 160).

" Many such false prophets have risen up against me, but the Lord hath blasted them " (p. 202).

" The God of heaven carried me over all in His power, and His blessed power went over all in His power " (p. 220).

" It came upon me about this time from the Lord to write a short paper and send it forth as

of the Lord broke through " (p. 94).

" I was sent to turn people from darkness to the Light, that they might receive Christ Jesus ; for to as many as should receive Him in His Light, I saw He would give power to become the sons of God ; which power I had obtained by receiving Christ " (p. 102).

" Moreover, when the Lord sent me forth into the world, He forbade me to put off my hat to any, high or low ; and I was required to Thee and Thou all men and women, without any respect to rich or poor, great or small " (p. 105).

" I asked them whether he that betrays Christ within himself be not one in nature with that Judas that betrayed Christ without " (p. 115).

" He had with him a silly young priest, who asked us many

an exhortation and warning to the Pope, and to all kings and rulers in Europe " (p. 222).

" For by the power of the Lord I was manifest, and sought to be made manifest to the Spirit of God in all, that by it they might be turned to God; as many as were turned to the Lord Jesus Christ by the Holy Spirit, and were come to sit under His teaching " (p. 224).

1656—Extract from a letter to all professors of Christianity :
" Let us be glad, and rejoice for ever ! Singleness of heart is come ; pureness of heart is come ; joy and gladness is come. The glorious God is exalting Himself ; Truth hath been talked of ; but now it is possessed. Christ hath been talked of ; but now He is come and possessed. The glory hath been talked of ; but now it is possessed, and the glory of man is defacing. The Son of God hath been talked of ; but now He is come, and hath given us an understanding " (p. 222, note).

" He told me I was a disturber of the nation. I told him I had been a blessing to the nation, in and through the Lord's power and Truth ; and that the Spirit of God in all consciences would answer it. Then he charged me as an enemy to the King, that I endeavoured to raise a new war, and imbrue the nation in blood again. I told him I had never learned the postures of war, but was clear and innocent as a child concerning those things ; and there-

frivolous questions ; and amongst the rest he desired to cut my hair, which was then pretty long ; but I was not to cut it, though many times many were offended at it. I told them I had no pride in it, and it was not of my own putting on " (p. 239).

" At another place, I heard some of the magistrates say among themselves that if they had money enough they would hire me to be their minister. This was where they did not well understand us, and our principles ; but when I heard of it, I said, ' It is time for us to be gone ; for if their eye were so much on me, or on any of us, they would not come to their own Teacher.' For this thing (hiring ministers) had spoiled many, by hindering them from improving their own talents ; whereas our labour is to bring every one to his own Teacher *in himself*" (p. 508).

" One, who had been a justice twenty years, was convinced, spoke highly of the Truth, and more highly of me than is fit for me to mention or take notice of " (p. 507).

" Amongst others came Nathaniel Batts, who had been Governor of

" Some came and asked me what I was. I told them, ' A preacher of righteousness ' " (p. 366).

" A blessed heavenly meeting this was ; a powerful, thundering testimony for Truth was borne therein . . . (p. 522).

" I am glad I was here. Now I am clear, I am fully clear ! " (p. 578).

of Captain Batts, and had been a rude, desperate man. He asked me about a woman in Cumberland, who, he said he had been told, had been healed by our prayers, and by laying on of hands, after she had been long sick, and given over by the physicians ; and he desired to know the certainty of it. I told him we did not glory in such things, but many such things had been done by the power of Christ " (p. 526).

while still in his storm and stress period at the very beginning of his ministry, he preached the possibility of a holy and sinless life as an actuality and not as a mere notion or theory such as that presented by the Ranters of his day.[1] Having felt that his spirit had been brought "through the flaming sword into the Paradise of God," he knew nothing "but pureness, and innocency, and righteousness ; being renewed into the image of God by Christ Jesus."[2] When he went forth to preach the everlasting Gospel, he had much joy in the message that he was to carry—the message of "that inward Light, Spirit, and Grace, by which all might know their salvation and their way to God"—for he "infallibly knew" it would never deceive any, but would lead them into all truth.[3]

Persecutions and imprisonments had no effect in lessening his entire confidence in his power to deliver his message. He told his persecutors that though they could confine his body and shut that up, they could not stop the Word of Life.[4] When on trial he was told that he was a disturber of the nation. But he unhesitatingly replied to Major Porter that he "had been a blessing to the nation, in and through the Lord's power and Truth ; and that the Spirit of God in all consciences would answer it."[5] Then he was charged with being an enemy to the King, and endeavouring to raise a new war ; but he replied that he "had never learned the postures of war, but was clear and innocent as a child concerning those things ; and therefore was bold."[6]

Such unlimited egotism, however, was no conceit

[1] *Journal*, p. 85.   [2] Ibid., p. 97.   [3] Ibid., p. 103.
[4] Ibid., p. 366.   [5] Ibid., p. 346.   [6] Ibid., p. 346.

in Fox. He was, as he said, bold because he knew
that when God doth work none can hinder it.[1] Once
having attained to the place where he knew experimentally that the power of God was in his life to direct
and control its every thought, word or deed, he knew
that to live in the same spirit as the apostles is as possible
to-day as it was hundreds of years ago. So his " secret
faith was stayed firm, and hope underneath held him,
as an anchor in the bottom of the sea, and anchored
his immortal soul to its Bishop, causing it to swim
above the sea, the world, where all the raging waves,
foul weather, tempests and temptations are."[2] He
never wavered in his faith in the absolute companionship and dynamic presence of God. As naturally and
directly as Jesus Himself spoke when He declared,
" He that hath seen Me hath seen the Father. . . .
Believest thou not that I am in the Father and the
Father in Me? . . . The words that I speak unto you
I speak not of Myself; but the Father that dwelleth
in Me, He doeth the works "; could George Fox
also without vainglory or affectation record, " The
mighty power of God wrought in a wonderful manner.
. . . The Lord's power broke forth gloriously to the
confounding of the gainsayers. . . . The Lord's power
sounded in their ears. . . . The Lord's truth went
over all. . . . The glorious God is exalting Himself;
Truth hath been talked of, but is now possessed. Christ
hath been talked of, but now He is come and possessed."[3]

A wholesome self-consciousness has attained in him
a strong type of self-assurance because he has come to

---

[1] *Journal*, p. 82.   [2] Ibid., p. 84.
[3] *Journal*, pp. 86, 110, 224, 503, and Letter : To All Professor of
Christianity ; cf. *Journal*, p. 222 (note).

that state of mind which is filled with harmony, unity, absolute goodness and absolute peace. His spirit within is ever calm, comforting, refreshing, quiet. His life has found its determinate centre. The Light Within has brought to him a consistency in the purpose and expression of his life, a rest that is not static but a poise in activity, a call that carries him to the service of his brothers.

The people of his day largely misunderstood him, and even imprisoned him for blasphemy. But he continued working with the courage of his convictions, and never in any spirit of self-aggrandizement. Personal praise was like a thistle in his flesh.[1] When Judge Fell told him that he had grown mightily in the truth, he put such commendation aside, commenting that indeed it was the judge himself who " was come nearer to the Truth, and so could better discern it." [2] In America the people were so pleased with his preaching that they spoke among themselves that " if they had enough money they would hire him as their minister." But as soon as he heard it he said, " It is time for me to be gone, for if their eye were so much on me, or on any of us, they would not come to their own Teacher." [3] His labour was to bring every one to his own Teacher *in himself*. Fox " knew the honour that cometh from God only, and sought that." [4] It was the God of heaven who carried him over all in His power.[5] As he would not accept any position of honour, so he would not accept for the Society any similar gift. When one ardent follower offered to buy Somerset House as a suitable place for the meeting of Friends, he put the suggestion

[1] *Journal*, p. 184.   [2] Ibid., p. 295.   [3] Ibid., p. 508.
[4] Ibid., p. 245.   [5] Ibid., p. 220.

aside without the slightest consideration.[1] Personal adoration he resented, and a silly woman who begged to cut a lock of his hair he ordered to cut down the corruptions in her own heart.[2]

With less of egotism and self-assurance, he would never have been able to found the Quaker religion. With more of self-seeking it would never have been as James says of it, " In a day of shams . . . a religion of veracity rooted in spiritual inwardness." [3]

Abnormality and Normality.

Tendencies which in another context of personality would have proved highly dangerous to the sanity of the possessor, in Fox worked together for good. With numerous abnormal traits, he was so constituted that he was yet able to retain essential self-control. He possessed an unusual psychical constitution. He was subject to profound transformations which deeply affected the functions of his body and mind, and which occurred independently of the will, but which were correlated with external events and happenings of momentous significance. They were usually times of stress and of unusual mental and emotional tension. He had the power of rare moral and spiritual penetration, which gave him power of leadership, as well as a prophetic sense and an ability to act intuitively toward instantaneous healings. He had an extraordinary power of sitting in rapt silence even for hours, and also an extraordinary power of expression in his eyes and at times in his entire person. Psychically he was most

[1] *Journal*, p. 328.   [2] Ibid., p. 293.
[3] James: *Varieties of Religious Experience* (New York, 1902), p. 7.

delicately organized, and at the outset most unstable. If near the end of his adolescent period he had not found a dynamic, constructive, and centralizing power, his being might never have become organized. His youth showed marks of hysteria when his blood would not flow, when he lost his sight and hearing, and when he lay in a trance for fourteen days much changed in countenance.[1] The marvel is that with such a constitution he ever became so sanely and practically organized. In manhood he was robust, virile ; ready to stand the world with its jeers, blows and prisons ; able to carry his message on foot or on horseback half-way round the world ; capable of influencing a Penn, a Barclay, a Penington ; with insight to organize a new type of religious society, to initiate far-reaching social and moral reforms ; strong to withstand flattery ; and with success in leadership. With a moral purpose, a spiritual earnestness that amounted to inward passion, an unswerving dedication and a fixity of will, he maintained a mental stability in which his life unfolded its moral and spiritual powers in harmonious parallelism with his development in physical and psychical power.

[1] *Journal,* pp. 73, 87, 95.

CONFLICTING TRAITS.

SANITY.

"The Lord taught me to be faithful in all things, and to act faithfully two ways, viz. inwardly to God, and outwardly to man; and to keep to Yea and Nay in all things. For the Lord showed me that, though the people of the world have mouths full of deceit, and changeable words, yet I was to keep to Yea and Nay in all things; and that my words should be few and savoury, seasoned with grace; and that I might not eat and drink to make myself wanton, but for health, using the creatures in their service, as servants in their places to the glory of Him that created them" (p. 66).

"Many Friends, that were tradesmen of several sorts, lost their customers at first, for the people were shy of them, and would not trade with them; so that for a time some Friends could hardly get money enough to buy bread.

"But afterwards, when people came to have experience of Friends' honesty and faithfulness, and found that their yea was yea, and their nay was nay; that they kept to a word in their dealings, and would not cozen and cheat, but that if a child were sent to their shops for anything, he was as well used as his parents would have been;—then the lives and conversation of Friends did preach, and reached to the witness of God in the people. Then things altered

PATHOLOGY.

"He would needs give me some physic, and I was to have been let blood; but they could not get one drop of blood from me, either in arms or head (though they endeavoured to do so), my body being, as it were, dried up with sorrows, grief and troubles, which were so great upon me that I could have wished I had never been born, or that I had been born blind, that I might never have seen wickedness or vanity; and deaf, that I might never have heard vain and wicked words, or the Lord's name blasphemed" (p. 73).

"When this man was buried a great work of the Lord fell upon me, to the admiration of many, who thought I had been dead, and many came to see me for about fourteen days. I was very much altered in countenance and person, as if my body had been new moulded or changed" (p. 87).

"As I was walking with several Friends, I lifted up my head and saw three steeple-house spires, and

15

so . . . Insomuch that Friends had more trade than many of their neighbours, and if there was any trading, they had a great part of it " (p. 198).

" One while they would have sent me up to the Parliament; another while they would have banished me to Ireland. At first they called me a deceiver, a seducer and a blasphemer. Afterwards, when God had brought His plagues upon them, they styled me an honest, virtuous man. But their good report and bad report were nothing to me; for the one did not lift me up, nor the other cast me down . . ." (p. 131).

" Thomas Lower also came to visit us, and offered us money, which we refused; accepting, nevertheless, of his love " (p. 265).

" Another time we asked the jailer what things were doing at the sessions, and he said, ' Small matters; only about thirty for bastardy.' We thought it very strange that they who professed themselves Christians should make small matters of such things " (p. 266).

" When some forward spirits that came amongst us would have bought Somerset House, that we might have meetings in it, I forbade them to do so " (p. 328).

" When Friends told me what a rage there was in the town, how they were threatened by the mayor and soldiers, and how unruly the soldiers had been the day before,

they struck at my life. I asked them what place that was. They said, ' Lichfield.' Immediately the Word of the Lord came to me that I must go thither. Being come to the house we were going to, I wished the Friends to walk into the house, saying nothing to them of whither I was to go. As soon as they were gone I stepped away, and went by my eye over hedge and ditch till I came within a mile of Lichfield, where, in a great field, shepherds were keeping their sheep.

" Then I was commanded by the Lord to pull off my shoes. I stood still, for it was winter; and the Word of the Lord was like a fire in me. So I put off my shoes, and left them with the shepherds; and the poor shepherds trembled, and were astonished. Then I walked on about a mile, and as soon as I was got within the city, the Word of the Lord came to me again, saying, ' Cry, " Woe to the bloody city of Lichfield ! " ' So I went up and down the streets, crying with a loud voice, ' Woe to the bloody city of Lichfield ! ' It being market-day, I went into the market-place, and to and fro in the several parts of it, and made stands, crying as before, ' Woe to the bloody city of Lichfield ! ' And no one laid hands on me.

" As I went thus crying through the streets, there seemed to me to be a channel of blood running down the street and the market-place appeared like a pool of blood.

" When I had declared what was upon me, and felt myself clear, I went out of the town in peace,

I sent for several Friends . . . and desired them to go to the mayor and aldermen, and request them, seeing he and they had broken up our meetings, to let Friends have the town hall to meet in. For the use of it Friends would give them twenty pounds a year, to be distributed among the poor, and when the mayor and aldermen had business to do in it, Friends would not meet in it, but only on First-days.

"These Friends were astonished at this, and said the mayor and aldermen would think that they were mad. I said, 'Nay; for this would be a considerable benefit to the poor.' And it was upon me from the Lord to bid them go. At last they consented, and went, though in the cross to their own wills.

"When they had laid the thing before the mayor, he said, 'For my part I could consent to it, but I am but one'; and he told Friends of another great hall they might have; but they did not accept, it being inconvenient.

"So Friends came away, leaving the mayor in a very loving frame towards them; for they felt the Lord's power had come over him " (p. 332).

and, returning to the shepherds, I gave them some money and took my shoes of them again. But the fire of the Lord was so in my feet, and all over me, that I did not matter to put on my shoes again, and was at a stand whether I should or no, till I felt freedom from the Lord so to do; then, after I had washed my feet, I put on my shoes again " (p. 132).

"It was upon me from the Lord to go and speak to the justices, that they should not oppress the servants in their wages. . . . But when I came in the morning they were gone and I was struck even blind, that I could not see. I inquired of the innkeeper where the justices were to sit that day; and he told me, at a town eight miles off. My sight began to come to me again; and I went and ran thitherward as fast as I could " (p. 95).

XI

A CHASM BETWEEN THE INNER
AND OUTER SELF

Torn between such contrasted characteristics, he was in a state of constant tension. As a child he had not felt the strain. His gravity, his sense of self-righteousness, his desire not to be like others, his apparently entire lack of any childish play impulse,[1] made him keep apart from others. As his mother was tender and indulgent to his eccentricities, he met with little difficulty. His inner life of piety was budding, but it had not yet grown sufficiently to thrust him into any marked break with his fellow-men. As he grew into the " gang age " the characteristics of adolescence made the struggle one of much more intensity for him than for one who was natively less individualistic than he. So at the period of storm and stress we find him torn far asunder. It seems as if his were a mind with a central organization that moved along entirely separated from an outward shell of social contacts.

His egotism, his feeling of self-confidence, his tough-mindedness, his negative suggestibility, his indifference to family, friends, or conventional social interactions, his censoriousness even in childhood, his

[1] The play impulse seems to show itself in Fox only in the tendency to try things out for himself, which tendency is at the basis of all play.

228

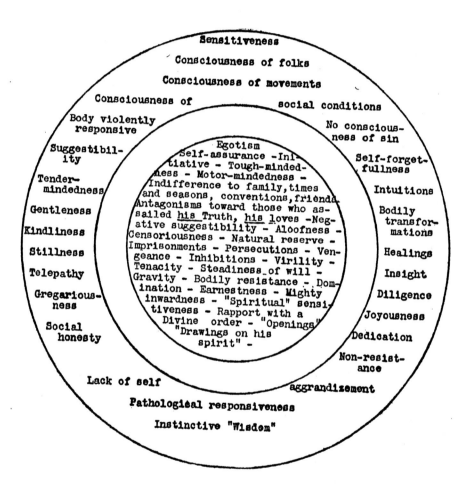

Sensitiveness

Consciousness of folks

Consciousness of movements

Consciousness of   social conditions

Body violently responsive   No conscious-ness of sin

Suggestibil-ity   Self-forget-fullness

Tender-mindedness   Intuitions

Gentleness   Bodily transfor-mations

Kindliness

Stillness   Healings

Telepathy   Insight

Gregarious-ness   Diligence

Social honesty   Joyousness

Dedication

Non-resist-ance

Lack of self   aggrandizement

Pathological responsiveness

Instinctive "Wisdom"

Egotism
Self-assurance - Ini-tiative - Tough-minded-ness - Motor-mindedness - Indifference to family, times and seasons, conventions, friends Antagonisms toward those who as-sailed his Truth, his loves - Neg-ative suggestibility - Aloofness - Censoriousness - Natural reserve - Imprisonments - Persecutions - Ven-geance - Inhibitions - Virility - Tenacity - Steadiness of will - Gravity - Bodily resistance - Dom-ination - Earnestness - Mighty inwardness - "Spiritual" sensi-tiveness - Rapport with a Divine order - "Openings" "Drawings on his spirit" -

natural reserve and aloofness—all these helped to turn him into himself and to keep him apart from his fellow-men. As he grew into young manhood the revolutionary changes in his physical being were driving him into contact with others. His sensitiveness, his tender-mindedness, his gentleness, his gregariousness, his virility, his consciousness of folks and of conditions, were drawing him sympathetically out to mingle with others. The conflict then becomes almost more than he can stand. We find him on the verge of a pathological separation into a truly divided self. But most fortunately for Fox, and for the world, his delayed reactions were very sure and his physical resistance was such that it enabled him to pass through this trying period and come out of it with his sanity surely established through its fiery testing. Those things that drove him into himself had pounded him till his inmost being was fine as tempered steel. Though it was plastic and adjustable to all circumstances, it was absolutely consistent in its loyalty and complete adjustment and responsiveness to his dominant centre—the Guidance of the Inner Light in his own heart. Becoming more centrally organized as he finds his mastery over himself and his work in the world, his life gives evidence of perfected pathways of co-operation between his inner and outer traits. His action and response are entirely normal, and bridge over a chasm between the inner and outer self. No longer torn apart, his inner depth of a mighty inwardness has gained a control that is sober, minute, laborious, humane and, most of all, consistent.

XII

THE LIBERATION OF A HIGHER SELFHOOD

NATURE always uses the most intense things of life for higher purposes if she may. Thus it is that habits are splintered off bits of old instincts. From the instincts the finer sentiments draw their very life-blood. The energy that might normally have gone into family relationships in his early manhood, Nature used in aiding him to carry each of his characteristics to a higher level. They all became so closely co-ordinated that he pulled himself apart from the tension of his divided self and found himself so unified that he seemed another person.

Not alone was his sexual impulse " long-circuited," to use G. Stanley Hall's phrase, but all his crude native instincts and endowments were kept on into a higher form. Fear became the essence of reverence for him. Penn says :

" The most awful, living, reverent frame I ever felt or beheld, I must say, was his in prayer. And truly it was a testimony he knew, and lived nearer to the Lord than other men ; for they that know Him most will see most reason to approach Him with reverence and fear."

[1] *Journal*, p. 54.

231

Leuba would do away with fear, and Coe would classify it as harmful and destructive, but Cannon has shown that it is one of Nature's most powerful ways of tuning the body up to a pitch necessary for emergency. When the lower forms of fear are held down, energy is liberated which seeks its own finer expression. "The fear of the Lord is the beginning of wisdom." Fox comes, through it, to lead a more alert life of reliance on the Lord.

Anger in Fox was as strong as in the most pugnacious of his fellow-men. But he had put such a curb of control upon it that, enraged at the incivility of a priest, he did not storm or fight, but was " wrapped up as in a rapture." [1] His refined instinct—torn asunder from coarser expressive reaction—could express itself in love even for personal persecutors. It could develop in him an attitude whereby he lived in the spirit that took away the occasion of all wars.[2]

George Fox's instinctive biological demands for food and drink blossomed out into a demand for spiritual rather than material values. You *can't kill an instinct*, and in him the physical thirst, which he refused to use in the conventional way for social drinking, became a double thirst. He thirsted for human companionship and for the presence of the Lord. So strong did this higher desire become that he says :

"If I had had a king's diet, palace and attendance, all would have been as nothing ; for nothing gave me pleasure but the Lord." [3]

He was happy in the possession of property sufficient to enable him to live his life and be no burden upon

[1] *Journal*, p. 92.   [2] Ibid., p. 128.   [3] Ibid., p. 84.

friends or relatives. Therefore his acquisitions took the form of gathering into his Truth a large following in whom he rejoiced. Men, not things, were the objects he garnered into his treasury. The appeal that beauty of clothing and such personal possessions made upon him became evident indirectly from his own insistence that the curly lock of his hair which he refused to have cut was not of his own putting on.[1] It shows, too, in the leathern breeches which he wore, perhaps in somewhat of an ascetic spirit ; in the scarlet cloak which he selected for his wife as a gift when returning from a journey ; in the white raiment that clad the people of his vision of Pendle Hill. His control and refinement of the natural love of property is shown in his insistence that his stepchildren should in no-wise lose, nor he gain, financially by his marriage with Margaret Fell ;[2] and also by his scrupulous honesty at all other times.

His youthful indignation at the priest who used his thoughts done over into sermons is but a cruder form of the instinct of rivalry which blossomed into a jealous guarding of " the Truth " and a bitter denunciation of all who assailed it. He was accused, apparently without foundation, a few times of jealousy toward some of the gifted ministers among his followers. His unconscious personal jealousy showed itself more in the harsh criticism of priest Lampitt.

His motor-mindedness at first had driven him from home merely to be as a stranger to all, with no objective point and purposive direction in his wanderings. On a higher level it became a definite moving to a clearly defined goal with a definite mission. He must go

[1] *Journal*, p. 239.   [2] Ibid., p. 469.

THE DEVELOPMENT OF THE PERSONALITY OF GEORGE FOX

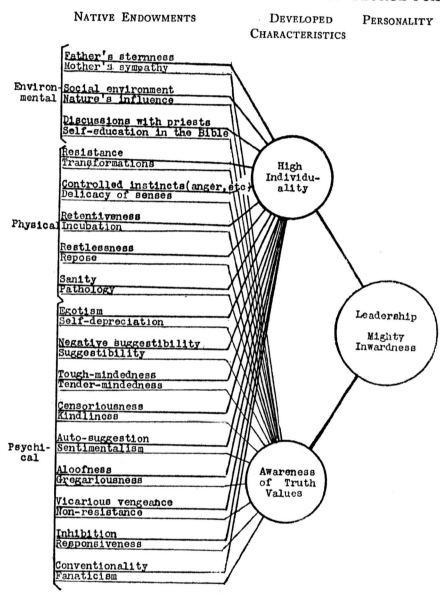

into Scotland to gather and strengthen the seed of God there. He must go to Barbadoes and to the American colonies to visit the Friends who had settled or had been exiled there.

His censoriousness became so heightened and impersonal that he exercised authority over evil, and evil alone, no matter where he found it, with nought of personal animosity, but with love, and gentleness and tenderness.

His aloofness became not a personal separating of himself from his fellow-men. Rather it was a drawing of his group so closely together that they drifted away from the conventional ways of the world until they developed into, and have ever remained, a peculiar people.

He had risen far above all conscious desire for vengeance, but his mind was still quick to detect vicarious vengeance in the "judgments" that were visited upon those who harmed him or his people, or his truth. He was also alert to predict and prophesy such approaching judgments.

Having thrown aside all trifling conventionality of minor customs and manners, his innate sense of propriety lets there be no question of too great familiarity in his co-operation with Margaret Fell through seventeen years of close friendship before their marriage. It developed in him an attitude in society which was, as Penn said, " civil beyond all forms of breeding." [1]

Such heightened instincts and characteristics, torn asunder from their cruder expression, show their influence in the development of Fox as a man of strong individuality and initiative, the natural leader of men.

[1] Penn : Preface to *Journal*, p. 59.

But other traits than those we have mentioned play as definite a part in the development of Fox as a mystic.

To no one element can mysticism be reduced than to the attitude of love. In religion, as in daily life, there are three sources of love : sex, gregariousness and nature. No higher thing is there in the world than true love between a man and woman, and much of the sordidness and grovelling of life is because people have not found the glory and beauty of human love. But I would not place it as the one source to which all other elements of the religious life are reducible, as some psychologists of to-day do. G. Stanley Hall and Freud would contend that all higher forms of love are but the irradiations of a smouldering sex impulse. With Morton Prince, rather, would I agree : that there is no more inhibition of the sex instinct than of any other, but that it, *with all others*, is conserved and refined and beautified. In Fox, beautiful, refined and ennobled as it was in his love for his wife, it was not alone in its religious influence. That which Ribot calls " gregariousness " and Guyan " sociality " is a tremendous factor. As a little child his very consciousness of folk impinged on him so hard that, in the interests of the integrity of his own selfhood, he drew apart and lived much alone. Wanton behaviour had repelled him in childhood, but in youth he still loved all who had a sense of good. He had sought out one after another, though repeatedly he found that they were all miserable comforters. Growing into manhood, his life had become so co-ordinated that it had found its determinate centre. No longer did he need to fear to allow his gregariousness free play. With all the might of his manhood he threw himself into the close

sympathy of human contacts in the life of fellowship
in the Society which grew up around him. Intending
to form no new sect,[1] the bond of union in the group
became so strong that spontaneously it felt a need for
a firmer organization whereby to protect itself from
the persecutions of the world. Irrespective of sex,
they worked side by side in loving companionship.
Friendly visiting was found to be such a source of
helpfulness that homes were opened so hospitably that
their contemporaries predicted that they would soon
eat each other out.[2] If it be true that greater criterion
of love there is not than that a man lay down his life
for his friend, then the Society of Friends gave full
evidence that they so loved each other. Had they
not offered themselves as substitutes in the prisons
for those who were perishing there? But their love
stretched even to their persecutors. Their offer had
been made also to shield the persecutors from the
responsibility of causing the death of innocent persons.[3]

Fox felt instinctively that " the strength of the wolf
is in the pack, and the strength of the pack is in the
wolf," as Kipling would have put it. When a single
member ran off into fanaticism, he was merciless in
his denunciation. Out of such close co-operation
Fox developed not only a sort of tribal self, wherein
he suffered and rejoiced with the whole, but through
it he developed his own higher selfhood.

Yet even with all the strength that social and sexual
love have in Fox, it is to the third source of love that
we find Fox turning when he seeks for some way to
express that closest and most fundamental element
in his mystical life. Then he uses no term of social

---

[1] *Journal*, p. 349.   [2] Ibid., p. 197.   [3] Ibid., p. 323.

or biological life. Rather he turns to general or more inanimate nature. He speaks in terms of its beauty : Light, Seed. Just as primitive man has so often found the direct source of his religion in the heavens and the earth, personifying the Dawn or the Sun or Fire, so Fox finds these the best symbols whereby to express the Inexpressible. He who had lived in the heart of Nature had found that these are wonderful, glorious, beautiful, majestic, fit symbols of the God-life which he found surging as an ocean of light through his own being. Just as the amœba gets fulfilment in sunlight, in warmth, in chemical environment, so Fox got a sense of values in his inner life which he objectified in terms of a Light Within that burns in the fastnesses of his heart. Through it his characteristics moulded together into a mighty inwardness.

After a boyhood of self-consciousness, of self-regard, of aloofness, of egotistic sensitivity and responsiveness, of subjectivism, he finds himself torn by the strain and tension of an adolescent period of temptation and torment. Separated from his family and friends, he has to fight out in the arena of his own heart the battle between a self-centred and a God-centred existence. Comte has said that as religion progresses to monotheism it becomes less intense and personal. Fox, with his warmhearted dominant impulse for gregariousness, had to learn to be willing not alone to recognize, but to rejoice in, the supremacy of the one God. He must seek no longer in men for his deliverance, but must rely on the Lord alone. Then only could he regain his faith in men by the realization that the Infinite Divinity is not only without, but also within the heart of man.

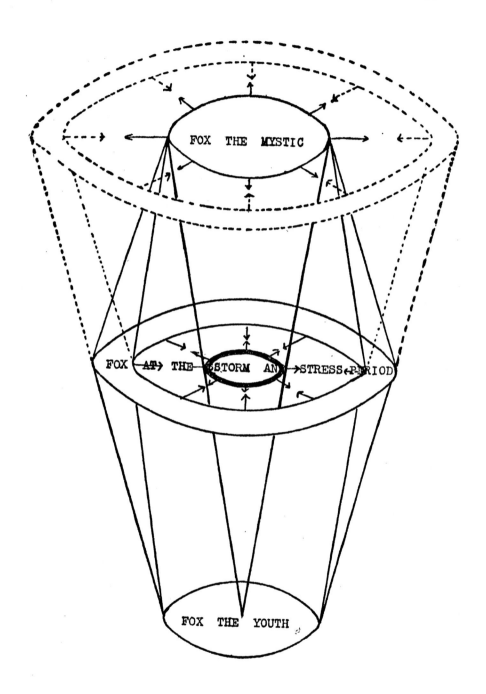

Not by casting aside a single trait, be it good or evil, did he mount. No purgation washed his pathway. Ennobled, refined, developed until it could find emancipation in liberty, each characteristic of the youth, torn and sorrowful, is retained in the man whose very presence expressed a religious majesty. Thus alone did he gain for himself that liberation of his higher selfhood, as a mystical leader of men, as a practical mystic.

PART FOUR

THE IMPLICATIONS OF FOX'S
MYSTICAL LIFE AND TEACHINGS

THE IMPLICATIONS OF THE LIFE AND MYSTICISM OF FOX

WE have traced the sources from which Fox drew the truth values of his mysticism. We found that they arose from normal mental procedure and not from any special spiritual sense, nor from any supernatural store of energy. Fox lived better than other people just in that he used to better advantage his normal faculties. From a youth with a manifold of conflicting traits, he developed into a unified personality. Out of an individualistic and self-righteous boyhood, he became the leader and founder of an intensely social fellowship. It now remains as part of our task to develop, if we may, the varied implications of his type of mysticism.

XIII

PHILOSOPHICAL IMPLICATIONS

Fox was not a philosopher. The problems of philosophy were not his problems. He begins with the demands of life and its ideals, but he never moves on to look for a reconciliation of these with the orderly procedure of Nature. Instead he very naïvely supposes that the orderly procedure of Nature is the resultant of the orderly procedure of life, which for him is life lived in accord with *his* ideals of its good ordering. Even of so apparently fickle a manifestation of Nature's good order as the weather he writes :

" So far as the Truth was spread, there was rain enough and no drought." [1]

He reprimands Cromwell for proclaiming a fast for rain instead of accepting the Truth as he preached it, for, had he done so, " Nature would have favoured him and his nation."

" It is not necessary to be a philosopher," says Royce, " in order to be a person ; and often enough, as human nature goes, abstract ideas may be permitted so much to stand in the way of concrete devotion, that a given individual may appear all the more doubtfully to be a person by virtue of the fact that he has let himself become a philosopher." [2]

[1] *Journal*, p. 282.
[2] Josiah Royce : *The Conception of God* (New York, 1897), p. 316.

George Fox was at all times the most concrete of persons. If in his writings he attempted to argue out a position, he became repetitious, involved, and lacking in clearness of expression. But his purpose was always clear as crystal, and so his thought and message carried over without ever being philosophized. However, there are evident in his mystical life and teachings certain central things which, had he been a philosopher, he might readily have used as the basis of a philosophical system, instead of merely as concrete practical principles for ethical living. The most prominent of these is his feeling of oneness with the total of Reality to which he responded so immediately.

In his youth Fox had rebelled at the hollowness of the social life about him. It is with childlike directness and simplicity that he finds the voice of God speaking in his own heart. Fox, with no introspection of his own mental processes as such, takes such experiences at their apparent objective value. But a philosopher of the fine temper of Spinoza would search out his mental procedure and write :

" After experience had taught me that all the usual surroundings of social life are vain and futile ; seeing that none of the objects of my fears contained in themselves anything either good or bad, except in so far as the mind is affected by them, I finally resolved to inquire whether there might be some real good having power to communicate itself, which could affect the mind singly, to the exclusion of all else : whether, in fact, there might be anything of which the discovery and attainment would enable me to enjoy continuous, supreme, and unending happiness." [1]

[1] Spinoza : *On the Improvement of the Understanding* (trans. by Elwes).

Spinoza the philosopher seeks and finds the " real good having power to communicate itself." It is the Lord whose voice speaks to Fox the mystic in his dire distress and loneliness.

For both the philosopher and the religious mystic, worry, desires, and passions that distract, all pass away. Even at a tender age Fox knew himself to be free from passions or wrong desires ; he knew innocence and purity. He learned to love even his persecutors and his enemies. Again, Spinoza writes in clear language an analysis of the way by which we reach to such virtues :

" Thus we easily conceive what power clear and distinct knowledge of God, and nothing else, has over the emotions ; if it does not, in so far as they are passions, absolutely remove them, at all events it brings about that they constitute the least part of the mind. Furthermore it begets love toward that which is immutable and eternal, and which really we do not have within our power—a love which, consequently is not stained by any of the defects inherent in common love but can always become greater and greater, and take possession of the greatest part of the mind, and affect it everywhere." [1]

The problem of cosmology was not Fox's. His problem was the nature of man and the relation between God and man. The experience of Fox's heart led him practically, not rationally, into an attitude of a monistic conception of Reality. He started out with the primary fact that there is no necessary dualism between the Divine Spirit and human spirits. James Nayler formulated it perhaps more simply and with clearer

[1] J. Spinoza : *Ethics* (trans. by Fullerton), Part V, p. 20.

philosophical insight than Fox ever did. His words are :

"Christ filleth all places and is not divided ; separate God and man, and He is no more Christ." [1]

Fox remained in no passive attitude of enjoyment of the inseparable unity of his spirit with the Divine. In fact, it was with conscious recognition that he felt the *power of God* within him as an energistic dynamic force expressing itself outwardly in words and deeds. It led him to an energizing sense of his call and his mission in life. Spinoza and Fox both conceive of God as the power which produces, organizes and governs the universe from within outwardly. He is in all things and all things are in Him. In Him every existing thing lives and moves and has its being. Though clothed in the language of concrete religious devotion by Fox, the conception is in effect much like the present-day energy concept of Reality.

Had Fox been a philosopher, we may conceivably imagine that he would have worked his way out philosophically until he had not only found the element of monism in his feeling of intense oneness with Reality, but also moved on to the conception that this inseparable Reality must be of an energistic dynamic kind.

Arising also from the conception of an internal force expressing itself in outward forms, he would have found himself recognizing the principle of each person's guidance as a doctrine of freedom very similar to that of Spinoza, or a doctrine of intuition similar to that of Bergson. The mystic Fox calls it the Guidance of

[1] James Nayler: *The Soul's Road to Damascus*, p. 317.

the Lord, but never questions how it operates, nor the forms which it takes.

Spinoza's logically reasoned-out doctrine of freedom [1] contributes to the service of life in four points entirely paralleled in Fox's unreasoned practical response to life. Spinoza says :

(1) "We act according to God's decree, and are participators in the divine nature ; and this the more, the more perfect the actions we perform, and the better we comprehend God. . . . Our highest felicity or blessedness consists only in the knowledge of God which leads us to do only those things which love and pity recommend."

No one could have been more conscious than Fox that God's decree was the rule of his life ; and blessedness and freedom from anxiety became his portion in proportion to that consciousness.

(2) Next Spinoza says this doctrine of freedom

"teaches us how to behave with regard to those things which depend upon fortune and which are not within our power ; that is, with regard to those things which do not follow from our nature."

It was the nature of man and his life that concerned Fox. The scientific and historical world of facts did not demand his attention. His behaviour was perhaps not always the best possible, but on the whole his response to life was meritorious.

(3) Thirdly, the doctrine of freedom is

"of service to social life in that it teaches to hate no one, to despise, to ridicule, to be angry at no one, to envy no one."

[1] Spinoza : *Ethics* (trans. by Fullerton), Part II.

(4) The last point which Spinoza makes as to the value of his insistence on freedom is also one which was evident in Fox's life. He could with entire honesty of conscience tell the judge that he had been a blessing to the nation. Spinoza says that freedom

"is of no little advantage to the State in that it shows how citizens ought to be governed and led ; namely, not so as to act like slaves, but so as to do freely what is best."

If Fox's Guidance resulted in such practical applications as these which Spinoza describes, it also gave much more a sense of knowledge that his spirit was reaching out beyond itself into the unknown. Fox says that it was *experimentally* that he knew that God worked through him. This fits in with Bergson's idea of a supra-intellectual intuition.

" If this intuition exists," says Bergson, " a taking possession of the spirit by itself is possible, and no longer only a knowledge that is external and phenomenal. What is more, if we have an intuition of this kind (I mean an ultra-intellectual intuition), then sensuous intuition is likely to be in continuity with it through certain intermediaries, as the infra-red is continuous with the ultra-violet. Sensuous intuition itself, therefore, is promoted. It will no longer attain only the phantom of an unattainable thing-in-itself. It is . . . into the absolute itself that it will introduce us." [1]

Philosopher and mystic alike thus arrive at the same goal of communion with the Divine.

A fourth point in Fox's system would be his recognition that each person, however mighty or humble, whether saint or reprobate, is part and parcel of the

[1] Henri Bergson : *Creative Evolution* (trans. by Mitchell), p. 360. New York, 1913.

divine life. This resulted in a conception of a divine community of Friends. They were bound by a common interest and a common interpretation of human nature, such as is recognized by the modern sociologists as essential to the unity of human groups. Charles A. Ellwood, leader of the social psychologists to-day, writes :

"In all conscious human groups it is the mental attitude of the individuals towards one another which is the final, decisive factor which decides whether a group shall maintain its unity or be disrupted. There are, for example, the feelings, sentiments, ideas, beliefs, and opinions of the group. Not only must these be similar within certain limits, but the members of the group must be more or less conscious of this similarity ; that is, they must develop mutual sympathy and understanding. From mutual sympathy and understanding, moreover, arise confidence and reciprocal trust which make possible still closer co-ordination between the members of a group." [1]

Together Fox's adherents developed into a people of upright life, of deep religious experience, of corporate serving the cause of the Lord. The Society of Friends waiting together in the silent worship of the Lord is a practical demonstration of Royce's doctrine of the communion of saints, a community of the children of God. Royce describes it partly thus :

"The true cause, the genuine community, the real spiritual brotherhood of the loyal is a superhuman and not merely a human reality. . . . The invisible Church, then, is no merely human and secular institution. It is a real and superhuman organization. It includes and transcends every form of the visible Church. It is the actual subject to which belong all the spiritual gifts which we can hope to enjoy. . . . It believes everywhere in the unity

[1] Charles A. Ellwood : *Social Psychology* (New York, 1915), p. 18.

of the Spirit, and aims to save men through winning them over to the conscious service of its own unity." [1]

It is just such a community of spiritual believers that Fox conceived the Church to be. In recounting an argument with a priest he says :

"I told him the Church was the pillar and ground of truth, made up of living stones, living members, a spiritual household, which Christ was the head of." [2]

To another he exclaimed :

"Alas, poor man ! dost thou call the steeple-house the Church ? The Church is the people, and not the house." [3]

"All philosophers," says James, "have conceived of the whole world after the analogy of some particular feature of it which has particularly captivated their attention." The naturalist's world, therefore, is constructed from the evidence of his senses alone ; the idealist's from the processes of his thought ; the philosophical sceptic's from "pure reason." But the world of a mystic like Fox is built out of the complete awareness of his entire experience. It is symbolized most of all by his sense of immediate rapport with a Supreme Being until he knows no difference between himself and God. He knows that he is not hermetically sealed from the complete Reality we call the Absolute. He is one with it. Fox soon learned to make no distinction between his own consciousness and the power of God which controlled him.

[1] Josiah Royce : *Sources of Religious Insight* (New York, 1914), p. 281.
[2] *Journal*, p. 93.　　　　　　　　　　[3] Ibid., p. 145.

A philosopher guesses and argues in the nice dialectic of many schools of thought. His religious life has become self-conscious and seeks to understand itself. Fox the mystic lived and looked and spoke the disconcerting language of first-hand experience directly. In him the love of truth of the philosopher becomes a personal passion to know, not *of* the truth, but to know the Truth at first hand. He does not dichotomize at all, but experiences the whole and makes his judgments that include intellect and intuition both in a combined whole of experience.

XIV

ETHICAL APPLICATIONS

Fox had no thought nor desire to start a new sect. In fact he denied that the Friends were a sect at all : " The Quakers are not a sect, but are in the power of God, which was before sects were." [1] He was a preacher of righteousness who believed that he had rediscovered a forgotten but essential fact of Christian thought and experience. He and his followers announced as their aim the revival of primitive Christianity. That remains the best definition of his work. Historically he is important as a leader of men into a " very insistently social religion." [2] Mysticism, not for the first time, proved itself to be a direct and powerful agent for the most practical issues of life. To Fox the life of a person must be a living testimony of his inner experience. An evil woman was told by him that " her heart was not right before the Lord, and that from the inward came the outward." [3]

Not only did his followers learn to speak the same religious language, but their religion found the same

[1] *Journal*, p. 349.
[2] Royce : " George Fox the Mystic," in *Harvard Theological Review*, January 1913, p. 38.
[3] *Journal*, p. 185.

consistent expression in a manner of life common to all. He asks :

"As concerning the Quakers ? . . . Do they not fear God ? and do they not walk justly and truly among their neighbours, and speak the truth, and do the truth in all things, doing to all no otherwise than they would be done unto ? and are they not meek and humble and sober ? and do they not take much wrong rather than give wrong to any ? And are they not such as delight in the ways of the Lord ? and do they not preach in the power of God, and reach to your conscience when you hear them ? and doth not the light in you answer that they speak the truth ?" [1]

However, their effort did not end in private lives of such morality. There is a dynamic force in the Quaker religion, as well as in Fox personally. Emerson writes : " An institution is the lengthened shadow of a man, as Quakerism of George Fox." So we find the work of the group as well as his personal life attended by moral awakening. The heightening of life brought with it an increase of energy to all whose hearts were reached by his message. The attainment of first-hand experience of Divine Reality brought a corresponding relaxation of the hold on forms, ceremonies and dogmas. Without any apparent pressure, those convinced took on, as if by natural instinct, the ideas, manners, practices, language and mode of worship which Fox had adopted.[2] Perhaps the consistency of Fox's expression of his personal realization of the truth, as he saw it, finds no better vindication

[1] George Fox : *Works,* vol. i, p. 24.
[2] Uniformity seems to be a characteristic of democracy wherever applied. Travellers already attest to such uniformity in the independent soviet governments of Russia and Siberia.

than in the fact that the most earnest of his followers, even to the present, can find few ways in which they can improve upon his practices. The " thee " and " thou " and the opposition to " hat-honour," which caused the early Quakers so much persecution, find to-day their modern expression in the directness of language and simplicity of apparel which are still approved among them. But more of the æsthetic side of life can be found to be in entire harmony with their truths. A greater strength, I believe, would come from such development.

The formality of the marriage procedure which Fox followed, gaining first the approval of the family and later of meetings of both men and women Friends, is one which, where still followed, results in a guarded care that prevents hasty and ill-advised marriage, and keeps it on a plane rarely invaded by divorce. The resulting home life, with its equality of the authority and responsibility resting in both parents, has made for a united home and an insistence on thorough and equal education for both boys and girls. The ideal has ever been an insistence on efficiency, but efficiency as a means to service and not to power.

The peculiar testimonies which Friends felt incumbent upon them to bear led them for a time into serious financial straits. Fox said :

" When they could not bow, or use flattering words in salutation, or adopt the fashions and customs of the world, many Friends that were tradesmen of several sorts, lost their customers at first, for the people were shy of them ; so that for a time some Friends could hardly get money enough to buy bread. . . . But afterwards, when people came to have experience of Friends' honesty and faithfulness and found their yea was yea, and their nay was nay ; that they kept to a word in their dealings, and would not cozen and cheat, but that if a child were sent to their shops for anything, he was as well used as his parents would have been ; then the lives and conversation of Friends did preach . . . insomuch that Friends had more trade than many of their neighbours. . . . Then the envious professors altered their note, and began to cry out, ' If we let these Quakers alone, they will take the trade of the nation out of our hands.' " [1]

It is interesting even to-day to see how much truth of fulfilment there has been to such an idle statement.[2]

Liberty, equality of opportunity, education, righteousness, truth, toleration : these were the causes for which Quakerism fought in the dark times of the Commonwealth. For the overthrow of evil, they fought in all realms of reform. It was natural that they who knew so much of the inside of prisons should be foremost in working for prison reform, as later they were for the abolition of slavery. In the cause of peace and healing the effects of war, they have been and are equally and constantly zealous.

Other people have believed in Divine Guidance in the lives of men, but the passion and fervour with which Fox applied this ideal practically and fearlessly is new. With such belief and faith in mankind as arose from his belief in the interpenetration of the God-life in humanity, the only consistent outcome is a democratic type of religious and social life. The principle not only involves an equality of the sexes, but gives a religious basis for democratic government as well. Such government is a far different thing from government by a

---

[1] *Journal*, p. 198.
[2] For instance, such well-known firms may be cited as Lloyd's, Rowntree's, Fry's, Cadbury's, Jacobs', etc.

majority vote, such as is to be found in " democratic "
governments as actually practised. It is still a far
call to raise humanity to a plane where real democracy
may be the safeguard of the world. But the Light
taught Fox " how to labour amid all the storms and
lurid hatreds of the day, not in vain, but humanely.
valiantly and beneficently.' [1]

[1] Royce : Op. cit., p. 59.

XV

RELIGIOUS IMPLICATIONS

IN a recent unpublished lecture by Dr. Starbuck,[1] he defined religion as "centring in one's total and whole-hearted reaction toward his most vitalizing feeling for that which has supreme and absolute worth or value—towards his most intimate sense of Reality." It is such an absolute religion of personal experience rather than a religion of faith alone which Fox insists upon as the only true religion. To such a God-centred religion as his was personally, he inspired the entire organization of the Society of Friends. It is no less truly a mystical religion because it does not tear itself away from the world. Everett says:

"There is more true religion in half an hour's question: 'What wilt Thou have me to do?' than in a whole lifetime of asking, 'What wilt Thou do for me?'"[2]

It is this dynamic type of true religion which Fox had found through the emancipation of his higher selfhood. He knew that he lived and moved and had his being in the very God-life itself.

George Fox had felt a direct and special call from

[1] Starbuck: Lecture delivered at the Conference of Religious Workers at the Summer School, University of Iowa, 1918.
[2] Everett: *Psychological Elements of Religious Faith*, chap. viii.

the Lord " to bring people off from the world's religions that they might know the pure religion." [1] Ralph Barton Perry, in *Present Philosophical Tendencies,* says that Kant led an idealistic revolution in philosophical thought that was really a counter-revolution through which the spectator again became the centre of the universe. [2] Fox also led an idealistic revolution that was really a counter-revolution. He turned the religious thought of the world back to the original gospel of a God-centred world. In it there can be no chasm between God and man. The " good news " he preached is the truth for which Jesus had lived and died. Before Christianity came to earth, the God-centred world gospel had been a vitalizing conception. Deussen writes of the religion of the Upanishads :

" If we hold fast to this distinction of the Brahman as the cosmical principle of the universe, the atman as the psychical, the fundamental thought of the entire Upanishad philosophy may be expressed by the simple equation :—

$$\text{Brahman} = \text{Atman}.$$

That is to say, the Brahman, the power which presents itself to us materialized in all existing things, which creates, sustains, preserves, and receives back into itself again all worlds, this eternal infinite divine power is identical with the atman, with that which, after stripping off everything external, we discover in ourselves as our real most essential being, or individual self, the soul. This identity of the Brahman and the atman, of God and the soul, is the fundamental thought of the entire doctrine of the Upanishads.

" We are unable to look into the future, we do not know what revelations and discoveries are in store for the restlessly inquiring human spirit ; but one thing we may assert with confidence— whatever new and unwonted paths the philosophy of the future

[1] *Journal,* p. 104.
[2] Ralph Barton Perry : *Present Philosophical Tendencies,* p. 104.

may strike out, this principle will remain permanently unshaken, and from it no deviation can possibly take place." [1]

God and humanity are so one and undivided that God can express Himself in human terms—even in human forms. Whoever will manifest the God-life within himself may become like God, even a very son of God. " Life on its highest level is nothing less than living a life in the flesh which reproduces in measure and degree that perfect, typical God-man life." [2] Fox writes of his preaching :

" It was proclaimed amongst the people that the day was now come wherein all that made a profession of the Son of God might receive Him ; and that to as many as would receive Him He would give power to become the sons of God, as He had done to me." [3]

England was filled in that day with many new and strange sects. Religious, or rather theological, discussions were of paramount interest, and great gatherings were often held for the purpose, not of religious service, but of general and public theological argumentation.[4] Fox's position led to a thorough theological reformation. Though he was often challenged to such public discussions, and at times did share in them, it was usually in a spirit of censorious disapproval. He was no systematic theologian. He formulated no creed, though his letter to the Governor of Barbadoes has frequently been quoted as such. He says :

[1] Paul Deussen : *The Philosophy of the Upanishads*, p. 39.
[2] Rufus M. Jones : *A Dynamic Faith*, p. 71.
[3] *Journal*, p. 195.
[4] Cf. *Journal*, p. 178. At the close of one such day's discussions " the cry was among the people that the Quakers had got the day, and the priests were fallen."

"I told them that all their preaching, baptism and sacrifices would never sanctify them, and bade them look unto Christ within them, and not unto men ; for it is Christ that sanctifies. Then they ran into many words ; but I told them they were not to dispute of God and Christ, but *to obey Him.*" [1]

Faith and baptism for him were not matters of reasoning and of outward observance. People "must find these things in their own hearts." [2] "God dwells not in temples made with hands, but in the hearts of men." [3] True believers in Christ "are passed from death to life ; and if passed from death, then from sin that bringeth death." [4] True faith, then, will give a victory over sin and death, and will purify the hearts and consciences of men. He took literally the command of Jesus, "Be ye perfect," because he believed in the Atonement, not as one historical event in the past, but as a continuous experience. The Indwelling Christ, the Light, the Seed of God in the hearts of men,

"who Himself was perfect, comes to make men and women perfect again, and brings them again to the state in which God made them.   So He is the maker-up of the breach and the peace betwixt God and man." [5]

No Second Coming of Christ did Fox prepare for, as did the Baptists and Fifth Monarchy Men. They looked for an outward reign.

"But Christ is come," said Fox, "and doth dwell and reign in the hearts of His people   Thousands, at the door of whose hearts He hath been knocking, have opened to Him, and He is

[1] *Journal,* p. 120.   [2] Ibid., p. 115.   [3] Ibid., p. 76.
[4] Ibid., p. 123.   [5] Ibid., p. 334.

come in, and doth sup with them, and they with Him ; the heavenly supper with the heavenly and spiritual man." [1]

The Doctrine of Predestination was one much discussed in those days. Of this Fox writes as follows :

" Now, the priests had frightened the people with the doctrine of election and reprobation, telling them that God had ordained the greatest part of men and women for hell ; and that, let them pray, or preach, or sing, or do what they would, it was all to no purpose, if they were ordained for hell. Also that God had a certain number elected for heaven, let them do what they would ; as David was an adulterer, and Paul a persecutor, yet still they were elected vessels for heaven. So the priests said the fault was not at all in the creature, less or more, but that God had ordained it so.

" I was led to open the falseness and folly of their priests' doctrines, and showed how they, the priests, had abused those Scriptures they quoted. Now, all that believe in the Light of Christ, as He commands, are in the election, and sit under the teaching of the grace of God, which brings their salvation. But such as turn this grace into wantonness are in the reprobation ; and such as hate the Light are in the condemnation.

" So I exhorted all the people to believe in the Light, as Christ commands, and to own the grace of God, their free teacher ; and it would assuredly bring them their salvation ; for it is sufficient." [2]

It is by his fearless attitude toward all the dogmas of the Church, and by his consistent application of the one underlying thought of the unity of man's soul with God, that Fox develops a practical, if unformulated, theology. It is principles of action and not logical formulations that are the basis of his religion.

The doctrine of the Inner Light, which is the cardinal

[1] *Journal*, p. 264 ; cf. pp. 156, 384.
[2] Ibid., p. 299 f.

principle of Quakerism, is Fox's real contribution to the progress of religious thought. He finds it as no new thing. For him it is the one great underlying thought of the entire Gospel as taught and exemplified in the life of Jesus. The Middle Ages seem to have lost sight of it in their insistence first on the authority of the Church, and then on the authority of the Scriptures as opposed to ecclesiastical control. Though men may fail to recognize it, or even may betray and violate it, this Inner Life, this Inner Guide, this Christ Within, yet " remains on God's side as an unbroken love and trust that ' will not let them go,' and on man's side as a haunting and unceasing longing." [1]

The early Quakers, being neither theologians nor philosophers, spoke out of their own intense and abundant experience. They knew that for them and for all men the supreme authority lay not in Church or Book, but in this Light Within. This they found

"sufficient to reprove and convince of every evil deed, word or thought, and by it they came to know good from evil, right from wrong, and whatsoever is of God, and according to Him, from what was contrary to God in motion, word and works. This Light gave them to discern between truth and error, between every false and right way, and it perfectly discovered to them the true state of all things. They found the Light to be a sufficient teacher to lead them to Christ. They needed no man to teach them, for the Lord was their teacher, by His Light in their own consciences, and they received the holy anointing."

To such, and such only, as had attained that same Spirit which they were in who wrote the Scriptures, could

[1] A. Barratt Brown: *The Universal Light : A Statement of the Quaker Faith.*

the Scriptures be intelligible. But having attained this Spirit, the Scriptures then become a confirmation of the truth to which the heart has reached.

No organization, no edifice, represents the Church to Fox. The Church is the group of men and women who worship together. Being all gathered into the same spirit in united communion with God, the worshippers can gain such corporate communion that the one speaks with authority in harmony with the witness in the souls of all the others.

The " Christ Within sufficient for all things, to teach them and to make them perfect as He is, and as God is," however, must not be identified with the historic Jesus only. Fox never seemed to feel that there was anything questionable in using the same term " Christ " for the living and saving presence which he felt in his own heart, and for the man who lived and died in Palestine sixteen hundred years before. His attempts, and those of his followers, to express their experience in words were often illogical, and even contradictory. However, as William James said :

"So far as our Christian sects to-day are evolving into liberality, they are simply reverting in essence to the position which Fox and the early Quakers so long ago assumed." [1]

That this Light, or God-life, is universal, and is to be found in all, good or evil, he does not hesitate to state very positively. It was a position that made Fox unintelligible and apparently blasphemous to those who held to a doctrine of original sin. " There is that of God in all men." " There is that of God in the children of disobedience and reprobation." But

[1] James: *Varieties of Religious Experience*, p. 7.

to become truly a " man," one must be reborn into freedom from sin.

" None come to the new birth, but they who come to the Light which every man that cometh into the world is lighted withal ; which *believing in* they are children of the Light. Believing and *receiving it,* they receive power to become the sons of God."

Plotinus had expressed much the same thought which Fox expresses here :

" We are always gathered around the Divine Centre of our being ; and indeed, if we could withdraw from it, our being would at once be dissolved away, and we should cease to exist at all. But, near as it is to us, often we do not direct our eyes to it. When, however, we do so direct our gaze, we attain to the end of desire and to the rest of our souls, and our song is no more a discord, but circling round our Centre, we pass forth a divinely inspired chorale." [1]

Though Fox gives no formal definition of religion, one finds that for him, as for Dr. Starbuck, the life of religion means just the whole-hearted total responding —not alone in feeling and mental conception, but in actual daily living—consistently and harmoniously, to this Reality which carries with it this intimate vitalizing sense of supreme worth and absolute value. Religion becomes a widening stream of conserved and objectified experience of value, cumulative through the years. It is not true religion until it calls forth the total response, the intimate and vigorous and meaningful response, of the whole life. It is this attitude which is the value of the mysticism of Fox.

Mysticism is a word that has been applied to all types of religion that emphasize man's personal experi-

[1] Plotinus.

ence of God, and perhaps rightly so. But in the general popular mind it seems somehow to have become associated only with those phases of mystical experience which have found expression in trance and ecstasy, and often abnormal and pathological manifestations. The adherents of such a type of mystical experience may be said to have followed a negative way, and to have climbed arduously by " mystical ladders of purgation, prayer, contemplation, illumination," [1] towards a far-off God. They have found their only fitting behaviour in a turning away, a withdrawal, from all that life in and of the world offers. They conceive of God as being all that the world is not.

But there is also that type, of which George Fox is a true exponent, which I prefer to call a truer mysticism. It is founded upon what I believe is a truer conception of the God to which the thought and insight of philosophy and science and a religion of experience lead directly. These mystics, who have enriched the content of religion, insist that true mysticism is neither passive nor negative, nor theoretical. The truest mystical experience concerns all the deep-lying powers of the personal life. It is not merely emotional, not merely intellectual, not merely volitional. It is rather that intense awareness of the entire man in his consciousness of God.

William James says of the Quaker religion, which Fox founded upon such a dynamic mystical faith :

" It is something which it is impossible to overpraise. In a day of shams, it was a religion of veracity, rooted in spiritual inwardness." [2]

[1] R. M. Jones: *A Dynamic Faith*, p. 53.
[2] James: *Varieties of Religious Experience*, p. 7.

Of Fox himself, his friend and co-labourer wrote :

" Thousands can truly say, he was of an excellent spirit and savour among them, and because thereof the most excellent spirits loved him with an unfeigned and unfading love." [1]

[1] William Penn : Preface to the *Journal*, p. 54.

PART FIVE

APPENDICES

I

IOWA UNIVERSITY STUDIES IN IMPERCEPTIBLE DIFFERENCES

An attempt was made at the University of Iowa to find if imperceptible differences did not sum up to affect judgments. Under the personal direction of Dr. Starbuck, and with consultations with Drs. Seashore and Williams, a test in pitch discrimination was used with a standard of difference much below the threshold of the observer.[1] The normal expectation would be that according to chance, 50 per cent. of the judgments would be correct. The result obtained was an average of 53 per cent. correct in 2,100 judgments. H. Woodrow [2] has shown that the nearer the absolute threshold is approached, the longer is the reaction time. So it is probable that where immediate judgments are given as in this test the real difference does not get itself disentangled in time to make its detection possible and the resulting specific judgment accurate. But the results, it seems to me, did warrant the conclusion that there may be some correlation between the feeling of certainty and correctness of judgment. A feeling of certainty is no criterion for the correctness of the

[1] The observer in almost all of these experiments was Clarence F. Hanson.

[2] H. Woodrow: "Cessation of Stimuli," in *Psychological Review*, vol. xxii, No. 6, November 1915.

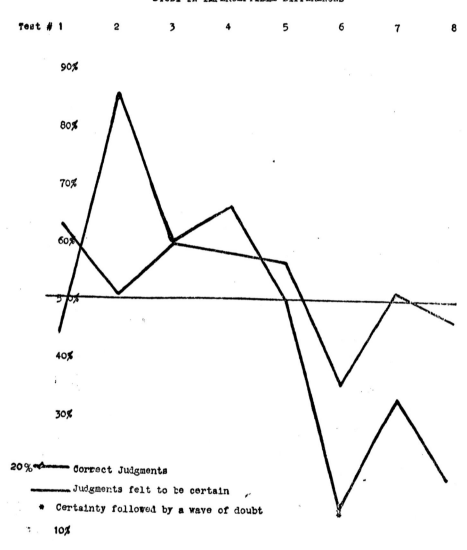

STUDY IN IMPERCEPTIBLE DIFFERENCES

CESSATION OF STIMULI

H. WOODROW
Psychological Review
XXII -No.6 -p.423
Nov.,1915

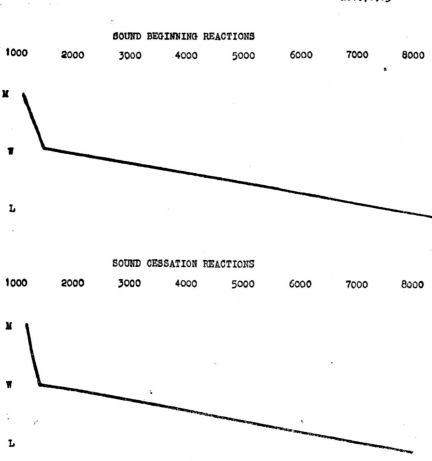

SOUND BEGINNING REACTIONS

1000 2000 3000 4000 5000 6000 7000 8000

M

W

L

SOUND CESSATION REACTIONS

1000 2000 3000 4000 5000 6000 7000 8000

M

W

L

M = medium stimuli
W = weak stimuli
L = lowest intensity which did fail to produce sensation

judgment, and it may just as readily be indicative of an unusually high percentage of wrong judgments as of right judgments. For instance, "Confidence followed by a wave of doubt" was the feeling tone accompanying a set of immediate judgments which were but 15 per cent. correct. Here the later reaction of doubt proves to be the more correct, which is in accordance with Woodrow's findings, though the certainty that there was a perceptible difference was correct throughout. E. A. Singer found through two hundred and fifty judgments in the location of equal or differing pressure stimuli that 12 per cent. represented the "percentage of times in which the subject was led by the presence of an unexpected difference to judge that an expected one was present." The judgment here also was right in its general, wrong in its specific, character.

II

FOX'S LETTER TO FRIENDS IN
BARBADOES, &c.

To Friends in Barbadoes, Virginia, Maryland, New England, and elsewhere.

Oh ! *Friends*, You all that have tasted of the *Power* of the *Lord God*, and of His *Truth* that is pure, and doth not admit of any impurity nor change : O ! therefore the *holy Truth* mind, which will let nothing that is unholy in you live : For nothing that is *unholy* can enter into the *Kingdom of God ;* and none that are disobedient to *Truth* must enter into the *Paradise* of *God ;* for, because of *Disobedience* was Man and Woman put out of Paradise. And therefore all everywhere, mind the pure *Power* of the *Lord God*, and the *Truth* which first Convinced you ; and whatsoever is gotten up through the *Carnal Reason*, and your *Eyes* going from the *Power* of *God*, and that which doth Convince you ; let that be purged out of your Hearts ; if not, it will lift up your Hearts to *Consultations, Subtilty, Questionings, Reasonings* and *Disputes.* Oh ! I feel too much of that which hath gotten up into the wrong understanding part, through which wrong Liberty gets up, which will bring a Plague into the Heart, which is worse than an outward Plague. O therefore consider, the *Life* and the *Power* of *God* hath not the

Supremacy in all your Hearts ; for I feel some *Minds*, and some *Bodies* have let in that which hath defiled them, and doth defile them. O *Cleanse, cleanse, cleanse,* and *joyn* to the pure *Immortal Power ;* for the *Power* of the *Lord God* will make room for itself, either in cleansing, or in vomiting, or casting out them, and that that doth not joyn to the *Power* of *God :* *Sodom* that Whorish and Adulterous Spirit, it must to the *Fire ;* and gainsaying *Core* into the *Earth.* And it will throw down that which hath been lifted up. The *Beesom* of the *Lord* is going forth to sweep, the *Candle* of the *Lord* is lighted to search every corner of your *Houses ;* for the *Just* walks in the *Path,* which is a *shining Light ;* which admits of no rubbish in it. O come out of all these things which you have entertained in your *Minds,* which you received not from them that came to minister unto you in the Beginning. O dwell in the *Power* of the *Lord God,* for to keep you low ; and take heed of getting up into *Conceitedness* and the *Air,* and to set up that which pertains not to the *Kingdom* of *God,* but to *Strife,* which never the *Apostles,* nor the *Saints* since, in the *Power* of *God* set up ; for if you do, the *Power* of *God* will sweep it and you all away. And O you that come to be *Vessels* of *Honour,* and *Vessels* of the *Mercies* of *God,* have esteem of your *Bodies ;* for such as defile their *Bodies* are neither *Vessels* of *Honour,* nor *Vessels* of the *Mercies,* but of *Wrath,* and are for the *Wrath.* Therefore keep out of *Strife,* keep out of *Fornication* and the *Adulterous Spirit ;* keep out of the *Lusts* of the *Eye,* the *Lusts* of the *Flesh,* and *Pride* of *Life, which is not of the Father ;* that *that* which is of the Father may be received, and have an entrance into every *Vessel.* O be not lifted up with a *vain Mind*; and let *Balaam's* Nature be slain, that erreth from the Spirit, and raileth Stumbling Blocks; and such as keep not their *First Habitation* in the *Power* of *God* and His *Truth*, become *Enemies* to such as are *Heirs* of the Kingdom, and the *Power* of an *endless Life*. Therefore all *Friends* and *People*, mind that which first convinced you, that *Power* of *God* which first awakened you, and arise and live in it, that all your *Eyes*, *Minds* and *Hearts* may be kept single and naked to God, and to one another; and uncloathed of all that which is contrary, and is got up since : For the *Seed* and the *Life* of *Christ Jesus* reigns and rules, Glory to Him for ever.

I have been uncapable to write or receive Writing a long time, or to speak, or bear to be spoken to, but have been as a Man buried alive, for else I should have writ to you before now; and therefore, O *Dear Friends*, give no occasion of stumbling; keep tender; for hardness of *Heart* is worse than an outward *Plague*, for that brings *Destruction* many ways; And so grieve not the Spirit in others, nor in yourselves. And whatsoever is decent and comly follow; honest and of a good report; that makes for *Peace*, and not for *Strife* under pretence of *Love*, for that's not of *God :* For *God*, who is *Love*, is not the *Author* of *Strife* and *Confusion*, but of *Peace*.

So, I desire you to let Copies of this be sent into Virginia, Maryland, and New Zealand, to be read amongst Friends in all their Meetings. Things are pretty well here, Friends being in Love and Unity, and the Dread of the Lord God is amongst us, who reigns, and will reign.

G. F.

III

BIBLIOGRAPHY

I GEORGE FOX AND THE SOCIETY OF FRIENDS.

1. *Journal of George Fox.* Edited by Norman Penney from the MS. Introduction by T. Edmund Harvey, 2 vols. Cambridge University Press, 1911.
2. *George Fox: An Autobiography.* Edited by Rufus M. Jones. London, Headley Brothers, 1904.
3. BARCLAY, ROBERT : *Apology for the True Christian Divinity.*
4. BRAITHWAITE, WILLIAM CHARLES : *The Beginnings of Quakerism.* Introduction by Rufus M. Jones. London. Macmillan, 1912.
5. BRAITHWAITE, WILLIAM CHARLES, and HODGKIN, HENRY T. : *The Message and Mission of Quakerism.* Philadelphia, John C. Winston Co., 1912.
6. GRUBB, EDWARD : *Authority and the Light Within.* London, Headley Brothers, 1908.
7. JONES, RUFUS M. : *Spiritual Reformers in the Sixteenth and Seventeenth Centuries.* London, Macmillan, 1914.
8. JONES, RUFUS M. : *Quakerism, a Religion of Life.* Swarthmore Lecture. London, Headley Brothers, 1908.
9. JONES, RUFUS M. : *Quakers in the American Colonies.* London, Macmillan, 1911.
10. JONES, RUFUS M. : *A Dynamic Faith.* London, Swarthmore Press, Ltd., 1900.
11 ROYCE, JOSIAH : "George Fox the Mystic," *Harvard Theological Review,* January 1913.
12. SEWELL, WILLIAM : *History of the Rise, Increase and Progress of the Christian People called Quakers* 2 vols. in one.
13. STEPHEN, CAROLINE E. : *Light Arising.* London, Heffer, 1908.
14. THOMAS, ALLAN C., and THOMAS, RICHARD H. : *History of the Society of Friends in America.*

278

II. MYSTICISM.

15. BOEHME, JAKOB : *The Signature of All Things.* Everyman's Library. New York, E. P. Dutton, 1912.

16. CHANDLER, ARTHUR : *Ara Cœli: An Essay in Mystical Theology.* 5th ed. London, Methuen & Co., 1912.

17. HERMANN, E. (Mrs.) : *The Meaning and Value of Mysticism.* London, Clark & Co., 1916.

18. HÜGEL, FREDERICK, BARON VON : *Mystical Element of Religion as Studied in St. Catharine of Genoa and Her Friends.* 2 vols. London, 1909.

19. INGE, WILLIAM RALPH : *Christian Mysticism.* Bampton Lecture. New York, Scribners, 1899.

20. INGE, WILLIAM RALPH : *Light, Life and Love : Selections from the German Mystics of the Middle Ages.* London, Methuen, 1905.

21. INGE, WILLIAM RALPH : *Studies of English Mystics.* St. Margaret Lectures. London, J. Murray, 1906.

22. JONES, RUFUS M. : *Studies in Mystical Religion.* London, Macmillan, 1909.

23. NORDAU, MAX S. : *Degeneration.* Ed. 7, pp. 45–249. London, Heinemann, 1895.

24. PACHEU, JULES : *Psychologie des Mystiques Chrétiens.* Paris, 1909.

25. PREL, CARL DU : *Philosophy of Mysticism.* 2 vols. London, 1889.

26. RÉCÉJAC, E. : *Essay on the Bases of Mystical Knowledge.* New York, Scribners, 1899.

27. SHARPE, A. : *Mysticism : Its True Nature and Value ; with a Translation of the " Mystical Knowledge " of Dionysius and of the Letters to Caius and Doroyheus.* St. Louis, Herder, 1910.

28. STEINER, RUDOLF : *Mystics of the Renaissance.* London, Theosophical Society, 1911.

29. UNDERHILL, EVELYN : *Mysticism.* London, Methuen & Co., 1911.

30. VAUGHAN, R. A. : *Hours With the Mystics.* Ed. E. Routledge, 1879.

31. CONYBEARE, FREDERICK CORNWALLIS : *Myth, Magic and Morals.* London, Watts & Co., 1910.

32. RUSSELL, BERTRAND : *Mysticism and Logic.* London, Longmans, 1918.

33. NEWTON, R. H. : *Mysticism of Music.* New York, 1915.

III. THE PSYCHOLOGY OF RELIGION.

34. CAIRD, EDWARD : *The Evolution of Religion.* Gifford Lectures. Glasgow, Maclehose & Sons, 1899.

35. COE, GEORGE A. : *Psychology of Religion.* New York, Houghton Mifflin & Co., 1916.

36. EMETT, C. U. : *Psychological Elements of Religious Faith.* Edited by E. Hale. 1902.

37. FRAZER, J. G. : *The Golden Bough.* 2 vols. London, Macmillan, 1890.

38. GUYAU, MARIE JEAN : *The Non-Religion of the Future.* Tr. from the French. New York, Holt & Co., 1897.

39. HOCKING, W. E. : *The Meaning of God in Human Experience.* Oxford University Press.

40. HÖFFDING, HARALD : *Philosophy of Religion.* Tr. from the German by B. E. Meyer. London and New York, Macmillan, 1906.

41. JAMES, WILLIAM : *Varieties of Religious Experience.* Edinburgh, Longmans, 1902.

42. PATTEN, S. N. : *Social Basis of Religion.* New York, 1911.

43. PRATT, J. B. : *Psychology of Religious Belief.* New York and London, Macmillan, 1907.

44. ROYCE, JOSIAH : *Sources of Religious Insight.* Edinburgh, T. & T. Clark, 1912.

45. SANTAYANA, GEORGE : *Reason in Religion.* Vol. iii. in *Life of Reason.* London, Constable, 1905.

46. STARBUCK, EDWIN D. : *Psychology of Religion.* London, Walter Scott Publishing Co., 1899.

47. STEVENSON, JOHN GILCHRIST : *Religion and Temperament.* London, Cassell & Co., 1913.

48. STRATTON, G. M. : *Psychology of the Religious Life.* London, George Allen & Unwin, Ltd., 1911.

49. STRONG, A. L. : *The Psychology of Prayer.* 1909.

50. MENZIES, A. : *History of Religion.* New York, Scribners,